South of San Francisco

SOUTH OF SAN FRANCISCO

A Guide to the San Mateo Coast, Santa Cruz,
Monterey, Carmel, Big Sur and Hearst Castle

*Alan Magary and
Kerstin Fraser Magary*

HARPER & ROW, PUBLISHERS, New York
Cambridge, Philadelphia, San Francisco, London
Mexico City, São Paulo, Sydney

1817

FIRST EDITION

Maps by George Colbert

Library of Congress Cataloging in Publication Data

Magary, Alan.
  South of San Francisco.

  Includes index.
  1. California—Description and travel—1981–
—Guide-books. 2. Coasts—California—Guide-books.
I. Magary, Kerstin Fraser. II. Title.
F859.3.M34 1983   917.94′0453   82–48520
ISBN 0–06–091035–6 (pbk.)

83 84 85 86 87 10 9 8 7 6 5 4 3 2 1

*To Frances Fraser
and Laura Magary
with our love*

Contents

TO BEGIN:
Notes
to the Reader

This book is a travel guide to the counties south of San Francisco: San Mateo ("Coastside" only; "the Peninsula" is along San Francisco Bay), Santa Cruz, and Monterey. This is an area of sunny strands and foggy coves, rolling hills and agricultural plains, rugged shore and gentle dunes, Spanish adobes and Victorian houses, artichokes and grapes, championship golf courses and redwood state parks, covered bridges and elephant seals, fishing villages and recreational shopping centers. This coast is versatile: it has places for beachball, places for growing things, and places for contemplation. There's an international city at one end, a dream castle at the other, a long, scenic highway in between, and always the Pacific Ocean in various moods and views.

This is primarily a sightseeing guide, but Part IV is as helpful and wide a listing of accommodations and restaurants as our time and resources allowed us to put together with confidence. We actually include far more places, in minireviews and informational listings, than any competitive guidebooks. The sightseeing sections, as you will see, are also far more personal, interpretive, and opinionated than most travel guides.

Interested residents and visitors should also see the companion guide to the counties north of San Francisco: *Across the Golden Gate* (Harper & Row, 1980). A guide to San Francisco and the Bay Area is in manuscript.

CHAPTER ORGANIZATION

Most chapters follow this pattern:

- "Highlights," a brief, uncritical list of principal attractions, with page numbers (this section extends the table of contents);
- an introduction to the area covered;
- "What to See and Do," touring information organized linearly (mostly north to south), almost always along and off California Highway 1; "What to Do" on the Monterey Peninsula is gathered in Chapter 10; and
- "Practical Information," a tail-end section covering transportation and giving signposts to the hotel and restaurant listings in Part IV.

SIGHTSEEING RATING SYSTEM

Like the Michelin green guides, we apply one, two, or three stars to attractions—or omit them—so that the reader has some way to judge how worthwhile one place is in relation to another:

   ***"worth a journey" or "highly recommended";
    **"worth a detour" or "recommended";
     *"interesting";
no star interesting but perhaps only to read about as you travel on (such things add texture) or to visit if you're a specialist or California resident with time to spare.

A relativity is involved in this system: the significance of the number of stars depends on where you are. To take an example outside this book, if you're planning a trip to California from New York or Knoxville or Phoenix, **Yosemite National Park***** means that this large area is worth including in a trip of hundreds or thousands of miles. Once you're in the park, **Yosemite Valley*****

means that's among the most important areas smaller than the entire park. And when you're in Yosemite Valley, **Yosemite Fall Trail******** means that is one of the most worthwhile things within the valley. Quite obviously, one would not rush across the continent just to walk on this trail, though the visitor could do a lot worse. It is assumed that even a one-day, one-stop tourist will take in a number of sights, at least casually.

PRICES

Inflation makes authors of travel guidebooks shy away from quoting prices. We say "small admission fee" or something similar if admission to a state park or other attraction is (at this writing) less than about $2.50 per adult, $1.50 or less per child. The introduction to Part IV describes the four-level price-category system ($:budget, $:intermediate, $:expensive, $:luxury) that we devised for indicating relative costliness of hotels and restaurants.

MAPS

The traveler should obtain some good maps to the area south of San Francisco. Good luck in your search. American mapmaking hasn't yet reached the heights of clarity, detail, interest, and color achieved by the British Ordnance Survey or the French Michelin maps. The U.S. Geological Survey and other government agencies produce some fine special-interest maps, but many are lamentably old and with sparse detail on the man-made landscape. Commercial maps for tourists are, on the whole, wretched.

That leaves the old standbys: the occasionally good, often indifferent maps produced by Rand McNally, the American Automobile Association, and a couple of other companies. While good on road detail these have little topographical information. The AAA has these maps for members: *California; San Francisco; Peninsula Points* and *Sequoia* (adjoining regional maps for sections south of San Francisco); *San Mateo County; Santa Clara and Santa Cruz Counties; Santa Cruz* (city map); *Monterey and San Benito Counties;* and *Monterey Peninsula Cities.*

The Big Sur Coast in particular lacks a good map. You'll have to use a combination of the AAA *Monterey and San Benito* map and the Forest Service's *Los Padres National Forest* (northern section) map to get a sense of the many small things—rocky points, back roads, redwood creeks, hiking trails, picnic grounds, tiny settlements, pocket beaches—that make up Big Sur.

TOURIST INFORMATION

There's no central tourist authority as there is in the "Redwood Empire" north of San Francisco. Here are the local sources of tourist information:

Capitola: Capitola Chamber of Commerce, 410 Capitola Ave., Capitola 95010; (408) 475-6522.

Carmel: Carmel Business Association, Vandevort Court (San Carlos between Ocean and 7th), P.O. Box 4444, Carmel 93921; (408) 624-2522. "A Guide to Carmel-by-the-Sea" (annual) is $1. Tourist Information Center (also room-finder service), Mission near Ocean, Carmel 93921; (408) 624-1711.

Half Moon Bay: Half Moon Bay Chamber of Commerce, 625 Miramonte Rd., Half Moon Bay 94019; (415) 726-5202.

Monterey Peninsula: Monterey Peninsula Chamber of Commerce—Convention and Visitors Bureau, 380 Alvarado St., P.O. Box 1770, Monterey 93940; (408) 649-3200. *Monterey Peninsula Review* is one of the most thorough and informative (but not critical) tourist weeklies we've seen. If the visitor's bureau doesn't send you one, send $1.50 to the *Review,* P.O. Box G-1, Carmel 93921. *Key* and a number of other periodicals are collections of ads and articles that, uncannily, echo the ads.

Pacific Grove: Pacific Grove Chamber of Commerce, Forest and Central, P.O. Box 167, Pacific Grove 93950; (408) 373-3394.

Pebble Beach: Pebble Beach Company, Resort and Recreation Division, Pebble Beach 93953; (408) 624-3811.

Salinas: Salinas Chamber of Commerce, 119 E. Alisal, Salinas 93901; (408) 424-7611. Ask for their *Steinbeck Country Starts in Salinas,* a pamphlet describing four one-day tours.

San Juan Bautista: San Juan Bautista Chamber of Commerce, 37 Mariposa St., San Juan Bautista 95045; (408) 623-2454.

San Mateo Coastside: San Mateo County Convention and

Visitors' Bureau, 888 Airport Blvd., Burlingame 94010; (415) 347-7004.

Santa Cruz: Santa Cruz County Convention and Visitors' Bureau, Church and Center, P.O. Box 921, Santa Cruz 95060; (408) 423-6927. The *Country Crossroads Map* can be obtained from the Santa Cruz County Farm Bureau, 1469 Freedom Blvd., Watsonville 95076.

State parks and Hearst Castle information: State Department of Parks and Recreation, P.O. Box 2390, Sacramento 95811; toll-free (800) 952-5580. (For castle reservations, see pp. 188–190.)

Watsonville: Watsonville Chamber of Commerce and Agriculture, 444 Main St., Watsonville 95076; (408) 724-3849.

OTHER SOURCES OF INFORMATION

California, Coast

Architecture: Gebhard, David, et al. *A Guide to the Architecture in San Francisco and Northern California.* Rev. ed. Santa Barbara: Peregrine Smith, 1976. The standard tall, fat guide to buildings large and small.

California in general: Hart, James D. *A Companion to California.* New York: Oxford University Press, 1979. A–Z listings, from art to zoos.

Coast in general: Sunset editors. *Discovering the California Coast.* 2nd ed. Menlo Park: Lane, 1978. The usual superb color pictorial.

Coastal beaches, walkways, viewpoints: California Coastal Commission. *California Coastal Access Guide.* Berkeley: University of California Press, 1981. A must for the coastal explorer.

Coastal conservation: California Coastal Commission, 631 Howard St., San Francisco 94105; (415) 543-8555. California Coastal Conservancy, 1212 Broadway, Oakland 94612. Big Sur Land Trust, 3785 Via Nona Marie, Carmel 93921; (408) 625-5523. Commission and conservancy are state agencies.

History, sites: Hoover, M. B., et al., *Historic Spots in California.* Revised by W. N. Abeloe. 3rd ed. Stanford: Stanford University Press, 1966. No levity here.

Place-names: Gudde, Erwin G. *California Place Names*. 3rd ed. Berkeley: University of California Press, 1968. Anecdotal but informative.

Outdoors, Natural History

Birds: Cogwell, Howard L. *Water Birds of California*. Berkeley: University of California Press, 1977.

Ecology: Bakker, Elna. *An Island Called California: An Ecological Introduction to Its Natural Communities*. Berkeley: University of California Press, 1972. Quiet, well-written.

Elephant Seals: Le Boeuf, Burney, and Kaza, Stephanie. *The Natural History of Año Nuevo*. Pacific Grove: Boxwood Press, 1982.

Fishing: Cannon, Ray, and Sunset editors. *How to Fish the Pacific Coast*. Menlo Park: Lane, 1978. Covers all fishing techniques, describes 202 fish. Squire, James L., Jr., and Smith, Susan E. *Angler's Guide to the United States Pacific Coast*. Washington, D.C.: National Marine Fisheries Service, 1977; order from Superintendent of Documents, Washington, D.C. 20402—Publication 003-020-00113-1, $7.50.

Foraging: Howorth, Peter. *Foraging Along the California Coast*. Santa Barbara: Capra, 1977. Stalking the wild grunion.

Marine mammals: Orr, Robert T. *Marine Mammals of California*. Berkeley: University of California Press, 1972. Otters, gray whales, seals, and lions of the sea.

Monterey Bay: Gordon, Burton L. *Monterey Bay Area: Natural History and Cultural Imprints*. Pacific Grove: Boxwood Press (183 Ocean View Blvd., Pacific Grove 93950), 1974.

Plants: Dawson, E. Yale. *Introduction to Seashore Plants of Northern California*. Berkeley: University of California Press, 1966.

Redwoods: Anthrop, Donald F. *Redwood National and State Parks*. Happy Camp: Naturegraph (P.O. Box 1075, Happy Camp 96039), 1977. Iacopi, Robert, and Sunset editors. *Redwood Country and the Big Trees of the Sierra*. Menlo Park: Lane, 1969.

Sea otters: Friends of the Sea Otter, 3750 The Barnyard, Carmel 93921; (408) 625-3290. Woolfenden, John. *The California Sea Otter: Saved or Doomed?* Pacific Grove: Boxwood Press (183 Ocean View Blvd., Pacific Grove 93950), 1979.

Seashore life: Taber, Tom. *From Bodega Bay to Monterey.* San Mateo: Oak Valley Press, 1977. Hedgpeth, Joel W. *Introduction to Seashore Life of the San Francisco Bay Region and the Coast of Northern California.* Berkeley: University of California Press, 1962. Companion to Dawson's plant book describes denizens of tidepool and marsh.

Tidepools: Ricketts, Edward F., and Calvin, Jack, ed. by Joel W. Hedgpeth. *Between Pacific Tides.* Stanford: Stanford University Press, 1968. Bulky but standard, written by *Cannery Row*'s "Doc." Braun, Ernest, and Brown, Vinson. *Exploring Pacific Coast Tidepools.* Happy Camp: Naturegraph (P.O. Box 1075, Happy Camp 96039), 1966. Less texty.

Trees: Watts, Tom. *Pacific Coast Tree Finder.* Berkeley: Nature Study Guild (P.O. Box 972), 1973. One of several very clever field identification guides; others help you identify coastal berries and redwood forest wildflowers.

Wildflowers: Munz, Philip A. *Shore Wildflowers of California, Oregon, and Washington.* Berkeley: University of California Press, 1964.

History, Literature, People

Big Sur: Lussier, Tomi Kaye. *Big Sur: A Complete History and Guide.* Monterey: Big Sur Publications (P.O. Box 1562), 1979. Four colors. Miller, Henry. *Big Sur and the Oranges of Hieronymus Bosch.* New York: New Directions, 1964. A memoir as meandering as the coastal highway. John Steinbeck's short story "Flight," in *The Long Valley,* is set on the coast. Lillian Bos Ross's *The Stranger* (1942), out of print, is a novel worth looking up.

Cannery Row: John Steinbeck's *Cannery Row* (1945) and *Sweet Thursday* (1954) are the two fables that started it all. *Travels with Charley* (1962) includes a late visit. Knox, Maxine, and Rodriguez, Mary. *Steinbeck's Street: Cannery Row.* Novato: Presidio Press, 1979. Complete history, numerous photographs.

Carmel literary history: Walker, Franklin. *The Seacoast of Bohemia.* Santa Barbara: Peregrine Smith, 1973.

Hearst Castle: Aidala, Thomas R. *Hearst Castle, San Simeon.* Photographs by Curtis Bruce. New York: Hudson Hills Press, 1981. A new interpretation of Hearst's complex edifice. Swanberg,

W. A. *Citizen Hearst.* New York: Charles Scribner's Sons, 1961; also paperback edition. Biography by a storyteller.

Indians: Margolin, Malcolm. *The Ohlone Way: Indian Life in the San Francisco and Monterey Bay Areas.* Berkeley: Heyday Books (P.O. Box 9145), 1978. Evocative account of a long-gone population. Heizer, Robert F., and Whipple, M. A. *The California Indians.* Berkeley: University of California Press, 1951. Scholarly.

Jeffers, Robinson: Robinson Jeffers Tor House Foundation, P.O. Box 1887, Carmel 93921; (408) 624-1813. The foundation, which owns Tor House and Hawk Tower, gives guided tours by reservation, has a shelf of Jeffers's works for sale, and has published a leaflet, *Jeffers Country,* poetry itinerary to the Big Sur Coast. An out-of-print book also titled *Jeffers Country,* originally published by Scrimshaw Press, has words by Jeffers, photographs by Horace Lyon. A comprehensive collection of his poetry is *The Selected Poetry of Robinson Jeffers* (New York: Random House, 1938); a short paperback selection of lyrical poems is *Robinson Jeffers: Selected Poems* (New York: Vintage, 1965). Bennett, Melba. *The Stone Mason of Tor House.* Los Angeles: Ward Ritchie, 1966. A biography. Carpenter, Frederic I. *Robinson Jeffers.* New York: Twayne, 1962. Brief biography, criticism.

Monterey history: Fink, Augusta. *Monterey County: The Dramatic Story of Its Past.* Fresno: Valley Publishers, 1978. Reese, Robert. *A Brief History of Old Monterey.* Monterey: City Planning Commission, 1969. Johnston, Robert B. *Old Monterey County: A Pictorial History.* Monterey: Monterey Savings, 1970. Mathes, W. Michael. *Vizcaíno and Spanish Expansion in the Pacific Ocean.* San Francisco: California Historical Society, 1968. Dana, Richard Henry. *Two Years Before the Mast.* Boston, 1840. Robinson, Alfred. *Life in California Before the Conquest.* New York, 1846. Colton, Rev. Walter. *Three Years in California.* New York, 1850.

Monterey adobes: Monterey History and Art Association, 550 Calle Principal, Monterey 93940; (408) 372-2608. Their *Old Monterey* is an abode guidebook. Ley, Gaston, ed. *Monterey's Adobe Heritage.* Photographs by Wynn Bullock. Monterey: Monterey Savings, 1965. Much the same as *Old Monterey* booklet. State Department of Parks and Recreation, Monterey State Historic Park, 210 Olivier St., Monterey 93940; (408) 649-2836. The park has several museums and/or adobes but no big guidebook.

Santa Cruz architecture: Koch, Margaret. *The Walk Around Santa Cruz Book*. Santa Cruz: Western Tanager, 1979. Chase, John. *The Sidewalk Companion to Santa Cruz Architecture*. Santa Cruz: Paper Vision Press (1111 Pacific Ave.), 1979. The Santa Cruz Convention and Visitors' Bureau has a free walking-tour brochure.

Steinbeck Country (Salinas and Valley): John Steinbeck's *East of Eden* (1952), "The Red Pony" (1937), *The Long Valley* (stories, 1938), and *The Pastures of Heaven* (stories, 1932) are his major works of interest to the literary pilgrim to the Salinas Valley. *Of Mice and Men* (1937), *To a God Unknown* (1933), and *In Dubious Battle* (1936) are more or less set in the valley but the place plays no real role. *Tortilla Flat* (1935) takes place in Monterey. *The Grapes of Wrath* (1939) is *not* set in the Salinas Valley, rather the San Joaquin Valley. *Travels with Charley* (1962) records his journey through 40 states, ending in his home territory. *Steinbeck Country* (Palo Alto: American West, 1975) has terrific photographs and interpretive prose by Steve Crouch, quotations from Steinbeck. Kiernan, Thomas. *The Intricate Music: A Biography of John Steinbeck*. Boston: Little, Brown, 1979. Steinbeck, Elaine, and Wallsten, Robert, eds. *Steinbeck: A Life in Letters*. New York: Viking, 1975; also Penguin paperback. French, Warren G. *John Steinbeck*. New York: Twayne, 1961. Brief biography, criticism.

Stevenson, Robert Louis: The Monterey past is summoned up in RLS's "The Old Pacific Capital," "San Carlos Day," and "Simoneau's at Monterey," collected with other California writings in *From Scotland to Silverado,* ed. by James D. Hart (Cambridge, Mass.: Harvard University Press, 1966). There are several biographies, including modern ones by J. C. Furnas, David Daiches, James Pope Hennessy, and Jenni Calder.

Wine country: Hinkle, Richard Paul. *Central Coast Wine Book, from San Francisco to Santa Barbara*. Illustrated by Sebastian Titus. St. Helena: Vintage Image (1335 Main St., 94574), 1980. Describes nearly all of the Central Coast's wineries, whether big and industrial or pocket-sized and intimate. Magary, Alan and Kerstin F. *Across the Golden Gate*. New York: Harper & Row, 1980. Part I is a comprehensive introduction to California wine. Thompson, Bob. *The Pocket Encyclopedia of California Wines*.

New York: Simon & Schuster, 1980. Thompson, Bob, and Sunset editors. *Guide to California's Wine Country*. Menlo Park: Lane, 1979.

EVENTS

It's difficult to travel by calendars of events. More likely, you'll arrive somewhere and find yourself in the middle of something. But for those who definitely want to attend the Crosby Pro-Am or the Carmel Bach Festival or whatever, here's a nondefinitive list. Details from the visitors' bureaus listed above.

January: Bing Crosby Pro-Am Golf Championship (Pebble Beach); Ye Olde English Market (Monterey County Fairgrounds); gray-whale watching begins (coastal promontories, also boat trips from Half Moon Bay, Monterey); elephant-seal watching continues (Año Nuevo State Reserve).

February: Gray-whale and elephant-seal watching continues.

March: Kite Flying Contest (Carmel); Victorian House Tour and Good Old Days (Pacific Grove); Steinbeck Birthday (Salinas); Rugby Tournament (Pebble Beach).

April: Adobe House Tour (Monterey); Fremont Peak Day, April 25; Polo Matches (Pebble Beach or Monterey County Fairgrounds); Moss Landing Marine Lab Open House; Antiques Fair (Bolado Park, south of Hollister); Wildflower Show (Pacific Grove Museum).

May: International Auto and Motorcycle Racing begins (Laguna Seca Raceway); Garden Tour (Monterey Peninsula); Commodore's Regatta (Pebble Beach); West Coast Antique Aircraft Fly-In (Watsonville); Del Monte Kennel Club Dog Show (Pebble Beach); Santa Cruz Spring Fair; Shark Derby (Moss Landing); Defense Language Institute Open House (Presidio of Monterey); Hunter Trials (Pebble Beach); Portuguese Chamarita (Pescadero, Half Moon Bay).

June: Merienda—Monterey's Birthday Celebration; Antiques Show (San Juan Bautista); Dressage Championship (Pebble Beach); Fiesta de los Padres (San Carlos Cathedral, Monterey); Miss California Pageant (Santa Cruz); San Benito County Rodeo and Saddle Horse Parade (Bolado Park); Steinbeck Festival (Salinas).

July: California Rodeo (Salinas); Sloat Landing Reenactment

(Presidio of Monterey); Carmel Bach Festival; Clint Eastwood Invitational Celebrity Tennis (Carmel Valley); Feast of Lanterns (Pacific Grove); Fiesta Rodeo (San Juan Bautista); Parade of Champions Drum and Bugle Corps Show (Seaside); Antique Street Fair (Moss Landing); Big Balloon Race (Cannery Row, Monterey); La Honda Days (La Honda); Japanese Obon Festival (Monterey County Fairgrounds); Bass Derby (Pacifica); Highland Games (Monterey Peninsula College); Multihull Classic (Monterey Bay); Hidden Valley Masters Festival of Chamber Music (Carmel Valley).

August: Cabrillo Music Festival (Aptos); Monterey County Fair; Flea Market (San Juan Bautista); Arts and Crafts Festival (Monterey); Concours d'Elegance (Pebble Beach) and Historic Auto Races (Laguna Seca); Frisbee Championships (Aptos); Highland Games (Pebble Beach); National Horse Show (Monterey County Fairgrounds).

September: Artichoke festivals (Castroville, Pescadero); Great Sand Castle Contest (or October; Carmel); Mission fiestas (Santa Cruz, Carmel, Soledad); Monterey Jazz Festival (Monterey County Fairgrounds); National Begonia Festival (Capitola); Morse Sailboat Regatta (Pebble Beach); Santa Cruz County Fair (Watsonville); Arts and Crafts Show (San Juan Bautista); Santa Rosalia Festival (Fisherman's Wharf, Monterey); Outrigger Regatta (Monterey Bay).

October: San Benito County Fair (Bolado Park); California International Airshow (Salinas); Pumpkin Festival (Half Moon Bay); Robinson Jeffers Tor House Festival (Carmel); Grand Prix Formula 5000 (Laguna Seca); Monterey History and Art Association Antique Show and Sale (Monterey Conference Center); Polo Matches (Pebble Beach); Vintage Festival and Wine Stomp (Monterey Peninsula Winery); Butterfly Festival (Pacific Grove).

November: Peak of monarch butterfly migration (Pacific Grove, also Santa Cruz); California Wine Festival (Monterey Conference Center); Marching Band Festival (Pacific Grove).

December: Festival of Trees (Monterey County Fairgrounds); gray-whale watching begins (coastal promontories, boat trips from Monterey, Half Moon Bay); Singing Christmas Tree (Pacific Grove); Old Alta California Christmas (San Juan Bautista); elephant-seal season begins (Año Nuevo State Reserve).

TO COMMENCE THE JOURNEY:

San Francisco to the Ocean

To begin with
The sea is a sound
A down and around pound of sound
A lot of swish and plish
The smell of something big.

—WILLIAM CARLOS WILLIAMS
(attributed)

Certainly, it is a good thing to travel the Big Sur Coast, to bide a wee in Carmel, to walk around San Juan Bautista, to find the fugitive summer sun in Santa Cruz. We encourage everyone to do it. But half of this good thing is that you're not in San Francisco.

Don't get us wrong. We live in San Francisco, work in San Francisco, shop in San Francisco, do things and enjoy ourselves in San Francisco. One of us was even *born* in San Francisco *(rara avis)*. San Francisco is, in a word, terrific.

But sometimes it is too much.

So we pack a small car and go to a rustic cabin under some tall trees and write books like this about places that are not San Francisco. Useful perspective on big buildings, a rural view of city streets, time to think about urban connections. The words come out better, sometimes.

And here you are, from Pittsburgh or Denver, Greenville or Reno, Minot (North Dakota) or Lufkin (Texas). You've peeled the Big Artichoke (prickly outside, tender and tasty inside). You've seen gold bars at the Old Mint and gold-laméd transvestites at Finocchio's, walked sticky sidewalks in Chinatown, eaten walk-away shrimp salad with sourdough at Fisherman's Wharf, seen a

Rembrandt at the de Young and a homer at Candlestick Park.
You've seen the view from atop Twin Peaks, experienced the bore-
dom of standing in line somewhere, stretched your calf muscles
walking up Nob Hill, taken a subterranean high-speed ride under
the Bay on BART, attended mass at Mission Dolores, aped a go-
rilla at the Zoo, tuned in to whateverthehell the local news was.
You've done special things, too: a friend took you to some ad agency's private cocktail party on the 48th floor of the Transamerica
Pyramid, and you've eaten at the Mandarin, Tadich's, Balboa
Café, Sam Wo's, Ernie's, and a hole-in-the-wall Salvadorean restaurant in the Mission. You've zipped up the glass-enclosed elevator at the St. Francis and you even found some time to take an
afternoon nap. You took a breath of fresh air on the Sausalito
ferry, two drinks at Perry's, three rides on the cable car, four minutes to call home and check with your house-sitter, five tries to get
some tickets to the opera or the 49ers, six fortune cookies before
you found one to put in your wallet, seven minutes to read Herb
Caen.* Whew.

It's terrific, but San Francisco has a lot of muchness.

So you leave. A rental car with your bags haphazardly packed, a
plastic bag of laundry and a brown bag with a selection of cold cuts
and picnic goodies. Somewhere the on-ramp, some ta-pocketa-
pocketa on a rough city freeway, lots of little houses stuck together,
then a merge right into Highway 1, more little houses.

And there's the Pacific Ocean coming into view.

More terrific.

The Central Coast of California—for that's where you're
going—has the smell of something big. From the Golden Gate to
William Randolph Hearst's idiosyncrasy at San Simeon, the coast
is not one bland beach after another, no acres of untidy bungalows
under too much sun. No, here the ocean is unkind and the continent must push back when the ocean bumps into it. The land and
the sea consequently define and describe each other in unequivocal
terms. Against the land the sea exhibits itself to best advantage,
with spectacles of long, parallel combers running in toward the
shore, or breakers furiously thrashing some lonely, never-dry rock.

---

*If you don't know who Herb Caen is (our New York editor didn't), pick up
the morning *Chronicle* when you get to San Francisco.

Even on a calm day, when the ocean is willing to be big and blue and sparkling, it still looks like it's waiting for a moment to surge and rush and dash itself against the land.

From the other point of view the ocean uses superior stagecraft to create a setting for itself: solitary sea stacks; tunnels and blow-holes drilled into a resisting shore; angular headlands; sheer bluffs; sculpted rock shelves pocked by tide pools, strands, plages, shingle and pocket beaches, mudflats and marshes; hidden coves ideal for smuggling whiskey (or driving a golf ball across); inland dunes that roll like waves; flat coastal terraces; and narrow river valleys where coastal fog creeps among giant trees or hangs low over fertile land.

Perhaps being on the shore puts us in touch with our origins in the primeval ooze. Of course, it is also nice to race yachts into the wind, sink one's feet into hot beach sand, roast hot dogs, drink beer.

The principal attractions are varied: beaches and seashore reserves, as you might guess, but also several redwood state parks in the Santa Cruz and Santa Lucia mountains; the university town of Santa Cruz and rich playgrounds of Carmel, Pebble Beach, and Monterey; well-preserved Franciscan missions at San Juan Bautista, Carmel, and San Antonia (Santa Cruz and Soledad are replicas); Pinnacles National Monument; the Big Sur Coast, identified with ruggedness and spirituality; and Hearst's house.

The fast way up and down the Central Coast is U.S. Highway 101, but you won't see the ocean unless you take California Highway 1, a mostly two-lane route that hugs the continent very closely. Bring an extra roll of film, a sweater or windbreaker, a coat and tie for dining out on the Monterey Peninsula, some money for something handmade, more money for sheer existence. Oh, don't forget to make reservations for Hearst Castle.

SOUTH OF SAN FRANCISCO

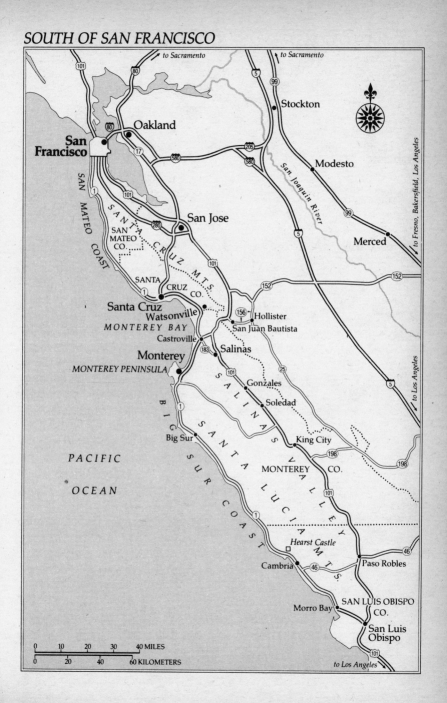

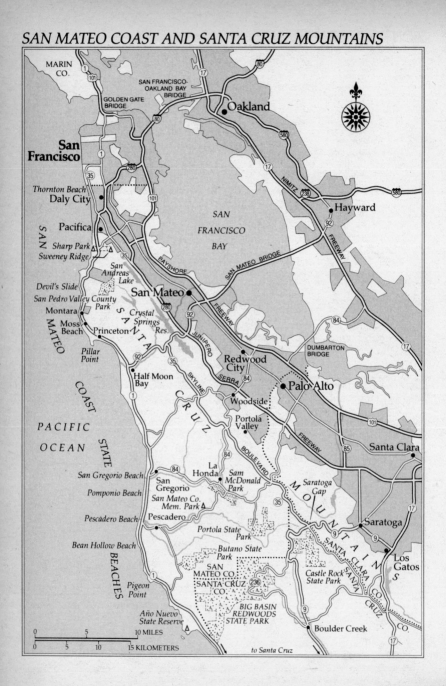

SAN MATEO COAST AND SANTA CRUZ MOUNTAINS

MARIN CO.

SAN FRANCISCO-OAKLAND BAY BRIDGE

GOLDEN GATE BRIDGE

Oakland

San Francisco

Thornton Beach
Daly City

SAN FRANCISCO BAY

Pacifica

Hayward

Sharp Park
Sweeney Ridge

San Andreas Lake

BAYSHORE

SAN MATEO BRIDGE

Devil's Slide
San Pedro Valley County Park
Montara
Moss Beach
Princeton

San Mateo

Crystal Springs Res.

JUNIPERO

NIMITZ FREEWAY

Pillar Point

FREEWAY

DUMBARTON BRIDGE

Half Moon Bay

SKYLINE

SERRA

Redwood City

Palo Alto

Woodside

PACIFIC OCEAN

COAST

Portola Valley

BOULEVARD

FREEWAY

Santa Clara

La Honda
Sam McDonald Park

San Gregorio Beach

Saratoga Gap

San Gregorio

Pomponio Beach

San Mateo Co. Mem. Park

STATE

Pescadero Beach

Pescadero

Portola State Park

Saratoga

Bean Hollow Beach

Butano State Park

SAN MATEO CO.
SANTA CRUZ CO.

Castle Rock State Park

Los Gatos

BEACHES

Pigeon Point

Año Nuevo State Reserve

BIG BASIN REDWOODS STATE PARK

Boulder Creek

MOUNTAINS

SANTA CLARA CO. SANTA CRUZ CO.

to Santa Cruz

0   5   10 MILES
0   5   10   15 KILOMETERS

SANTA CRUZ MOUNTAINS AND COAST

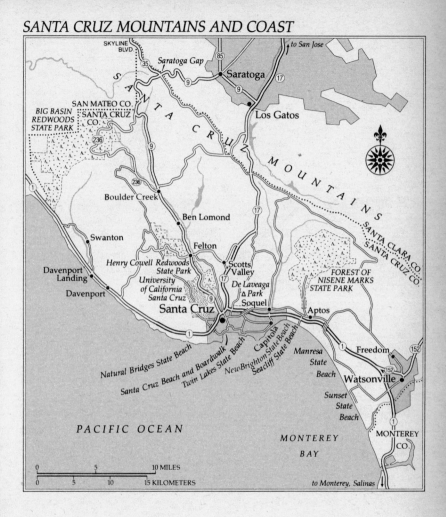

MONTEREY BAY SHORE

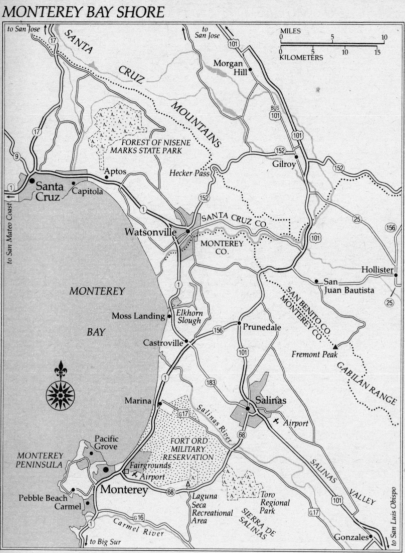

to San Jose

SANTA CRUZ MOUNTAINS

17

to San Jose
101

Morgan Hill

BUS
101

FOREST OF NISENE
MARKS STATE PARK

101

152

Gilroy

152

9

17

Aptos

Hecker Pass

152

Santa
Cruz

Capitola

1

25

156

SANTA CRUZ CO.

Watsonville

MONTEREY
CO.

101

Hollister

San
Juan Bautista

25

MONTEREY

Moss Landing

Elkhorn
Slough

Prunedale

156

SAN BENITO CO.
MONTEREY CO.

BAY

Castroville

101

Fremont Peak

183

GABILAN RANGE

Marina

G17

Salinas River

Salinas

Airport

FORT ORD
MILITARY
RESERVATION

68

SALINAS VALLEY

Pacific
Grove

MONTEREY
PENINSULA

Fairgrounds
Airport

Monterey

68

Laguna
Seca
Recreational
Area

Toro
Regional
Park

SIERRA DE
SALINAS

101

G17

Pebble Beach
Carmel

G16

Carmel River

1

to Big Sur

Gonzales

to San Luis Obispo

to San Mateo Coast

MILES
0   5   10
KILOMETERS
0   5   10   15

BIG SUR COAST

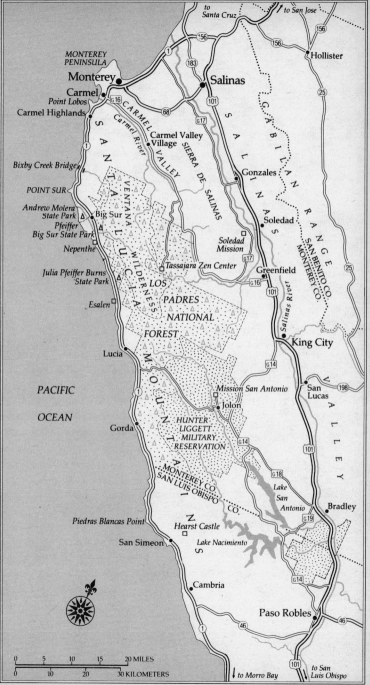

MONTEREY
PENINSULA

Monterey
Carmel
Point Lobos
Carmel Highlands

Bixby Creek Bridge

POINT SUR

Andrew Molera
State Park
Pfeiffer
Big Sur State Park

Nepenthe

Julia Pfeiffer Burns
State Park

Esalen

Lucia

PACIFIC

OCEAN

Gorda

to
Santa Cruz

to San Jose

Hollister

Salinas

Carmel Valley
Village

Carmel River

SANTA LUCIA MOUNTAINS

VENTANA WILDERNESS

LOS
PADRES
NATIONAL
FOREST

Big Sur

Tassajara Zen Center

Gonzales

Soledad

Soledad
Mission

Greenfield

SIERRA DE SALINAS

CARMEL VALLEY

SALINAS VALLEY

GABILAN RANGE

SAN BENITO CO.
MONTEREY CO.

Salinas River

King City

San
Lucas

Mission San Antonio

Jolon

HUNTER
LIGGETT
MILITARY
RESERVATION

MONTEREY CO.
SAN LUIS OBISPO
CO.

Piedras Blancas Point

Hearst Castle

San Simeon

Lake Nacimiento

Cambria

Lake
San
Antonio

Bradley

VALLEY

Paso Robles

PACIFIC

OCEAN

to Morro Bay

to San
Luis Obispo

| 0 | 5 | 10 | 15 | 20 MILES |

| 0 | 10 | 20 | 30 KILOMETERS |

MONTEREY PENINSULA

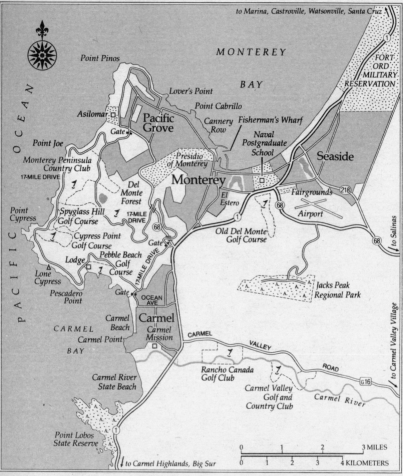

to Marina, Castroville, Watsonville, Santa Cruz

FORT
ORD
MILITARY
RESERVATION

MONTEREY

BAY

Point Pinos

Lover's Point

Point Cabrillo

Cannery
Row

Fisherman's Wharf

Asilomar

Pacific
Grove

Gate

Naval
Postgraduate
School

Seaside

Point Joe

Presidio
of Monterey

Monterey Peninsula
Country Club

Del
Monte
Forest

Monterey

17-MILE DRIVE

El
Estero

Fairgrounds

218

Point
Cypress

Spyglass Hill
Golf Course

17-MILE
DRIVE

68

Airport

to Salinas

Cypress Point
Golf Course

Old Del Monte
Golf Course

68

Lone
Cypress

Lodge

Pebble Beach
Golf Course

Gate

Jacks Peak
Regional Park

Pescadero
Point

Gate

OCEAN
AVE

to Carmel Valley Village

Carmel
Beach

Carmel

CARMEL

Carmel
Mission

CARMEL

VALLEY

Carmel Point

BAY

Rancho Canada
Golf Club

ROAD

G16

Carmel River
State Beach

Carmel Valley
Golf and
Country Club

Carmel River

Point Lobos
State Reserve

1

to Carmel Highlands, Big Sur

0   1   2   3 MILES

0   1   2   3   4 KILOMETERS

MONTEREY

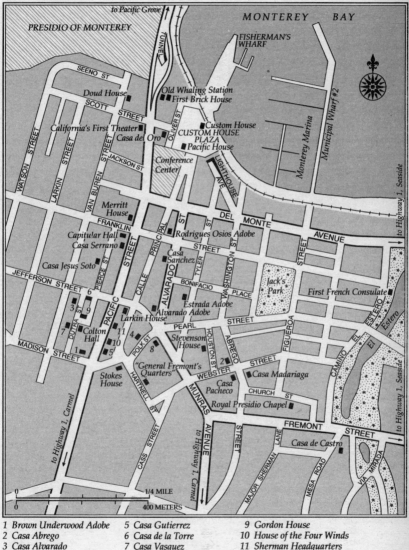

1 Brown Underwood Adobe
2 Casa Abrego
3 Casa Alvarado
4 Casa Amesti
5 Casa Gutierrez
6 Casa de la Torre
7 Casa Vasquez
8 Cooper Molera Adobe
9 Gordon House
10 House of the Four Winds
11 Sherman Headquarters

CARMEL

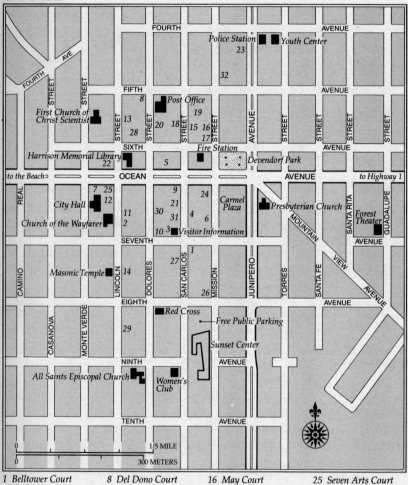

FOURTH AVENUE
Police Station
23 Youth Center
32

FIFTH
8 Post Office
First Church of Christ Scientist
13 19
28 20 18 15 16
17

SIXTH
Harrison Memorial Library
22 5
Fire Station
Devendorf Park

to the Beach → OCEAN AVENUE to Highway 1

7 25 9 24
City Hall 12 21 Carmel Plaza
11 30 4 Presbyterian Church
Church of the Wayfarer 2 31 6 Forest Theater
10 3 Visitor Information

SEVENTH
1
Masonic Temple 14 27
26

EIGHTH AVENUE
Red Cross
29 Free Public Parking
Sunset Center

NINTH AVENUE
All Saints Episcopal Church
Women's Club

TENTH AVENUE

0 ——— 1/5 MILE
0 ——— 300 METERS

Streets: FOURTH AVE, FOURTH STREET, STREET, CAMINO, REAL, CASANOVA, MONTE VERDE, LINCOLN, DOLORES, SAN CARLOS, MISSION, JUNIPERO, TORRES, SANTA FE, MOUNTAIN VIEW, SANTA RITA, GUADALUPE

 *Part I*

San Mateo Coast, Santa Cruz, and Inland Monterey County

CHAPTER 1:

San Mateo Coastside

HIGHLIGHTS

The 55-mile Pacific shore of San Mateo County is often called Coastside to distinguish it from the heavily urban Bayside on San Francisco Bay.* Not merely by contrast, Coastside *is* a rural area and occasionally looks quite desolate: there are dangerous places where the sea bullies the land, and the land slides into the ocean;

---

* The Bayside suburbs comprise "the Peninsula." Curiously, San Francisco, which is at the tip of the Peninsula, is not included in the term. But that is typical of San Francisco—to designate a potential rival with something like a diminutive. Even the Spanish did this, calling the mainland to the east *contra costa,* "the coast opposite" our metropolis. One of the East Bay counties is Contra Costa County.

vast stretches of blufftop agriculture without trace of habitation; waterless hills and densely forested valleys of the Santa Cruz Mountains (part of the Coastal Range). Yet only 5, 10, 15 miles away from wilderness and coastal shelf are the 4.5 million people of two of the largest metropolitan areas in the United States.

Thus Coastside is a close, convenient place to be alone. Besides 10 scattered units of the San Mateo County State Beach, Coastside includes a dozen other coastal accesses, several redwood parks, a few towns (two with an interesting Portuguese background), a sprinkle of restaurants and art galleries.

There are places to watch the gray whales go by in the winter; reserves where you can investigate tide pools and list shorebirds; a dune area where both elephant seals and people congregate in herds; beaches for various purposes, including pebble hunting, hang gliding, and shedding all clothes; fields of flowers, both wild and cultivated for vases; the nation's second tallest lighthouse; and opportunities to see what one of the world's great faults, the San Andreas, can do to the land.

WHAT TO SEE AND DO

An interesting way to begin a coastal tour is in San Francisco. From the Golden Gate Bridge toll-plaza vista point, take Lincoln Boulevard southwest through one of the most scenic military posts existing, the Presidio of San Francisco, then El Camino del Mar through the exclusive Seacliff neighborhood and into Lincoln Park. From there, in front of the Palace of the Legion of Honor, take the park drive out to Clement Street, turn right and go several blocks, joining up with Point Lobos Avenue in the vicinity of the Cliff House, which overlooks Seal Rocks with their barking sea lions. Now turn directly south, following the Great Highway along the western edge of San Francisco, along Ocean Beach, past Golden Gate Park (at this end you can see the restored Murphy Windmill and the interesting Beach Chalet), along the edge of the Sunset district to the San Francisco Zoo. At the zoo the Great Highway joins Skyline Boulevard (Highway 35), which goes between the Fort Funston dunes and Lake Merced before it leaves San Francisco behind.

From Golden Gate Bridge to the city limit, all the shoreland (except for parts of Seacliff) is part of the **Golden Gate National Recreation Area** (GGNRA), established in 1972. This 100,000-acre federal park is extremely linear, beginning 30 miles north at Point Reyes. We mention it here because of legislation, not yet implemented, that could extend it south to include 23,000 acres of the San Mateo Coast. Information: GGNRA, Fort Mason, San Francisco 94123; (415) 556-0560.

Skyline Boulevard*** is worth a trip if you're a resident or a second-time visitor. While the northern end is urban, and the central section partly overlaps the beautiful **Junipero Serra Freeway** (Interstate 280), from Highway 92 south it's a winding, very scenic excursion road along the crest of the Peninsula's hills. It terminates at Highway 17, the road between Los Gatos and Santa Cruz—either one a destination for a good day-trip. There are lots of redwoods along the road, and turnoffs to several state and county parks where you can picnic.

But we'd encourage first-time visitors to this area to take the coastal road south. So take Skyline only as far as the junction with Highway 1.

Thornton State Beach

South of San Francisco is The City's closest, least interesting suburb, **Daly City.** This was John Daly's dairy ranch until the 1906 earthquake and fire. San Francisco refugees put up cottages on small lots. **Thornton State Beach*** is for picnicking, kite flying and hang gliding (it's windy here), and hiking on the **George R. Stewart Nature Trail,** named for the California historian. There is some discreet "environmental camping": walk in and take care. Information: (415) 755-5255.

Thornton is the first unit of the **San Mateo County State Beach**** system. Swimming at this beach and others is not recommended because of undesirable water conditions—undertow and frigid temperatures, crosscurrents and "sneaker waves"—and the absence of lifeguards. In any case, summer fog lasts until mid-morning and returns in the afternoon. In short, these are windbreaker and headscarf beaches, useful for a variety of interesting purposes but not watersports. (Surfers with wetsuits are the occasional exceptions.) Parking charges apply at the most popular units (Francis, San Gregorio, Pomponio). Information: 95 Kelly Ave.,

Half Moon Bay 94019; (415) 726-6238.

At Northridge Avenue (a loop road) you can get to both small Northridge City Park, a playground overlooking the sea, and **Daisaku Ikeda Trail.**** This steep half-mile trail down Wildman's Gulch, with a midway vista point, has been extensively planted with Monterey cypress and pine by the Buddhists of the Nicheren Shoshu Academy. At the bottom you can walk along the beach a mile north to Thornton and a mile south to Mussel Rock. One hundred and fifty feet up the cliff are the remains of an old section of Highway 1, abandoned after the 1957 Daly City earthquake caused slippage and washouts.

Jutting out from the beach, **Mussel Rock*** is a sea stack composed of greenstone basalt. Low-tide access is only for the foolhardy. A park being developed on landfill here will no doubt beautify the area. Just south, through another set of sea stacks, a tunnel was bored to accommodate a stage road; because of earth slippage it was never used.

San Andreas Fault

We've mentioned two earthquakes and several instances of earth movement. That's because you're standing in the **San Andreas Fault Zone.** The fault comes ashore south of Mussel Rock and shoots south through San Mateo, Santa Clara, and onward. This was near the epicenter of the 5.3 magnitude quake in 1957, the last Bay Area temblor to cause any significant damage. A V-shaped cut in the cliff at the end of Westline Drive (off Palmetto Drive) marks the fault line. Note the landfill and the tract homes; man triumphs over nature.

The San Andreas is a strike-slip fracture in the earth's crust. The 20-mile-deep, 600-mile-long fault separates the Pacific Plate (south of Mussel Rock) from the North American Plate (north, including San Francisco). Locally, the Salinian Block (Point Arena to Santa Barbara) tends to move both north and vertically. These giant plates have been slipping along the fault for millions of years, at the rate of about two inches a year. The slipping has created what geologists and botanists have termed "islands in time": rock and vegetation on one side of the fault may not match that on the other side. Studies at Pigeon Point (see p. 15) indicate that the rocks there originated near Acapulco on Mexico's west coast, 2,000 miles away. Anaheim and Marin will merge in only another 20 million years.

Northern Californians can see the most dramatic impact of the fault in two places. In Marin County, Tomales Bay, a flooded rift valley 16 miles long and thin as a knife, nearly cuts Point Reyes peninsula from the continent; nearby Olema was the epicenter of the 1906 quake. And southeast of here, alongside Interstate 280, the rift is again filled with water, Upper and Lower Crystal Springs and San Andreas Lake. (The fault was named for the lake; the lake, in 1774, for Scotland's St. Andrew.)

Further along in this tour, when you're near Portola and other redwood parks, you can take an earthquake walk. At Los Trancos Open Space Preserve, Page Mill Road a mile east of Skyline Boulevard, the 13-stop self-guided **San Andreas Fault Trail** loops around slips and sag ponds. When you get to San Juan Bautista, in Chapter 4, you'll see the fault again.

Continuing down the coast, veer off Skyline onto Highway 1 into **Pacifica,** a collection of former villages (Pacific Manor, Edgemar, Sharp Park, Vallemar, Rockaway Beach, Pedro Point, and Linda Mar) incorporated rather uneasily into a city. Several of the villages began as stops on the Ocean Shore Railroad (1898–1920), an ill-fated venture through earthquake country. Vallemar railroad station is now a restaurant; another station is a private house.

Paloma Avenue will take you to Beach Boulevard and **Sharp Park State Beach,*** a strand with a 1,300-foot pier that is very popular with fishermen; crab, Pacific salmon, halibut, and striped sea bass are the catches in season (local information from the bait shop at the land end). Open 5 A.M. to 9 P.M. during Daylight Savings Time. At the ocean end you may be able to see a gray whale cruise by January to March; they're drawn close to shore by the extra food in the vicinity of a sewage outfall beyond the pier. Advanced surfers try the waves here.

Sweeney Ridge

Up above Pacifica is **Sweeney Ridge,** a 1,063-acre open space that includes the **San Francisco Bay Discovery Site.**** Here, on a ridge of Montara Mountain some 1,100 feet above the water, Gaspar de Portolá and his men stood on November 4, 1769, and saw the big blue harbor and narrow Golden Gate entrance that numerous voyagers for 200 years had completely missed. (Chapter 5 recounts the similar difficulty explorers had finding Monterey Bay.) "We once more came to climb an extremely high hill," wrote Miguel Costanso, "and shortly descried from the height a large arm of the sea, or extremely large estuary, which . . . may be four or five leagues in width. . . . About a league and a half or two leagues from where we were, some mountains were made out that seemed to make an opening. . . ." The trailhead, at the end of Fassler Avenue, may be marked for restricted access for Sweeney Ridge is still in the process of being added to the Golden Gate National Recreation Area. (Congress voted to acquire the land, President Carter signed the bill, but President Reagan's Interior Department refused to go through with the purchase.) Ring Pacifica City Hall, (415) 877-8650, if a trail permit is necessary. **Sweeney Ridge Skyline Preserve** at the north end is a small park, formerly a Coast Guard radio station; it's accessible via Skyline College, off Highway 35.

East off the highway near **San Pedro Beach** (good for beginning surfers, okay for swimmers), Linda Mar Boulevard goes up to two points of interest. The **Sanchez Adobe** ** is a two-story, verandahed house, the only one of the period either in San Francisco or on the Peninsula that is open to the public. Set in a five-acre garden, the museum-house was built in 1842–46 and owned until 1862 by Francisco Sanchez, *alcalde* (mayor) of San Francisco and captain of the port. Open, free, Wed.-Sun. 10-12, 1-4. Information: (415) 359-1881. Sanchez's backyard was the 9,000-acre Rancho San Pedro, part of which is now **San Pedro Valley County Park*** further up the road. A 2.5-mile loop trail goes up the creeks (where steelhead spawn) into grassy hillside meadows with views of the ocean and local peaks (San Pedro, 1,050 ft., and Montara, 1,898 ft.). Portolá camped in the canyon. Archaeologists have searched the area for both an Indian village and an outpost of the Mission Dolores. Park information: (415) 355-8289.

Devil's Slide

Highway 1 now leaves Pacifica behind. It may also leave itself behind, for this is the **Devil's Slide** area, a beautiful, notorious three-mile stretch of slipping cliff; the highway is 400 feet up—at the moment. Devil's Slide has been the scene of horrific accidents, murders, and so much other mayhem that a local occultist believes it is the Bay Area Trapezoid, not unlike the Bermuda Triangle.* Caltrans engineers may also believe the Devil is at work here, and are planning either a mammoth moving job (pushing three million cubic yards into the sea) or an expensive bypass.

Down below are **Edun Cove** (clothing optional) and **Gray Whale State Beach,** accessible by private stairway and trail. Be careful crossing the highway from the parking area.

Past Devil's Slide and down on the shore, **Montara State Beach** is long and sandy but the water is treacherous. Just south, in a Victorian house at the base of the old, squat **Montara Lighthouse,** is a 30-room hostel (see Part IV). Next door is the three-mile stretch of eroded limestone shelf prized for its marine life, the **James W. Fitzgerald Marine Reserve,*** otherwise called Moss Beach. If you've never witnessed the activity in a tide pool, here's the place to do it, certainly at low tide (check the papers ahead of time). A naturalist on duty daily till 5 P.M. occasionally leads tide-pool walks. Seashore life displays, trails, picnicking. No specimen collecting; don't harass the anemones. Parking is at the end of California Street. Information: (415) 728-3584.

The reserve ends at a hook of land, **Pillar Point,** where the breakwater has created a recreational boat harbor snuggled into the north end of Half Moon Bay. **Johnson Pier,** 500 feet, offers pier fishing for rockfish while party boats go out for deep-sea fishing and gray-whale watching. Information: Pillar Point Fishing Trips, P.O. Box 658, Half Moon Bay 94019; (415) 728-3377. Launch or moor your boat or park your RV here, if you have either. Information: (415) 726-4723. The town on the harbor is small but interesting **Princeton-by-the-Sea,*** which has a couple of good restaurants and a fresh-fish market.

* The Spanish bestowed "Diablo" on a number of places but the Americans have scattered "Devil" prodigally in California, with 150 to 200 occurrences. Erwin Gudde, the state's place-name authority, wrote that "probably no other state can equal this number. We have not only many forbidding places in mountains and forests where he [the Devil] might abide, but also an assortment of weird formations of basalt, sandstone, and lava, as well as numerous evil-smelling pools and wells." The names range from 10 Devil's Gates and 3 Devil's Backbones to a Devil's Half Acre, Devil's Hackle, Devil's Paradeground, Devil's Mush Pot Cave, Devil's Bathtub, and Devil's Inkstand.

Half Moon Bay

Stretched out along the shallow bay's shore, **Half Moon Bay***** is either a small, quiet, very livable town with good recreation and an interesting historical background or it's a farm town, ambitious to be a city, caught in the throes of a classic conservation versus development struggle. Founded in the 1860s by Portuguese and Italian farmers and fishermen (some of whom hauled whales ashore at Pillar Point), the settlement was first called Spanishtown. An early attempt by the Ocean Shore Railroad ("It Reaches the Beaches") to bring holidaymakers and commuters failed because of the 1906 earthquake and continual slippage of the roadbed. So Half Moon Bay remained a distant farming community. Brussels sprouts, squash, pumpkins, cut flowers all grew so well in the coastal fog that half the county's agricultural income came from Half Moon Bay.

But by the 1960s urbanization had arrived. Seven thousand residents (half the Coastside population) and city visitors were pressing in on the farms within city limits: some 1,600 acres along six miles of coastal shelf. Farmers tried to cope with trespassers and vandals, restrictions on pesticide use, rising taxes. Many wanted to cash in and retire; Westinghouse bought a lot of the land and drew blueprints for tract houses, planting some among the sprouts.

But after 1972, when Californians approved the Coastal Act, the trend went the other way: conservation was closing in on the city. Empowered to protect open space and prime agricultural land, the Coastal Commission denied permit after permit. The farmers (and developers) countered with sob stories that made the city papers: An elderly ailing farming couple couldn't farm and couldn't sell. A 14-acre farm made only $2.62 profit. A 21-acre farm had volunteer labor for 12 years and still couldn't earn a dollar. The town, wanting to be a real city, proposed to triple its population. That would mean widening Highway 92 (the main access to Bayside San Mateo), bypassing Devil's Slide, building sewage facilities, importing more water.

Half Moon Bay was united. But the Coast Commission had the backing of conservation groups and Californians who already lived in areas too thickly developed. After a nine-year fight the issue seemed to be reaching a head in early 1982 when the Commission would vote for houses or farms. But it knocked down the city's plans and sent its own staff back to draw up a compromise plan, perhaps featuring five-pumpkin houses or condos cantilevered over the squash. You can tune in to the latest developments when you visit.

It *is* a place to visit. The cut-flower fields are photogenic, the acres under greenhouses impressive, the town dotted with interesting buildings. Among the latter are several buildings on Main Street; the Victorian Gothic **Community Methodist Church,** Johnson and Miramontes; and the turn-of-the-century **San Benito House** inn and restaurant, Main and Mill. **Spanishtown,** 501 San Mateo Rd., has 16 shops and galleries. The **Pilarcitos Cemetery,** first occupied in 1820, and the adjacent **IOOF Cemetery** give an idea of the early Coastside population.

Three Events

For a small town Half Moon Bay has three real crowd-attracting events. First is the **Pumpkin Festival,**** a mid-October weekend affair attracting up to 200,000 people to carve jack-o'-lanterns, eat pumpkin ice cream, handpick pumpkins in the fields, and judge which is the fairest pumpkin of them all. Half Moon Bay vies with Manteca as pumpkin capital of California, and both look askance at Circleville, Ohio, which claims the world title. Using secret formulas, farmers get the vegetables up to nearly 500 pounds.

The July Fourth weekend sees the **Coastside County Fair,** rodeo and livestock and produce displays. The big event in old Spanishtown is the **Chamarita,*** formally the Holy Ghost and Pentecost Festival, held seven weeks after Easter. The festival includes a traditional crowning and a free barbecue. The fiesta supposedly originated in the Azores when a foreign ship loaded with food miraculously docked at an island whose inhabitants were starving. The captain, refusing money, gave away the food.

Half Moon Bay has several fine beaches. **Dunes Beach,**** big and sandy, is good for families, **Francis Beach*** for picnickers and campers (full facilities), **Dunes** and **Venice** beaches for horseback riding through the surf and along the bluffs. Local stables are Friendly Acres, (415) 726-9871, and Sea Horse Ranch, (415) 726-2362; reservations advised. You can walk on continuous beach at low tide for three miles from Pillar Point to Miramontes Point.

Half Moon State Beach information: (415) 726-6238.

An interesting local institution is the **Bach Dancing and Dynamite Society,** 311 Mirada Rd., on the Miramar beachfront. This nonprofit group offers a series of Sunday afternoon jazz, classical, and international music concerts. Information: Box 302, El Granada 94108; (415) 726-4143.

At Half Moon Bay is the turnoff for the main connector to Bayside, **Highway 92.** This scenic road goes east over the hills of San Francisco's watershed (property of the city) and between **Lower and Upper Crystal Springs,** the city's two big reservoirs. These are mainly fed by a giant pipeline from a drowned valley named Hetch-Hetchy in Yosemite National Park. The **Pulgas Water Temple**** on La Cañada Road south of the junction of 92 and I-280, is a Greco-Roman temple built over the pipeline terminus, where the Sierra water rushes through.

The coast south of Half Moon Bay now becomes wild and beautiful. It's sparsely settled and there aren't any public beaches until San Gregorio. Landowners ignore innocent explorers in a couple of places. More shoreline will open up at Purisima Ranch, and connectors are planned between San Gregorio, Pomponio, and Pescadero Beaches. **Martin's Beach** at Lobitos is a private fishing cove at the mouth of Tunitas Creek; this is as far as the Ocean Shore Railroad got. You can surfcast for smelt April through November. A left turn on Tunitas Creek Road takes you to Skyline Boulevard and a couple of undeveloped redwood parks, Huddart and Wunderlich.

Three Redwood Parks

South of Tunitas, look for an inland turnoff into **Stage Road,** a parallel country lane through sweet farmland to Pescadero. The next turnoff, at San Gregorio, is **Highway 84,** or La Honda Road, which leads east to three developed redwood parks. First along, on Pescadero Road just south of 84, is **Sam McDonald County Park.**** The 850-acre park came to the public courtesy of a Stanford University janitor. Included is 37-acre **Heritage Grove***** of virgin redwoods. **Ridge Trail**** loops four miles to ocean views and back. **Towne Trail*** goes 1.5 miles to a Sierra Club hiker's hut (small fee; reservations 415/327-8111). Park entry is free. Information: (415) 747-0403.

To the southwest along Pescadero Road is the oldest county

park, 325-acre **San Mateo County Memorial Park.**** There's camping (140 spaces) and picnicking. **Homestead Trail***** goes two miles along Pescadero Creek (springtime waterfalls) through the redwoods, alders, azaleas, maples, and huckleberries. Information: (415) 879-0212.

To the east, off Alpine Road (off Pescadero Road), is the 1,700-acre **Portola State Park.**** Ten miles of trail wander through the once-logged redwoods up to the higher forest (Douglas fir, tan and live oak, madrone; undergrowth includes ferns, azaleas, and oxalis) into open chaparral. Most of the park once belonged to a Pony Express rider named Chris Iverson; his cabin still stands along **Iverson Trail.** A nature trail goes to the **Shell Tree,** a true survivor: burned time and again, heartwood gone, it's still alive at the crown. The long **Slate Creek Trail** goes east to the site of old Page Mill. Park has small day-use fee. Information: (415) 948-9098.

The small town way under the trees wishes to stay hidden but we'll mention it anyway. **La Honda** may be remembered as the hangout of author Ken Kesey and the Merry Pranksters. Many privacy seekers of the counterculture are making a last stand here, but there are a couple of crafts shops and woodsy bars; **La Honda Days** in mid-July draws a modest crowd.

Descending to the coast again, you'll come to **San Gregorio,** a very early fishing and hunting resort; century-old San Gregorio House is now private. The town has a delightful but quite functional general store, **Peterson & Alsford's** (1889). It's the market, hardware store, gas station, coffee shop, bar, bookstore, post office, and town hall. The old Petersons and Alsfords have been succeeded as owners by a Stanford MBA and philosophy Ph.D.

San Gregorio State Beach* is a sandy cove below eroded bluffs. Swimming isn't recommended (though there is sometimes a lifeguard in summer). Portolá camped here on his way to San Francisco. Small parking charge. Just north, marked by a white gate and perhaps an orange flag, is a private clothes-optional beach, usually open on weekends.

Next beach along is **Pomponio State Beach,**** one of the most popular because of its photogenic cliffs, marshy lagoon, picnic tables, and firepits. Small parking charge. Pomponio was a mission-converted Indian who converted back and became a bloodthirsty renegade. The noble savage was captured and executed in 1824.

Pescadero Beach, Preserve, Town

Pescadero State Beach,* a mile long but quite rocky, adjoins **Pescadero Marsh Natural Preserve.**** The marsh is a lagoon created by the junction of the Pescadero and Butano Creeks. A 1¼-mile trail through the 400-acre preserve offers very good birdwatching; look for great blue herons, egrets, sandpipers, phalaropes, marsh wrens, marsh hawks, redwing blackbirds, and yellow-throated warblers. Best times are late fall and early spring. Keep to the trail and don't annoy the rangers. Information: (415) 726-6203.

Nearby **Pescadero Road** goes up the creek valley to a nestled town, **Pescadero.**** The name translates either as "fishing place" or "fisherman," but there is no harbor on the shore, the town is inland, and the largely Portuguese population doesn't fish but grows 'chokes, sprouts, and strawflowers (these are arranged on wires and then crisped in ovens for florists everywhere). Pescadero has a New England appearance because of its site, the many white frame houses, and pointy-steepled **Pescadero Community Church** (1868) and **St. Anthony's Church** (1870). Tradition has it that the Coastside shipwreck of the *Columbia* fortuitously yielded a cargo of white paint that was used for decades.

Pescadero has a **Chamarita** dance, parade, crowning, barbecue, and auction. **Williamson's** general store is worth a peek and **Duarte's** a bite.

Stage Road north and Cloverdale Road south are both excellent for bicycling. Cloverdale runs to **Butano State Park,**** a 2,200-acre park with camping (21 car spaces, 19 walk-in) and 20 miles of trails. **Año Nuevo Trail**** takes you to a viewpoint of the coast south to Año Nuevo Island. **Creek Trail*** goes up Little Butano Creek, and you can return on a fire road. The longest loop, okay for bicycles, covers the perimeter on the **Butano** and **Olmo Fire Trails.** The new **Indian Trail** goes a mile to a trail camp. Day-use fee. Information: (415) 879-0173.

At Pescadero Point is one of the more absorbing units of the county beach system, **Pebble Beach.***** The small cove is a natural collector of agates, carnelians, jasper, serpentine, and other colorful varieties from an offshore reef of quartz. The pebbles have been tumbled and polished by the sea, and wet pebbles are truly jewels. Getting down on your knees and elbows for an hour of careful selection or admiration has been popular for the last century. We'd love to say, "Take all you want"—but better toss them back and go away with a memory of an hour well spent.

From Pebble Beach you can walk about a mile south to **Bean Hollow State Beach,** ** exploring tide pools (no collecting of invertebrates), observing harbor seals, identifying coastal wildflowers and grasses. Bean Hollow is so called from the local creek, Arroyo de los Frijoles, which runs into an appropriately named little lagoon, **Lake Lucerne.** The beach is a quiet, sandy bit of shore where, once again, picnicking is safer than swimming.

The next point along has the nation's second tallest lighthouse, **Pigeon Point Lighthouse** (1872). The tower is 115 feet high, 28 feet in diameter at the base, 16¼ feet at the top; the walls are up to 3 feet thick. The point was named for the clipper ship *Carrier Pigeon,* which broke in two here in 1853. The crew made it to shore safely, but the salvage ship *Sea Bird* came to grief nearby, on Año Nuevo Point. Because the cove was used for whaling operations and lumber loading (via aerial cable), many other ships experienced misfortune. Congress finally voted money for a lighthouse in 1869. Bricks were shipped around the Horn and cabled ashore. A steam-operated whistle was succeeded by a Fresnel lens, 9 feet in diameter, with a history of its own. Made in Paris in the 1850s, it was installed at Cape Hatteras, N.C., then removed and buried in the sand at Fort Sumter for protection during the Civil War. Rescued and shipped to Pigeon Point, the 1,008 pieces were reassembled in 1872. Only one more ship went on the rocks in the next 102 years. The light was replaced by an automatic beacon on an outside platform in 1974. The buildings at the base house a youth hostel (see Part IV) and an oyster hatchery. The grounds are open for day visitors.

Año Nuevo State Reserve

There's a fishing access at the mouth of **Gazos Creek,** and at low tide you can walk two miles along the beach. The main attraction is further down the highway, near the Santa Cruz county line. It's **Año Nuevo State Reserve,** *** dune fields on either side of **Año Nuevo Point** that have become a firmly established **elephant-seal rookery** in the last decade. Mating season, mid-December through March, has become a spectacle.

The large, lumbering elephant seal, noted for its drooping proboscis, was in the last century nearly hunted to extinction. When whalers couldn't find whales, they went "elephanting." Each seal has about six inches of blubber that can be flensed (stripped off) and put in a try pot, where it renders into some 150 gallons of fine lubricant, second only to whale oil in quality. The seals were so easy to catch that few were spotted after the 1850s.

In 1907 a group was discovered on Guadalupe Island, off Baja California. As it seemed to be the last herd, a museum expedition killed 14 in order to preserve them for display. The Mexican government protected the survivors, and by 1922 another expedition counted 264 males. Since then the elephant-seal population has roared back. Migrating north they established rookeries in the Coronado Islands near San Diego by 1929, the Channel Islands by 1938, Año Nuevo Island by 1955, the Farallon Islands off San Francisco by 1972. Scientists now estimate a total of 60,000 elephant seals along the western coast.

The seals mated on Año Nuevo Island without much public notice. The males driven away by dominant bulls would come ashore on "Loser's Beach" and make a lot of noise; in those days you could stroll freely among them. Then, in 1975, a cow came to the mainland dunes and gave birth to a pup called Blues. This seemed to be a unique event, but the next year there were 4 pups, the next year 15, then 84, then 97.

The crowds of people multiplied even more dramatically, and park rangers had to restrict open access during the season and set up guided walks. Naturalists now take 20-person groups on a three-mile, 2½-hour walk and explain things. Walks begin at 8:15 A.M. and leave every 15 minutes until 3 P.M.

Reservations are taken beginning October 1 and are booked up rapidly. There are two combinations of transportation and reservations. If you are planning to go by car, reserve a day by calling (415) 879-0227 or -0228 beginning October 1; on the day, get there early enough to line up for a parking space (small charge) and tour (free). There's a standby list for those without reservations; no guarantees. If you want to go by SamTrans bus, call (415) 348-SEAL, receive a reservation form, send it in with your payment; on the day, take a bus at 8:30 or 9:30 A.M. from the Hillsdale shopping center, San Mateo; the round trip takes five hours, with costs for the bus only. The Santa Cruz Metropolitan Transit District has a similar service from Capitola Mall; call (408) 425-8600.

Observing the Elephant Seals

What will you see? To start with, the seals are physically impressive. The bull measures 16 feet and weighs three tons—but monsters are 20 feet and four tons. The season begins when the bulls arrive, in early December. A pecking order determines who gets to have a harem and therefore mate most often. Strong bulls establish their dominance by fighting and driving off weaker bulls and staking out a territory, usually closest to the tideline. Then the cows— a mere 11 feet long and 1,500 to 2,000 pounds—begin coming ashore and are coralled into harems. Beach masters run large harems, lesser bulls small ones. Bachelors prowl the perimeters, eyeing available females and seizing opportunities to mate.

The result is, in a word, bedlam. The bulls charge and fight and mate with deafening bellows and roars and squeals. In this pandemonium, pups from last year's mating are born, mostly in January. The lumbering bulls and cows can move fast but are somewhat careless: about 15 percent of the pups are squashed. The survivors put on 25 pounds a day from mothers' milk and, 24 days after birth, are abruptly weaned, mostly in February. The females then rejoin the fray; no wonder they spend most of their lives pregnant.

The adults leave the beach one by one during March, the juvenile pups by the end of April. The life of the seals in the ocean is mysterious: they appear to swim north, mostly alone, and feed on noncommercial fish before returning to southern rookeries in December. The cycle begins again and the crowds return. Don't miss it, but reservations are as necessary as at Hearst Castle. Incidentally, the dunes are also used by California sea lions and harbor seals.

The rest of the year you can go into the reserve on your own. After a half-mile walk to the beach, there's picnicking, hiking, and birdwatching (five habitats, 60 species of fall migrants, plus the usual pelicans, gulls, cormorants, plovers), surfing (intermediate; the summer waves are popular). No swimming. Small parking charge. Information: (415) 879-0227 or -0228.

Año Nuevo Point was so named by Sebastián Vizcaíno, who

sailed by on New Year's Day, 1603. He actually named what is now **Año Nuevo Island** (closed to the public); in the last 150 years the San Gregorio Fault and erosion have made the old point an island.

PRACTICAL INFORMATION

Getting There, Getting Around

This is a coastal route, so Highway 1 is the logical road, but don't neglect the possibilities of a loop excursion offered by Skyline Boulevard (Highway 35) and such laterals as Highways 84 (Woodside–La Honda) and 92 (Belmont–Half Moon Bay).

SamTrans runs the local bus service, but it's not frequent enough for good sightseeing. Five times a day Mon.-Fri. the 1-A goes between the Daly City BART station, Palisades, Pacifica, Montara, Moss Beach, and Half Moon Bay, serving many beaches. On Saturday the 1-A originates at the Transbay Terminal, San Francisco, but doesn't run on Sunday. The 90-H runs from San Mateo across 92 to Half Moon Bay, going south to Miramontes Point and north to Moss Beach. Information: San Mateo County Transit District, 400 S. El Camino Real, San Mateo 94402; (415) 761-7000 (San Francisco), 871-2200 (north county), 348-8858 (central county), 726-5541 (Coastside). There's an elephant-seal excursion bus; see p. 16.

Light planes can land at Half Moon Bay Airport.

Where to Stay and Eat

Accommodations and restaurants are listed in Part IV under the heading San Mateo Coastside; see also Santa Cruz and Coast and Santa Cruz Mountains.

CHAPTER 2:

Santa Cruz Mountains

HIGHLIGHTS

Like the Big Sur Coast, the Santa Cruz Mountains are two places. The automobile-enclosed traveler may hurry through the mountains on Highways 9 or 17 and observe briefly, "Gee, there sure are a lot of redwoods." But for the many who have established mountain retreats, where they can quietly tend their own gardens and hand-hew an alternative way of living, the mountains and forests offer the possibility of living a sane rural life—though near many urban centers.

The thing for the sensible traveler to do, of course, is not rush through here from the Bay Area to Monterey Peninsula. The back roads are worth exploring for the occasional glimpses of hideaway cabins and the dedicated backwoods folk. And there are destinations, mostly along Highway 9: several redwood state parks, long-established resort towns, covered bridges, a steam excursion train, arts and crafts shops, and lots of outdoors.

WHAT TO SEE AND DO

The coastal redwoods (*Sequoia sempervirens,* different from the Big Trees of the Sierras, *Sequoiadendron giganteum*) begin right outside Santa Cruz: 1,737-acre **Henry Cowell Redwoods State Park***** doesn't have the tallest coastal redwoods, but with a height of 285 feet and girth of 51 feet, **Giant Tree** isn't exactly small. [The world's tallest tree, in Redwood National Park (north of Eureka, CA, and about 55 miles south of the Oregon border) is 367.8 feet, while the "biggest" around, the General Sherman in Sequoia National Park, is 101 feet in girth. For more on redwoods, see our *Across the Golden Gate,* Part III: Redwood Country.] Much of this land along the San Lorenzo River was never logged because two of its original owners, Joseph Warren Welch and Henry Cowell, Sr., outbid the lumbermen for the Rancho Cañada del Rincón in 1867. Welch sold the **Redwood Grove** and 80 additional acres to the county in 1930. In 1954 that land and another 1,500 acres given by the Cowell heirs were transferred to the state.

The day-use entrance, at the northern end of the park off Highway 9, takes you to the **Redwood Grove Trail***** loop, and nearby are picnic facilities. Off Graham Hill Road is a 51-site campground, located in a stand of ponderosa pine. Fishing is good in the San Lorenzo November to February. Fifteen miles of trail serve the semiwilderness south and west of the campground. One takes you to the **Cathedral Redwoods,**** a ring of trees growing from a single base. In the hollow **General Frémont Tree,** then Lieutenant John C. Frémont is said to have slept when the rainy weather kept him from exploring in 1846. When asked to confirm this later, Frémont said, "It is a good story; let it stand." Other trees are named for Grant and Sherman—or their bigger namesakes in the Sierra. **Giant's Top** is so named because you can actually see the top of one of these giants, usually lost in the canopy. For comparison a dawn redwood **(Metasequoia),*** a cousin of the coastal redwood in another genus, has been planted in Cowell Park. Information: Henry Cowell Redwoods State Park, Box P-1, Felton 95018; (408) 335-4598.

Felton

Nearby **Felton**** has a number of things to attract your attention. The most popular is the **Roaring Camp & Big Trees Narrow-Gauge Railroad,*** whose depot is a half-mile along Graham Hill Road from town; (408) 335-4484. A 1912 locomotive, the *Dixiana Shay,* or an older Heisler (both geared), hauls passengers in three open yellow cattle cars and a caboose on a mile-plus excursion up what the proprietors say is the steepest railroad grade in the country, across Indian Creek, through Grizzly Flats and Deer Valley, into Spring Canyon, then up an 8.5 percent grade onto the last remaining corkscrew double trestle in the country, then stops on top of Bear Mountain to let you look around, hike, or have a picnic. The Saturday night Moonlight Steam Train ends up with a barbecue dinner, entertainment, and dancing.

The story behind the name of this short line is that it was the subject of Bret Harte's 1868 story, "The Luck of Roaring Camp." Not likely, for there wasn't any gold to be found in these parts. If there was a "Roaring Camp" here (it hasn't been positively identified in the Sierra foothills) it was probably a lumber camp: in 1842 a Kentuckian named Isaac Graham started one of California's first power saw mills, on Zayante Creek 500 yards north of Roaring Camp Depot. Tall historical tales aside, enjoy the ride with the Japanese, German, French, and American tourists. Open: daily; during the summer, the steam train runs five times daily; Labor Day–April, once during weekdays, three to five times a day weekends and holidays. Closed Christmas. Admission: adult—$6.75, child (3–15)—$4.50. Note: during the week in the off-season, a railway track car, the *Jackrabbit,* may substitute for the steam train. Information: Roaring Camp RR, Felton 95018; (408) 335-4484.

A genuine relic of the last century is Felton's 186-foot **covered bridge,***** said to be the tallest one in the country. Constructed in 1892 of local redwood, the span was superseded in 1938 by a concrete bridge nearby, but townspeople were so fond of the old one that they kept it and hold an annual Bridge Benefit Ball (a pancake breakfast) to raise maintenance funds. It's located across the San Lorenzo River just south of the Graham Hill Road bridge, near Highway 9. (The county has two other covered bridges: one is in Santa Cruz's De Laveaga Park, while the **third covered bridge**** is south of Cowell Redwoods in the town of Paradise Park. The latter, 180 feet long, was put up in 1872 and is the only one still in regular use.)

You will see signs in Felton that there are craftsmen active there. The best place to see what they're making is at the **Felton Guild,**** an ambitious, still-developing complex intended to have working and gallery space for woodworking, woodcarving, stained glass, jewelry, ceramics, photography, typography, printing, and other arts and crafts. The main building has exhibitions and a casual restaurant. It's at 5455 Highway 9, south of the Cowell Redwoods Park entrance; (408) 335-3464. North of Felton, at **Cliff Short Redwood Products and Sculpture,** 7064 Highway 9, is a 21-foot-tall statue called "Universal Man," with a revolving light at night. You can't miss it.

The next town along, **Ben Lomond,** is so named because someone in the 1860s fancied that the mountain to the northwest looked like Scotland's well-known peak. How fitting, therefore, that the local man-made recreational lake is **Loch Lomond** (fishing, picnicking) and across the hills is **Bonny Doon.** Being carried away by all this, one Robert Howden in 1926 built **Weatherly Castle,** a miniature turreted house on the bank of the San Lorenzo River, southwest of the highway on the north side of town. It's open for tours 1-6 weekends and holidays. In the fierce winter storms of January 1982 Love Creek turned into hate, landslides pulled down half a dozen homes and killed as many people. Similarly Aptos Creek in Aptos ripped homes and lives apart. Nature wreaked havoc that winter.

Big Basin Redwoods Park

At the next large collection of summer cottages, fishing-tackle shops, general stores, crafts shops, and gas stations, **Boulder Creek,** turn left off Highway 9 onto Big Basin Way (Highway 236) in order to get to California's oldest state park, **Big Basin Redwoods State Park.*****

The Indians and the Spanish ignored the redwood forests, but the Americans, when they arrived, weren't awed enough to lose much time in exploiting them. In the 1860s and '70s, William Waddell, the first to log the Big Basin area, had a horse tram to haul lumber from his sawmill just outside the park five miles down the Waddell Creek canyon to his ocean wharf, which was located about where the county line is. Nature in the guise of a grizzly ended Waddell's custodianship in 1875, but by that time a couple of dozen sawmills in the Big Basin–San Lorenzo Valley region were cutting upward of 34 million feet of lumber a year.

The forests seemed inexhaustible to all but a handful of people. One of them, a San Jose photographer named Andrew P. Hill, spent a lot of time here before the turn of the century; one logger, perhaps sensing trouble with early-day environmentalists like John Muir, demanded $100 to allow Hill to photograph one tree. In 1900 Hill brought some friends camping in Big Basin and, at the base of Slippery Rock founded the Sempervirens Club to campaign for a Big Basin national park. Congress was reluctant but the state legislature in 1901 created the State Park and Recreation Commission to acquire Big Basin (it was then named California Redwood Park). The first 3,800 acres were purchased for $250,000 in 1902. At the time it was not the oldest state park but it is now; Abraham Lincoln in 1864 had signed a law turning over Yosemite Valley and Mariposa Grove to California as a state preserve, but the state returned Yosemite to the federal government in 1906.

A fire nearly destroyed the new Big Basin park in 1907—and the danger was not over, for the state forester then allowed a timber operator to cut thriving redwoods as "dead and downed" trees left in the wake of the fire. The Sempervirens Club stopped that outrage. Today's Sempervirens Fund (reorganized in 1968) campaigns for more land to be added to both Big Basin, which now totals nearly 13,000 acres in the Waddell Creek watershed, and 1,300-acre Castle Rock State Park to the northeast. The goal is to add enough to Big Basin and Castle Rock to form an "ecological entity," connecting the two by trail. Information: P.O. Box 1141, Los Altos 94022.

Today's Big Basin is the most popular state park in the Santa Cruz Mountains. Much of the activity is on the Opal Creek flatlands at the bottom of Big Basin. The **Nature Lodge*** (1938) there has numerous natural and park history exhibits, including early logging machinery and tools and the Andrew Hill photographs that helped create the park. Nearby is **Redwood Inn*** (ca. 1915), well visited until about 1950; in 1942 the Fred MacMurray–Paulette Goddard movie *The Forest Rangers* was set here. A few steps away is the **Campfire Center,** dating back 50 or 60 years as a hub of activities.

The self-guiding **Redwood Trail,***** beginning at headquarters, is the easiest of the 35 miles of hiking trails in the park, and will take you to such named redwoods as the **Mother Tree,** once thought to be the world's tallest (because redwoods grow so tall and so close together, finding *the* tallest tree wasn't achieved until 1964 in Redwood National Park). Also along the trail are the **Father of the Forest,** the **Animal Tree,** and the **Chimney Tree.** From headquarters the **Opal Creek Trail** goes alongside a creek that is opalescent in hue not because of pollution but because of plant and mineral action. Many of the redwoods through here were fire-scarred in 1907. Near **Commissioners' Grove** the trail connects to one of the oldest trails, **Trail Beautiful,***** which loops by **Sempervirens Falls*** and **Slippery Rock Memorial*** (the rock was a hauling route for tanbark) back to headquarters. A trail along Hihn Hammond Road goes up to **McAbee Mountain Overlook,*** offering a view of the coast. A longer trail goes the five miles to **Berry Creek Falls**** and on to **Golden Galls Cascades** and **Silver Creek Falls.**

Skyline to the Sea Trail

The most ambitious hikers, with several (four) days, can tackle the recently completed **Skyline to the Sea Trail.***** Starting from the trailhead parking lot at rugged **Castle Rock State Park** on Skyline Boulevard (Highway 35), the trail goes half a mile to the trail's high point, **Castle Rock,***** an 80-foot landmark at 3,214 feet above sea level, then winds down through chaparral and knobcone pine groves, mixed forest of madrone, California nutmeg, wax myrtle, and oak, into protected canyons where redwood and Douglas fir thrive, then up one of the last ridges before the drop down to sea level at Highway 1 near Waddell Beach. Six backpacking camps are spotted along the trail (reservations to park headquarters, small fee).

Big Basin also has picnicking, camping (362 sites), fishing, stream wading and splashing, guided walks, campfire programs, and riding (a 15-mile bridle path will eventually form a loop).

There is a store and restaurant. Information: Big Basin Redwoods State Park, Big Basin 95006; (408) 338-6132.

Castle Rock Park, save for the parking lot and trailhead, is mostly undeveloped, as are two others in these mountains: **Fall Creek State Park,** located on the inland side of the mountains between Big Basin and Cowell Redwoods, and the 10,000-acre **Forest of Nisene Marks.** The latter, named for the mother of the donors of the land, is in the Aptos Creek watershed north of Aptos and was heavily lumbered and even clear cut, 1875–1925, but has second-growth redwoods that are about 70 years old and some virgin redwoods that were left standing as "mavericks" because they wouldn't have made good lumber. Trails, including a 6.5-mile loop, meander through the redwoods, oaks, ferns, an old lumber camp, and along an abandoned railroad bed.

There is little of interest on the main highway across the mountains to the Bay Area. In Scotts Valley is an amusement park, (formerly **Santa's,** now **The Village**), where among other things there are refurbished children's rides, a gingerbread house, and a duck that plays the piano. Open: 10- or 11-5 daily in summer and Nov.-Dec.; weekends and holidays rest of year. Admission, not including rides: adult—$1.75, child 4-16—75¢. Plans are for 135 acres, including restaurants, an outdoor amphitheater, crafts square, and shops. Santa will visit at Christmas time.

PRACTICAL INFORMATION

Getting There, Getting Around

If you want to see anything, avoid Highway 17, especially during the rush hour: fully 27 percent of Santa Cruz County's working population commutes to and from jobs outside the county. The principal road up the San Lorenzo Valley, through the mountain resort area, is Highway 9, but even that can be busy. An alternative that goes in the same direction, from Santa Cruz to near Big Basin Park, is charmingly named **Empire Grade,** which goes through the new University of California campus and past Fall Creek Park, up and down Ben Lomond Mountain, and connects to other rural roads into Big Basin. Masochistic backroaders may want to try twisty **Skyline Boulevard–Summit Road–Loma Prieta Road–Summit Road,** along the county line and the top of the Coastal Range all the way to Mt. Madonna, a Santa Clara County park.

The only public transit in the San Lorenzo Valley is the hourly #15 bus of Santa Cruz Metropolitan Transit District, on Highway 17 and Mt. Hermon Bypass Road to Highway 9, thence through Felton to Cowell Redwoods Park, then doubling back up to Ben Lomond and Boulder Creek. From there alternate buses go up Big Basin Way as far as Forest Pool. The Village is served by the #20 bus. Information: (408) 425-8600.

By the way, we don't advise anyone, especially solo females, to hitchhike in the Santa Cruz Mountains.

Where to Stay and Eat

Accommodations (including camping) and restaurants are listed in Part IV under the heading Santa Cruz Mountains; see also Santa Cruz and Coast.

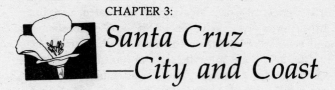

CHAPTER 3:

Santa Cruz
—City and Coast

HIGHLIGHTS

Giant coastal redwoods, a bank of broad beaches, some of the best weather on the Central Coast, a steam-train excursion, a famous roller coaster on the California coast's last boardwalk, fishing wharves, begonias, and tide pools—all that alone would make the Santa Cruz coast and its forested mountains an attractive place to visit. But anyone who visited Santa Cruz before 1965 would now see that since then a revolution, a sociological whirlwind, has swept into the deteriorating retirement community and changed its appearance and character forever, making it a university town and a capital of the counterculture—or whoever the descendants of the 1960s are.

The shaking up of Santa Cruz began in a dignified meeting room of the University of California Regents in 1961: upon the question of where a full-fledged University of California campus for the South Bay–Central Coast area should be located, San Jose was passed up in favor of Santa Cruz. UCSC was established in trailers in mud beneath redwoods on the old Cowell Ranch (some say those were the best years to be there) and has grown to eight Oxford-style undergraduate colleges, with an attendance of 6,100. Half the impact was caused by the burgeoning of a university fringe community. Starting with a few pioneer urban refugees, aging surfers, rural poets, and Ken Kesey's Merry Pranksters (who had moved from La Honda in San Mateo County to Soquel near Santa Cruz), the community grew not in one location but over the whole county. Funky beach rental units, hidden mountain cabins, and, in time, many old Victorian houses became populated by what a consultant to the town fathers and old-timers—who were fighting a rear-guard action—called the "undesirable transient element." Sweatshirts emblazoned with "UTE" promptly appeared, and the mellow population elected a poet to the county board of supervisors on the UTE ticket.

But that was a good sign, for the laid-back folk were obviously settling down. In the hidden redwood glens, down timber trails named Ice Cream Grade and Last Chance Road, people may have handcrafted domes and hexagons and treehouses without electricity or plumbing, but many became commuting suburbanites of a different sort, trekking by VW bus on the steep Highway 17 grade to straight jobs in the Santa Clara Valley. Hitchhikers on the way to Big Sur flooded through, but many stayed to weave, to carve, and to handcraft jewelry and stained glass, ceramics and leather.

The old population and the new (90 percent of the population is under 30 or over 45) have made their peace. The creative energies of the new and the commercial instincts of the old led to the conversion of declining Pacific Avenue into the winding Pacific Avenue Garden Mall: the revived stores, selling all manner of goods, are booming; the old courthouse, now Cooper House shopping gallery, is the scene of public musical performances; and the sidewalks are crowded with students, pensioners, street people, and tourists.

The owners of the Santa Cruz Boardwalk spent $10 million and spruced it up to keep the family crowd and hordes of adolescents on spring vacation. So many Victorian gingerbread houses were lovingly restored and gaily painted that the Chamber of Commerce published a walking-tour booklet (so did Watsonville down Highway 1).

There was also an alliance on the growth issue. The retirees, in their conservatism, and the newcomers, in their appreciation of the redwoods and the shoreline, had similar fears of Santa Cruz becoming a suburb of San Jose if Highway 17 were made a freeway, or becoming a smoggy sprawl if the population kept soaring (between 1970 and 1976 alone the number of people in the county jumped more than 31 percent, from 124,500 to 162,700). Despite complaints that the I've-got-mine elite were now closing and barring the gate, an antigrowth movement cooperated with the State Coastal Commission to halt the subdividing along the north shore and block a convention center in Lighthouse Field, and also discouraged the state from widening Highway 17.

It would take a hardhearted conservative to deny that the UTEs have brought energy to Santa Cruz, but even some newcomers became alarmed at what emerged when rocks were lifted up. Between 1970 and 1973 three different mass murderers killed a total of 24 people. One LSD freak carried out 13 sacrificial murders to keep the San Andreas Fault from cracking; another murdered a family of five as "persons who destroy the natural environment." Magazine articles have since noted that two of these chaps were local kids who, if Santa Cruz had remained asleep, might have found their victims in some other place, like Los Angeles. The owner of a popular gathering place called the Catalyst dismissed any fancy theories: Santa Cruz, he said, "is a benign place, and the dingbats like nice weather just like everybody else."

The traveler need not fear, for the only mystery these days is at the Mystery Spot, a tourist attraction where trees and people and rocks allegedly defy gravity, particularly its tendency to keep things vertical and level. So maybe Santa Cruz is a little out of kilter in certain respects, but to the greater degree it is beautifully eccentric: a large university campus, the antithesis of the Berkeley multiversity, is secluded in the redwood trees; an old-fashioned beach-side amusement park has held its own; the population of craftspeople and rural folk celebrate self-reliance and privacy with community, and small enterprise; and a town has been renewed and revitalized without much blockbusting urban renewal. "ODDS AND ENDS MAKE OUR TOWN EVEN," said the headline in a local paper. The traveler will agree with delight.

WHAT TO SEE AND DO

The southern part of San Mateo Coastside and the northern Santa Cruz coast comprise one of the loneliest, most remote reaches of undeveloped coastline in California. The shoreline is irregular, with pocket beaches below steep cliffs. These are often hidden from travelers on the highway, which passes on top of the coastal benches or ancient beaches that have been raised a step. Santa Cruz's fertile coastal shelf and the creek valleys that drain into the Pacific, together with farms on San Mateo Coastside and the Monterey Bay shore, produce some 95 percent of the nation's Brussels sprouts. Remarkably, only four dozen farmers and 680 acres are responsible for the 60-to-65-million-pound crop. This is actually a small crop. As one farmer in Watsonville says, "If Americans ate sprouts like the British do, California would be up to its ears in Brussels sprouts."

Across the fields are occasional access trails to the shore. **Greyhound Rock** is a state fishing access, popular with rock fishermen, surf netters, and skin divers.

What buzzing metropolitan activity there is along here is in the little inland town of **Swanton,** location of a couple of potteries, and **Davenport,** on the land side of the highway. The latter is actually two places. One is old **Davenport Landing,** which was a whaling station for 20 years from the 1850s. It was Captain John P. Davenport's idea to harpoon whales at sea and tow them to the cove for blubber removal; remains of Davenport's 450-foot-long pier are still visible, and there's reportedly good abalone diving. New Davenport has grown up a mile south, around a coal-powered cement plant.

Just past Davenport is **Bonny Doon Road,*** the first access road to the Santa Cruz Mountains redwood parks and resort area.

Highway 1 curves gently toward the point where the Pacific Ocean may be said to end and **Monterey Bay** begin. The state obtained jurisdiction over the bay waters by convincing the federal government that it was a real bay and not a shallow scallop in the coast.

On Meder Creek about four miles west of Santa Cruz is the **Wilder Ranch,** purchased about 1978 by the state, on the grounds of which (left side of the road for southbound travelers) are the remains of the **Rancho Refugio adobe,** built about 1839 by an interesting early settler, José Antonio Bolcoff, a Russian who deserted his ship in 1815, married into the Castro ranching family, and was *alcalde* of Santa Cruz when the American flag was raised in 1847. Half of the building fell in some time ago; the rest is maintained.

When you cross the Santa Cruz City limits, urbanization suddenly begins.

Santa Cruz

Santa Cruz*** was formerly a distinct city but now forms the western part of a small urban mass with Capitola, Soquel, Aptos, and Rio del Mar. Coming through here in 1769, the Portolá expedition, which was trying to find Monterey Bay, bestowed the name Santa Cruz ("holy cross") on a small arroyo, perhaps Majors Creek, but left no settlers. The local Indians were able to continue their peaceful lives in the balmy climate until 1791, when the **Misión la Exaltación de la Santa Cruz** was founded.

Purposely sited between the Santa Clara and Carmel missions, number 12 in the chain of Franciscan missions, Santa Cruz Mission doesn't exist in its original form any longer. The first structure was moved because it was too close to the San Lorenzo River. The second mission was constructed 1793–94 in the shape of an open square around the **plaza**** at High, Emmet, Mission, and Sylvar Streets. Its heyday was scarcely 20 years. There were problems with the local Californios and in 1834 the mission lands were secularized (read "seized") by the Mexican provincial government. The church itself was weakened in the 1840 earthquake and fell down in the 1857 quake. The third structure was a frame church that lasted until 1889. The fourth and final church, the Gothic Revival **Holy Cross Church*** (1889), built of brick, still stands and was joined in 1931 by a half-size concrete **replica of the 1793–94 mission,*** the grateful gift of a pilgrim to Lourdes. The replica, 126 High St., (408) 426-5686, is open, free, 10-4 daily. Nearby, at 136 School St., is **Casa Adobe** (or **Neary-Hopcroft Adobe**),* the original mission's guardhouse, built about 1810 and, therefore, the oldest building in Santa Cruz. Bus: #1.

Across the San Lorenzo River, which still cuts the city in two, the Spanish in 1797 established the third and last of that regime's civil pueblos, naming it **Villa de Branciforte** in honor of the viceroy of Mexico. The site of the center of that town is marked by a monument on the school grounds at Water Street and Branciforte Avenue. Branciforte's settlers refused to settle down, annoyed the Mission Indians, and spent much time in the livelier pueblo at San Jose. In the end, the town of Santa Cruz, established by the Americans in 1849, grew up around the ruins of the Mission; in 1907 the city annexed Villa de Branciforte as a suburb. (The county, for a few months in 1850, was named Branciforte.)

Santa Cruz was initially a lumber port and manufacturing town but began its long career as a seaside resort in the late nineteenth century, actually being predated in that respect by neighboring Capitola. The big wooden Sea Beach Hotel of 1890 is long gone but the Boardwalk and its old-Fashioned Casino, Natatorium, and Ballroom, the basic structures designed in 1906 by William Henry Weeks (also an active builder at Watsonville), still stand.

The city has established a signposted 29-mile **Tree-Sea Tour*** that goes by most of the major attractions. If you're approaching Santa Cruz from the north along Highway 1, the most direct access to Santa Cruz Beach and Boardwalk is a right turn on Bay Street to Main Beach, but the far prettier access is by way of Natural Bridges State Beach. Just inside the city limits, turn right on Mission and again on Natural Bridges Drive. From the park you can then wind along West Cliff Drive past Lighthouse Point to the Boardwalk.

Natural Bridges

Natural Bridges State Beach** has a photogenic, formerly double-arched sandstone bridge (one arch collapsed in 1980 storms), naturally eroded by wave action; to keep the other from tumbling down any sooner than it eventually will, foot traffic is prohibited. Hikers are encouraged, instead, to use the **Monarch Butterfly Trail,**** if the migrating monarchs are in residence (see Chapter 7 for more on monarchs). At this first of a series of Monterey Bay beaches there's also picnicking, tide-pool watching, and fishing. Swimming isn't safe but surfers find curled waves here. Information: (408) 423-4609. Bus: #3C.

The drive along West Cliff is pleasant despite the rows of so-so houses on the landside. Bikers, joggers, and skaters like the two and a half-mile bike path along here. **Lighthouse Field**** is a pleasant, informal picnicking area, and in the **Light Station*** you can visit the small **Mark Abbott Memorial Museum,** open, free, weekend afternoons. Sea lions are at home daily on **Sea Rock.** Bus: #7.

Around the bend, off **Cowell Beach** and **Steamer Lane,*** you'll see beginning and expert surfers on some of the 6-to-10-foot waves that Monterey Bay is known for in the surfing world; the Western Surfing Association meets regularly here.

Beach and Boardwalk

Santa Cruz's wide, bright, mile-long, soft-sand **Main Beach***** begins at Municipal Wharf and runs along the front of the Boardwalk to the mouth of the San Lorenzo River. Because it is the closest thing to a Southern California beach one can find in Northern California, Santa Cruz Beach is a very popular place, not only for little kids, sunbathers, and surfers but also for swimmers (no lifeguards, however). Half-mile-long **Municipal Wharf**** (1913), roomy enough to allow cars, has picnic tables, rest rooms, facilities for pier fishermen (no license necessary), fish markets, snack stands, and some seafood restaurants; party fishing boats leave from here. The more physical thrills are found, however, on the **Boardwalk,***** whose 1923 **Giant Dipper** roller coaster offers a two-minute ride that some fans rank in the nation's top 10. There are also 23 other rides, including the German-built Jet Star, a log-chute ride, Ferris wheel, bumper cars, the centrifugalizing Super-Go-Round, and the tamer Merry-Go-Round, which has 62 handsomely Looff-carved horses, two Roman chariots, and a 342-pipe organ. The owners of this old-fashioned amusement park aren't letting it get dirty, tacky, or dangerous, and refurbished it and the Coconut Grove for $10 million. It's crowded on weekends. Admission: free; rides are modestly priced, with ticket books selling for $2.50, $4, and $5. Open: daily mid-May to mid-September, weekends and holidays the rest of the year. Information: (408) 426-7433. Bus: #7. Free beach shuttle bus.

While you're on the shore, there's another state beach a mile to the east: **Twin Lakes State Beach*** is so called for the two lagoons, one of them now dredged out to accommodate the **Santa Cruz Yacht Harbor*** (boat mooring and launching ramps), the other a wildfowl refuge; picnickers will like the fire pits, families the presence of lifeguards during the summer. Information: (408) 476-4992. Bus: #6, #67, #68, #7N.

A short walk from Twin Lakes along East Cliff Drive will bring you to the small **Santa Cruz Museum,*** which has collections of seashells and Indian costumes, among other things. It's open, free, 9-5 Mon.-Sat. Bus: #67.

Pacific Garden Mall

Santa Cruz's urban delights are the revived old commercial street, Pacific Avenue, and the old Victorian houses. With an activist named Chuck Abbott pushing, cooperating merchants taxed themselves and hired architect Kermit Darrow and landscape architects Harold Hyde and Roy Rydell to transform an uninteresting, straight, five-block stretch of Pacific Avenue from Water to Cathcart into **Pacific Garden Mall,***** a serpentine roadway (one-way north) with wider sidewalks, lots of street furniture, and lavish paintings (of some 40 species of trees), and equally diverse underplantings. Some of the buildings, drab in any other setting, now have a bit of interest. Two remarkable conversions were of the tan-brick 1894 courthouse (the county government has relocated across the river) into **Cooper House,**** a shopping gallery with a musical mural (one of many in town) and a sidewalk café that is the street's social center; and the People's Bank (1919), now the **ID Building,**** into a combination kitchen store, jewelry shop, and ice-cream shop (which is called the Ice Cream Bank, of course). There's free live entertainment most weekend afternoons at or around the Cooper House. Two generations—one college-age, the other on Social Security—meet along the new mall. The popular Santa Cruz **Spring Fair**—arts, crafts, entertainment, etc.—started on Pacific Mall but got so popular it was moved to a field next to the river. At the **Art Center,** 1001 Center St., you can watch weavers, potters, jewelry makers, clothes designers, and stained-glass workers. The **Art Museum of Santa Cruz,** 224 Church St., is open Tues.-Sun. 12-5 (Thur. to 9 P.M.), and has primitive to contemporary art.

Victorian Architecture

Also making a comeback in the last few years has been Victorian architecture. The old-timers among the residents and visitors may shake their heads with wonder, but a young generation of urban pioneers here, as elsewhere in the country, has taken the architecture of the last century to its heart, delighting in restoring and painting the intricate millwork—barge boards, fishscale shingles, spindles, finials, brackets, columns, pilasters, cornices, balustrades—as well as the ironwork and etched and stained glass.

The city and local preservationists have outlined four 20-minute walking tours (brochure available from the Chamber of Commerce or the Public Information Office, City Hall, 809 Center St., Santa Cruz 95060). If you want to take one of the walks but don't have the brochure, here are the routes in brief.

Mission Hill Tour,*** is easy to take if you visit the Santa Cruz Mission. Bus: #3A, #3B, #3C. Route: High, then south on Sylvar, Mission, Green to Chestnut, then double back to Mission, Emmet, and School. Highlights: Mission Santa Cruz site and replica and Holy Cross Church (1889); 109 Sylvar, perhaps the oldest house (1850s) in town; 127 Green, a Victorian Gothic Revival house with some Greek Revival features (ca. 1867); 123 Green, once a Methodist Episcopal Church (1850), moved, converted, and remodeled (1880s); 207 Mission, one of the best Queen Anne–Eastlake mansions (1883–86), with what amounts to a four-story square tower; Mission Plaza, which appears as it did in the 1870s and '80s; the last piece of the old Mission, 130 School St.

Ocean View Tour:* Ocean View Avenue south from Broadway (this area is the only Victorian district east of the river). Bus: #67. Highlights: 407 Ocean View, well-restored Queen Anne–Eastlake cottage; #325 (late 1880s); #317 and #250, twins but the first has been simplified while the second, a Santa Cruz showpiece, has its original carriage house, spacious grounds, wooden Queen Anne fence; #245, a symmetrical house of mixed style from the 1880s.

Beach Hill Tour,* convenient if you're tired of the nearby Boardwalk. Bus: #7. Route: North on Cliff, 3rd to Front, double back to Main, south to Beach. Highlights: Cliff Crest, 407 Cliff; 417 Cliff, an 1899 mixture of Queen Anne and Colonial Revival; 912 3rd Street, originally a beached ship, converted into a boarding house for sailors; Golden Gate Villa or McLaughlin House (1891), 924 3rd, the most noticeable Victorian in Santa Cruz, a shingled Queen Anne structure with a tower whose open column-and-arch third floor has since been enclosed; 80 Front, a rambling building built as a hotel (1867), extended as a house, then remodeled and added to as a large villa (1883), home for a millionaire art collector in the 1890s; 1005 3rd, a nicely painted Stick-Eastlake cottage raised up to make a basement; 311 Main, a Queen Anne remodeled in 1897 as Colonial Revival; La Bahia Hotel, 215 Beach, with a Spanish courtyard.

Laurel Hill Tour,** in an area three blocks west of Pacific Garden Mall. Bus: #3A, #3B, #3C, #7. Route: From Center along New to Washington, Lincoln to Chestnut, Walnut back to Center. Highlights: Calvary Episcopal Church, 532 Center, a wooden Gothic Revival structure of 1864–65, oldest church in Santa Cruz; 619 and 621 Washington, similar in style but not size; 708 Washington, built in 1884 as the German Methodist Church; 412–20 Lincoln, row houses restored by the late Chuck Abbott, the photographer who started PROD in the 1960s to revitalize downtown Santa Cruz; Lindsay Cottage, 219 Walnut, a small Queen Anne (1895) with a big paneled front door, arched portico, and squat, conically roofed round tower.

The standard architectural guide to Northern California discusses several dozen other buildings of note in Santa Cruz. One not included in the walking tours above is a very large Queen Anne at 724 California. The **Records Building,**** Front and Cooper next to Cooper House, is an 1882 octagonal brick building that was, it is said, modeled on the U.S. 1855–56 gold piece; it is now open as the Santa Cruz Historical Museum. The guide fancies that the **Santa Cruz City Hall,**** a 1937–38 WPA project done in Monterey Revival style, looks every inch the ideal small city hall. The **Cummings House,*** Cedar and Sycamore, is a Victorian with odd lines: a hexagon with the front door at one angle, a curved mansard roof, and big porch arches. The **Cedar Street Gallery,** 411 Cedar, is in a small, splendid, 1860s Gothic Revival and displays its paintings and graphics vividly.

There's actually not much open space in Santa Cruz once you leave the shore; like San Francisco, this town put nearly all its greenery in one space, redwooded **De Laveaga Park,** which tourists will want to visit either for a shady picnic or a look at one of the county's three **covered bridges,** this one an 83-foot span (1892) over Branciforte Creek, just off Branciforte Drive. If you're interested in commercial wonders, north of the park at 1953 Branciforte is the **Mystery Spot,** a 150-foot-wide area, discovered in 1940, that has "numerous variations of gravity, perspective, compass, velocity, and height." A guided tour either explains it—or leaves you well mystified. Open: daily 9:30-5. Admission: adult—$2.50, child—free or $1.25. A kitschy Santa Cruz attraction is a life-size wax-figure reproduction of Leonardo's **The Last Supper,** on display (with a 10-minute narration) at the Santa Cruz Art League, 526 Broadway, (408) 426-5787. Open 10-5 daily for any small donation. Bus: #68.

University Campus

The institution that has so radically changed the character of Santa Cruz isn't even visible downtown. The way to the **University of California–Santa Cruz Campus***** is indicated by hitchhiking students and the city's #1 bus (two or four times per hour) up into the hills northwest of town. There, on the 2,000-acre former Cowell Ranch (cattle, limestone quarry), in a setting too beautiful to be real, are striking buildings designed to fit the landscape, which is redwood forest and open coastal pastureland. The site plan for the campus was developed in 1962–63 by John Carl Warnecke and Thomas D. Church. What makes this campus educationally and architecturally different is its organization and design as small, residential, undergraduate colleges in clusters around large, shared facilities. This offers the advantages of collegiate intimacy and availability of university resources. The eight colleges have 400 to 800 students majoring in traditional liberal arts fields; some colleges have special interests, such as environmental, East Asian, women's studies, the performing arts, and Western civilization. Students take courses at their own college and elsewhere on campus. Each college has its own faculty of Fellows, but each professor belongs to a campuswide board of studies in his or her own field. Though the emphasis is on undergraduate education, PhDs are offered in such subjects as astronomy (this campus runs the Lick Observatory on Mt. Hamilton, above San Jose), physics, literature, and the history of consciousness (of which we're ignorant). Tom Lehrer even taught math here, and American musicals, in between Cambridge jaunts.

The eight colleges are scattered here and there along several hilly, forested roads. Entering campus at High Street and Bay Drive, you'll see some of the old **Cowell Ranch buildings:**** the barn is now the 178-seat Barn Theater, the cook house is the police station, and the carriage house is University Extension. Follow Glenn Coolidge Drive past a visitor-information kiosk (self-guided walking-tour maps available) then turn left on Hagar Drive. The student farm is on the left, the playing fields and **Field House** (Callister, Payne & Rosse, 1965) on the right. At the top of the ridge on the right are the first two residential colleges, **Cowell College*** (Wurster, Bernardi & Emmons, 1965), which has a coffeehouse and an art gallery, and **Adlai E. Stevenson College*** (Joseph Esherick & Assoc., 1966–67). Park on the left and walk to the **Redwood Building,**** which houses student activities and the Whole Earth Restaurant; the **Bay Tree Bookstore;** a central **Classroom Building** (Marquis & Stoller, 1972); the **Upper Quarry Amphitheater** (Royston, Hanamoto, Beck & Abey, 1968); **Central Services** (Ernest J. Kump & Assoc., 1965); and the 515,000-volume **McHenry Library**** (John Carl Warnecke, 1968), which has exhibits.

Hagar Drive ends at McLaughlin Drive. Above the latter are **Crown College** (Ernest J. Kump & Assoc., 1967) and **Merrill College** (Campbell & Wong, 1967–68). Merrill houses the Center for South Pacific Studies, and behind the two colleges is **Music East.** Take McLaughlin Drive to the left, passing the **Cowell Student Health Center** (John Funk, 1970) on the left. After the bridge, on the right, are the **Communications Building*** (Spencer, Lee & Busse, 1968) and **Applied Science** (Reid & Tarics, 1971), which houses the Coastal Marine Laboratory and has exhibits on rocks and minerals, sea shells, and earthquakes, including a seismograph. Park on the left and walk to the **Natural Sciences II**** complex (Anshen & Allen, 1965 and 1969), where the Lick Observatory has offices and exhibits, and **Social Sciences,** which houses the nonresidential **College Eight** (opened 1972) and environmental studies. Located in an old rock quarry on the campus is the **Predatory Bird Research Group,** which is dedicated to saving the Peregrine falcon, nearly extinct due to DDT.

McLaughlin Drive ends at Heller Drive. To the right Heller winds around to **Kresge College** (Moore & Turnbull—MLTW, 1966–71); while five of the colleges have residential dormitories and dining halls, Kresge has private apartments with kitchens. Go left on Heller, passing on the right **College Five** (Hugh Stubbins, Jr., 1969–70), which has a coffeehouse and an art gallery, and on the left **Performing Arts** (Ralph Rapson, 1971). Just before Heller leaves the campus at Empire Grade, you'll see the **Student Apartments** (Ratcliff, Slama, Cadwalader, 1971) on the right and **Oakes College** (MBT Associates, 1972) on the left. The **Arboretum** is along Empire Grade; features Southern Hemisphere plants and conifers, and is open 2-4, Wed., Sat., Sun.

Visitor information: at High Street entrance gate and at the Redwood Building; (408) 429-GATE. Bus: #1. Free campus shuttle bus during the academic year.

Though we've taken you here into the lower reaches of the Santa Cruz Mountains, see Chapter 2 for an excursion into the redwoods.

After you leave downtown Santa Cruz, the residential neighborhoods of stucco beach and retirement homes continue through Capitola and on southeast to La Selva Beach. Those communities are squeezed between the beach and the freeway (Highway 1), while north of the freeway, **Soquel** (pronounced So-KELL) and **Aptos** (Spanish version of a local Indian name) are more free to grow into the mountains.

Capitola

Founded in 1876 as a seaside resort, **Capitola**** has wonderful beaches; a community college, **Cabrillo College,** which hosts a music festival in Aptos every August; and such a blossoming begonia industry that the town's big celebration every September is the **National Begonia Festival,** with red, pink, yellow, and white begonia-covered floats and boats on parade down Soquel Creek plus barbecues and fishing derbies (information: Box 501; Capitola 95010). Ironically, the begonia showcase, **Antonelli Brothers' Begonia Gardens,** is located not in Capitola but in Santa Cruz, at

2545 Capitola Ave.; (408) 475-5222. The begonias bloom (without charge for visitors) June-November but are best in August-September. Bus: #69, #70.

Capitola has an attractive **city beach,*** usually good for swimming and especially so when low tides create a saltwater lagoon at the mouth of the creek (divers here go for ling cod, blue rockfish, kelp bass). In the 1870s visitors to "Camp Capitola" tented on the beach, soaking up the rays. Following the curve of the beach is the old turn-of-the-century **Esplanade,** being renewed, and across Soquel Creek **Capitola Wharf,** for fishing. Bus: #56, #58. Free beach shuttle and free bike shuttle, 10-8 summers, from Hill Street. The eastern end of Capitola is consumed by the state—that is, **New Brighton State Beach,**** which offers picnicking both on the 3,200-foot-long beach and 135 feet up on the bluffs. The water here is also gentle enough for family swimming. New Brighton has camping and summertime campfire programs. Information; (408) 475-4850. Bus: #56, #58.

Seacliff, Sunset, and Manresa State Beaches

The most popular Central Coast beach is just down the road in Aptos. **Seacliff State Beach***** has what park officials call the safest ocean swimming in the area off the two-mile-long beach. Fishermen like to drop their lines off the hulk of the World War I cement-hulled supply ship **Palo Alto,** around which perch, sole, flounder, halibut, and other fish swim; surf fishing is possible when there aren't crowds. There's also camping, picnicking, and hiking. Information: (408) 688-3222. The next beach along, **Manresa State Beach,** has no facilities but is used for beach play, surf fishing, and pismo clamming. Bus to Seacliff and Manresa: #54. Santa Cruz County's most southerly beach is 3.5-mile-long **Sunset State Beach,*** 4 miles west of Watsonville. Camping and picnicking can be done among the planted groves of Monterey pine and cypress. Swimming, fishing, pismo clamming are popular below the bluffs. Information: (408) 724-1266.

The area headquarters for all the Pajaro area Coast State Beaches is in Aptos, (408) 688-3241.

Watsonville

As you leave Santa Cruz County on Highway 1, watch for the exit to **Watsonville.**** Like Santa Cruz, Watsonville has so many landmark Victorian houses that a walking-tour brochure has been put together (Chamber of Commerce, 444 Main St., Watsonville 95076). Many of the houses, several schools and hotels, and commercial buildings, and **St. Patrick's Church,** 721 Main Street, were designed by the same man, William Henry Weeks, between 1894 and 1928; he was so prolific and well traveled that by 1915 he had designed 1,000 buildings in California. The best sampling of Victorians is along **Beach Street** (East and West), on **Maple** between Union and Marchant, and out **East Lake Street.** Bus from Santa Cruz: #70 or #71. On East Beach, look for the **IOOF Building** (1893), on the plaza; #124, a small house Eastlake built in 1893 for a banker; #128, a Queen Anne, the first house that Weeks built in Watsonville (1894); #134, one of the last remaining 1870s Italianates; #227, office of the Martinelli apple cider company, founded by an Italian-Swiss in 1868; #261, **William Volck Memorial Museum**** (open Sat. 1-4) of the Pajaro Valley Historical Association, in another Weeks house (1901); #302, a Queen Anne–Colonial Revival house built by Weeks (1900) for the 1906–10 California lieutenant governor; #332, the Bockius House, built for a town notable about 1870, an Italianate well set back in a garden. Three of the prize houses along East Lake Avenue are #723, the **Tuttle Mansion***** (Weeks, 1899), a three-story Queen Anne with corner tower and stone gargoyle rainspout, business offices (open to the public) of the real-estate and development partnership that restored it; #832, an 1867 farmhouse; and #1211 (Weeks, 1898).

The best example of old Spanish California architecture around is located on a hill about three miles northwest of downtown. The **Castro Adobe,**** 184 Old Adobe Road (off Larken Valley Road at Buena Vista Drive), is a large two-story house with a ballroom on the second floor and verandahs on both floors. Don José Joaquin Castro, who came to California with explorer Juan Bautista de Anza's party, built the house sometime in the 1840s on the two-square-league (9,000-acre) Rancho San Andrés. The adobe was tumbling down but has been restored as a private house.

Watsonville, settled in 1852, is the market town for the rich **Pajaro Valley,**** whose principal crops are apples, strawberries, lettuce, flowers, and nursery crops, mushrooms, and Brussels sprouts. Watsonville leads the state in apple production (the tart Newton pippin is the local specialty) and is center of the world's

largest strawberry-growing area. The town has a very large fro-
zen-foods industry. (While we're on the subject of agriculture, the
loganberry originated in Santa Cruz as an accidental hybrid, possibly a cross between a native blackberry and the red Antwerp rasp-
berry). **Acres of Orchids,** 2352 San Juan Road, about 2 miles off
Highway 101, gives tours of its 105 greenhouses, Sat., Sun., 10:30
A.M. and 1:30 P.M.; (408) 728-1747.

North of Watsonville, in what is now Pinto Lake Park, a mem-
ber of Portolá's 1769 expedition made the first recorded **discovery
of the California coastal redwood.** It is to be assumed that the
local Indians, the Zayantes, were keeping the secret to themselves.
Father Crespi, who kept the journal of the expedition, described
the redwoods as "very high trees of a red cedar, not known to us.
They have a very different leaf from cedars, and although the
wood resembles cedar somewhat in color, it is very different and
has not the same odor; moreover the wood of the trees that we have
found is very brittle. In this region there is a great abundance of
these trees and because none of the expedition recognizes them,
they are named redwood [*palo colorado*] for their color."

See Chapter 2 for the redwood parks above Santa Cruz.

PRACTICAL INFORMATION

Getting There, Getting Around

Greyhound and Peerless Stages provide the only public transit to
Santa Cruz County cities. Greyhound operates four or five times a
day on the San Francisco–Palo Alto–Saratoga–Los Gatos–Scotts
Valley–Santa Cruz route and once a day on the San Francisco–San
Jose–Gilroy–Watsonville–Salinas route. Peerless, with several connections to Greyhouse at Oakland and San Jose, operates four
times daily Oakland–Hayward–San Jose–Los Gatos–Santa Cruz.

San Jose Municipal Airport and Monterey Peninsula Airport
are about equidistant from Santa Cruz, with the former having
more commercial flights in and out. Watsonville has an airstrip
from private planes.

The Pacific Coast Bicentennial Bike Route follows Highway 1
into Santa Cruz, then takes city streets and Soquel Drive, Bonita
Drive, and San Andreas Road to the Monterey County line. The

route is on the whole fairly flat all the way to south of Carmel.

Driving here, Highway 1 is most scenic from San Francisco and Monterey. Highway 17, called "Blood Alley" by Santa Cruz residents, causes heartburn and boiled-over radiators from Santa Clara.

Thumbing is pretty common around Santa Cruz but some drivers are pretty creepy folks, as the D.A. will tell you. Luckily, there's The Bus, operated by the Santa Cruz Metropolitan Transit District, with routes up the San Lorenzo Valley and to Watsonville. The fare is only about 25 cents. The system has four "transit centers," the busiest being in Santa Cruz, Pacific Garden Mall at Soquel Avenue, where 25 routes, of 43, originate or terminate. In Capitola the center is at 41st Avenue and Capitola Road; in Aptos at Rancho del Mar; and in Watsonville at Crestview Center. These are linked by the twice-hourly #71 and #72 Watsonville–Santa Cruz bus. Generally speaking, you can get a bus at least every half-hour to most of the places highlighted above in "What to See," where route numbers were indicated. Buses stop running about 7 P.M. except on the #71 and #72 express routes, which stop about 10 P.M., and the #1 UCSC route. That bus to the campus runs every 15 minutes 7-7, then every half-hour until past midnight. Information: SCMTD, 111 Union, Santa Cruz 95060; (408) 425-8600 (in Watsonville, 408/688-8600). The Santa Cruz County phone book Yellow Pages has the SCMTD routes at the front.

Bicycle riding is *very* popular along the Santa Cruz coast. For local routes, send a stamped self-addressed envelope to Bicycle Program, County Governmental Center, 701 Ocean Street, Santa Cruz 95060. Bikes can be rented at **Dutchman,** 3961 Portola/41st, (408) 476-9555, and **Free Wheelin',** 302 Pacific, (408) 425-9278, both in Santa Cruz.

Where to Stay and Eat

Accommodations (including camping and hostels) and restaurants are listed in Part IV under the heading Santa Cruz and Coast; see also Santa Cruz Mountains.

CHAPTER 4:

Monterey Bay Shore and Inland—Steinbeck Country

HIGHLIGHTS

For reasons of topography, friendly Indians, climate, fertile soil, and some very early hype about California (Sebastián Vizcaíno in 1602 raved that Monterey had a "noble harbor . . . the best port that could be desired"), this flat coastal and valley land was ready-made for seafarers, pathfinders, road and railroad builders, missionaries, ranchers and farmers, makers of history, and a great American novelist.

Flat or gently rolling valley farmland that produces an epic bounty, a coastal plain where the rivers empty into Monterey Bay, some oak-dotted parallel ridges whose steepness on the oceanside has caused them to be named Big Sur (some inland crags were styled the Pinnacles), a shore rich in intertidal and marine life, some towns populated by well-to-do lettuce farmers and old and new Hispanic peoples: this is the country that John Steinbeck described in *East of Eden, Of Mice and Men, The Long Valley* (including "The Red Pony"), and other books—while Monterey became the setting of *Tortilla Flat, Cannery Row,* and *Sweet Thursday.*

Much of the first half of California's history dozed in or swirled around or galloped past or was plotted in Monterey and the circumjacent area. Monterey was capital of Alta California under several flags; trading port for furs, hides, tallow, and grain; and presidio and principal pueblo on El Camino Real, the King's Highway that connected the missions. The Franciscan padres established five missions in this region; some of the earliest ranchos—big or enormous parcels—were granted around Monterey. Monterey saw the coming of the first Americans: first a few sailors and merchants by sea, then mountain men like Jedediah Smith and adventurers like Frémont who came by land. There was some rallying and marching of troops, a small battle, and finally the American flag went up in Monterey and the first California constitutional convention was held.

If gold hadn't been discovered, Monterey would have remained important, but the glitter shifted the political, financial, and social centers elsewhere, and in a few years even San Juan Bautista, a principal crossroads, and Salinas, on the new railroad, were more important than Monterey. Meanwhile, the unfenced ranchos with their Spanish black cattle became American farms. The Salinas Valley, the "Salad Bowl of the Nation," and the Monterey Bay Shore are now major growers of lettuce, sugar beets, artichokes, grapes, and other crops worth more than half a billion dollars annually.

When Americans had a chance to think of something other than mining and agriculture, they discovered both a historical heritage in "old Monterey County" (which includes the present San Benito County) and the recreational possibilities of the Monterey Peninsula.

This chapter is about the hinterlands—the Monterey Bay Shore and the Salinas and parallel valleys. Very hot inland but foggy on the coast in the summer (all very good for various fruits and vegetables), this country displays the wonders of American agriculture and has a number of specific destinations: the mission and state historic park at San Juan Bautista, three other missions, Steinbeck's house and Oldenburg's "Hat," boating and fishing reservoirs, a richly populated wetland, and Pinnacles National Monument. Most are convenient to Highway 101, which as El Camino Real is California's oldest thoroughfare.

WHAT TO SEE AND DO

We'll pick up where we left off: on shoreline Highway 1 at the Santa Cruz–Monterey county line.

The concave shoreline of Monterey Bay leaves behind the sandy swimming beaches near Santa Cruz. Monterey County's beaches—**Zmudowski, Moss Landing,** and **Salinas River State Beaches**—are more popular with surf fishermen (perch, net for night smelt) and clam diggers (gaper or horseneck and Washington clams). Rock and jetty fishermen find fishing spots (for jacksmelt, striped bass, and halibut) in and around **Moss Landing,*** a miscellaneous-looking town not incapable of arousing one's interest. Though visually dominated by an awesome PG&E plant (the state's largest fossil-fuel-burning power plant), Moss Landing was to have been one of the state's first supertanker ports—a plan that fell through in 1980. The town is thoroughly oriented toward salt water and has had several maritime careers: it was founded (1865) as a harbor for shipping out wheat, produce, hides, and lumber—until the railroad took the commerce away; then had a brief career (1917–27) as an odoriferous whaling station—until health authorities eventually declared that a public menace; then was home for purse seiners—until the sardines in the bay disappeared in 1945; and now is a commercial fishing harbor (the catch is bigger these days: salmon, tuna, and similar), recreational boating marina, and marine biological station (**Moss Landing Marine Laboratory,** run by a consortium of state university campuses). A school of tackle shops cater to fishermen and clammers, and on Sandholdt Road (off Moss Landing Road) the **American Shellfish Corporation** sells live mussels, oysters, clams, lobsters, and Dungeness crab from its purified saltwater holding tanks. A colony of Vietnamese refugees uses small boats to fish close to shore; their use of gill nets—which results in bird kills—has aroused conservationist wrath. About the only nonnautical activity is in the 23 antique shops, a Mexican imports emporium, and a sort of flea-market shopping center. No decent restaurants, unfortunately.

Elkhorn Slough

Moss Landing is located at the ocean edge of **Elkhorn Slough,**** the second largest coastal wetland system in California and the first "estuarine sanctuary" to be protected. The State Fish and Game Department and the private Nature Conservancy between them own nearly 2,000 of the 2,500 acres that are enormously rich, natural food factories. Some 50 species of fish (including two-thirds of the varieties on the menu at restaurants), 100 waterfowl species (including sandpipers, herons, brown pelicans, and least terns), and 41 land-bird species (including golden eagles), 30 kinds of crabs and shrimp, 38 species of oysters, clams, and mussels, and numerous mammals (including harbor seals, gray foxes, weasels, and muskrats) make their home here all or part of the year.

Ironically, the slough was created only in this century, after 1908, when the Salinas River changed course to enter Monterey Bay some 4.5 miles further south of Moss Landing; subsequent diking and dredging have stabilized the wetland.

An interpretive center and nature trail are contemplated. Meanwhile, access can be gained three ways: through classes at the Marine Lab; on your own via skiff or canoe, which can be launched at Kirby Park, a fishing access four miles off Elkhorn Road in the northeast corner of the slough; and by the Nature Conservancy trail along the eastern edge from Kirby Park. Maps, information from the Conservancy, 156 2nd Street, San Francisco 94105; (415) 777-0541.

Highway 1 bends away from the shore and through prickly-looking fields of **artichokes,** a perennial vegetable of the thistle family that is in season March through September. **Castroville,*** the market town, has a proud banner across the highway: "Artichoke Center of the World." (Actually, Spain has three and a half times the acreage of the United States.) About 85 percent of the nation's artichokes—mostly the green-globe variety—are grown hereabouts; they flourish on these 8,900 acres because of the particular combination of soil and coastal summertime fog. Such roadside stands as **Mr. Artichoke** will sell you choice samples and even send gift packs to artichoke lovers you know. At the **Giant Artichoke*** in Castroville, artichoke fanatics can put together a complete meal: artichoke soup, artichoke salad, steamed artichokes, french-fried artichoke leaves with mayonnaise, topped off by artichoke nut cake.

Castroville has a major junction of roads: Highway 1 will take you into Monterey past nicely situated but esthetically dull **Fort Ord,** with its drab suburbs of **Marina, Seaside,** and **Sand City.** Note all the firing ranges on the dunes west of the road. Highway 183 goes to Salinas and Highway 101. And Highway 156 takes you to San Benito County.

San Juan Bautista

The last first. San Benito, which was formed in 1874 from the inland part of Monterey County, is simply constructed: the Gabilan Range on one side, the Diablo Range on the other, and San Benito River in the middle. Highway 101 dashes through one corner, just bypassing—and thereby preserving—one of the most delightfully preserved historic towns in California, **San Juan Bautista.*****

The quiet, unspoiled, but well-visited town—still almost a village with not quite 1,200 souls—grew up around the old **Mission San Juan Bautista***** (Misión de San Juan Bautista Precursor de Jesucristo), founded on the feast day of St. John the Baptist, June 24, 1797. The present church was begun in 1803 but, when Fray Felipe Arroyo de la Cuesta arrived in 1808, underwent an expansion: naves were built on either side of the altar, creating three aisles on the model of a large cathedral. In 1812, however, the arches through which the naves were reached were bricked up because the church was far too big for the Indian congregation and because of structural instability.

Fray Felipe died in 1833, on the eve of secularization of the mission. The next year, Mission San Juan Bautista lost its quarter of a million acres and the Indians drifted away, but the Mexicans established the judicial and administrative headquarters for the northern half of Alta California in the town, which was then renamed San Juan de Castro because members of that prominent family were prefects of the district. When the Americans came, San Juan (as it is often called nowadays) became an important crossroads stop for several stage lines, including the Butterfield Overland Mail (you can drive 17 miles of the unpaved **Old Stage Road** between here and Salinas). But, like Monterey, San Juan was bypassed when the railroad was built in the 1870s, and went into decline.

Meanwhile, the mission church, though it has never been without a Franciscan priest, fell into disrepair, but when Californians began preserving their heritage in the 1880s, San Juan Bautista was among the first missions to be restored. Unluckily, the 1906 earthquake tumbled the outer walls and there was some unfortunate remodeling.

Today's newly restored church is the largest of the 21 mission churches: 184 feet long, 72 feet wide, and 48 feet high. The naves have been reopened, the walls shored up, the roof retiled, and the photogenic 15-arch arcade of the 200-foot monastery wing (containing museum rooms) renewed. Most of the church furnishings, except for the pews, are original. The altar and the reredos (the ornamental screen behind the altar) were painted in 1818 by Thomas Doak, one of the first Americans to settle in Spanish California. David Gebhard's architectural guide remarks (see p. xv) that the mission's "simple forms," though not architecturally sophisticated, "became one of the major sources of the new Mission Revival of the '90s and early 1900s." The mission is open daily (donation requested); mass weekdays 9 A.M., Sat. 5:30 P.M., Sun. 9, 11 A.M., 1 P.M.

The mission, which still belongs to the Church, is encompassed by the **San Juan Bautista State Historic Park.***** The park, established in 1934, includes most of the buildings around the plaza (the mission is on the northwest side).

The open northeast side of the plaza, on the **San Andreas Fault Scarp,** frames a view of the lush San Juan Valley. On the southwest side the principal historic building is the **Castro House**** (1840–41), built for the most famous Castro in California, José Maria, prefect of the northern district, leader of revolts against two unpopular governors in 1836 and 1843, and commander of the Californio military forces. In 1848 the two-story adobe, with its second-floor verandah, was purchased by the Breens, fortunate survivors of the 1846 Donner Party, and occupied by that family until it became part of the historic park. The adobe has 1870s furnishings, complete with hair wreath and stereoscope.

Next door is the **Plaza Hotel***** built in 1858–59 by a former Louisiana chef, Angelo Zanetta, utilizing the walls of the old 1813–14 military barracks. Restored completely in 1982, at a cost of $1.2 million, it is likewise furnished in the style of the 1870s, when it was the stagecoach stop; a fanned poker hand laid out on a table makes it appear the players will be back in a moment. A period bar-restaurant is planned. A garden and orchard occupy the rest of the block.

On the southeast side of the plaza are the **Plaza Stables**** (1861), built to handle the stage traffic (a buckboard, surrey, chuckwagon, and other vehicles are now displayed inside); the **Zanetta House/Plaza Hall*** (1868), the first floor of which was used by the hotelkeeper and his family while the second was used for dances, political meetings, traveling shows, and similar; the **Blacksmith Shop, Granary, Wash House,** and other buildings, including a **Rapazzini wine-tasting room** (open daily 10-6).

Below the plaza is a portion of the original **El Camino Real,** a grand name for a nine-foot-wide wagon trail; between it and the church is the melancholy burial ground of some 4,300 Indians, none identified. There are several places to sit and picnic.

The park is open daily, 10-5, for a minor charge. Information: (408) 623-4881; the office is in the Castro Adobe.

The San Juan Bautista Chamber of Commerce (37 Mariposa St.; 95045) has published a walking-tour brochure that includes other adobe buildings and several other period structures, mostly along 3rd Street. The four restored adobe structures are the **Juan de Anza Adobe,** Franklin and 3rd; **Theophile Vaché Adobe** and **Tuccoletta Hall,** both at 3rd and Washington; and the **Native Daughters of the Golden West Parlour,** 4th near Washington.

Alfred Hitchcock filmed scenes for *Vertigo* here, and David Belasco's play *Rose of the Rancho* was set here. San Juan is now also the home of the only full-time, permanently housed Chicano theater in the United States, **El Teatro Campesino,** originators of the play and movie *Zoot Suit* (1982). Box office: (408) 623-2444 or -4505.

A winding county road south of San Juan will take you 11 miles to **Fremont Peak State Park,*** on Gabilan (Hawk's) Peak, 3,169 feet. This was the setting of an ambiguous but dramatic incident in the crucial year of 1846, when California was subtly being lost by the Mexicans and gained by the Americans.

The event involved a man who surely wanted to be the hero of an epic poem, John Charles Frémont, an erratic, impetuous, brave, imaginative adventurer who, as the husband of the ambitious Jessie Benton, was son-in-law of a prominent westward expansionist, Missouri Senator Thomas Hart Benton. Historians still debate Frémont's character and motivations: they generally give him credit for his explorations as "The Pathfinder" while often condemning the strange, belligerent role he played in California in 1846. Nonetheless that role helped make him one of California's first two senators and, in 1856, the Republican party's first presidential candidate (he lost to Buchanan by half a million votes).

Frémont, who had accomplished much on an initial exploration in California in 1843–44, returned in late 1845 as topographical engineer in charge of a rugged band of 60 armed "surveyors," Kit Carson among them. Despite an understanding with the Mexican authorities to stay away from the coast, Frémont in February 1846 abruptly left his winter quarters south of San Jose and moved into Monterey County, establishing himself on March 6 on Gabilan Peak in a log fort, over which he undiplomatically raised the U.S. flag. In reaction, General Castro, at San Juan Bautista, raised the Californio militia and brandished threats about ridding the area of this upstart invader, while Frémont replied in kind. But on March 9 Frémont peacefully decamped and, "slowly and growlingly" (his words), marched north to play a firebrand role in the Bear Flag Republic affair in July.

No trace of Frémont's fort remains. The state park takes in 244 acres of scrub oak, manzanita, and grassland that springtime decorates with poppies and lupines. Picnicking, camping (12 sites), a nature trail, and a windy view of Monterey Bay and Salinas Valley. Modest charge to enter the park. Information: (408) 623-4355.

Adjoining Fremont Peak is the **Hollister Hills State Vehicular Recreation Area.** Picnicking, camping (100 sites), hiking trail— and 100 miles of trails for motorbikes only. Information: (408) 637-4881.

South of **Hollister,** the San Benito County seat, at **Tres Pinos,** the famous *bandido* Tiburcio Vásquez committed his last robbery, killing three men, in August 1873. He was brought to bay in southern California, brought to justice in San Jose, and brought to his God March 19, 1895.

Pinnacles National Monument

Thirty-five scorching-summer miles south of Hollister is one of California's eight national monuments, **Pinnacles National Monument,** three square miles of jagged 23.5-million-year-old spires and crags rising from the otherwise rounded Gabilan Range. Because of the slippage of continental plates along the San Andreas Fault, the Pinnacles are 195 miles north of where they once were (near Lancaster in southern California). That same slippage will make the Pinnacles a set of offshore islands in about six million years. Erosion has made something besides the Pinnacles: talus caves, or covered canyons, created when boulders tumbled down and wedged between canyon walls.

This 23-square-mile national monument, one of the first established, in 1908, is primarily for hikers and climbers; those only desiring to get out of their cars won't see much besides chaparral-covered hillsides of the East Pinnacles area from the main (east) entrance off Highways 25 and 146. The West Pinnacles are reached by road (cars only) from Soledad in the Salinas Valley (Highways 101 and 146). There is no connecting road, only trails.

The **High Peaks Trail,*** 5.4 miles (which takes four to five hours to walk), rising 1,300 feet, goes from the East Pinnacles visitors' center 1.8 miles up along the Moses Spring Nature Trail to near the **Bear Gulch Talus Caves,*** then clockwise round by Scout Peak and the Tunnel Trail, and back to park headquarters; you'll walk along narrow ledges and get some panoramic views on this strenuous hike. Also from this side of the Pinnacles you can hike (an eight-to-nine-mile round trip) south by Bear Gulch Reservoir to the fire lookout on North Chalone Peak, 3,305 feet, or take a fairly level trail 3.2 miles north to the second (less exciting) set of talus caves, the **Balconies Caves,** located between the Balconies and Machete Ridge. If you're approaching from the West Pinnacles, the Balconies Caves are closer to the trailhead, and the new **Juniper Canyon Trail** connects to the High Peaks Trail.

You should wear some appropriate clothes for scrambling through the caves and on some of the rocks; a flashlight is also useful. Because of summer heat and winter rain, park rangers advise that spring and autumn visits are best—and weekdays are less crowded down below. There's picnicking and camping. Information: Pinnacles National Monument, Paicines 95043; (408) 389-4578.

Mouth of Salinas Valley

Well, all that is pretty good for such a small county. Now backtrack to Monterey County (unless you're either still there, or at home in your armchair), to the mouth of the **Salinas Valley,**** an alluvial lowland through which flows the **Salinas River,** called the "upside-down river" because it not only flows from south to north but is fed principally from underground sources, not from tributaries . . . and in the summer it flows, for part of its course, only underground.

Between San Juan Bautista and Salinas, a bronze plaque near the intersection of the old stagecoach road, **San Juan Grade,*** and Crazy Horse Road marks the site of the only noteworthy battle of that tumultuous year 1846 that occurred in Northern California: the Battle of Natividad, November 18, 1846. An American recruiting and foraging party led by Captains Charles D. Burrass and Bluford K. Thompson was on its way to Monterey with 500 horses for Frémont's California Battalion (which was involved in some larger set-tos in southern California) when it was intercepted by a Californio force led by General Castro's brother, Manuel de Jesús. There were several casualties on each side, including Burrass and two of his men, who are buried nearby.

Salinas

The roads around here mostly take you to **Salinas,*** an overgrown farm town that was the birthplace and boyhood home of Nobel Prize winning novelist John Steinbeck (1902–1968).

Salinas had a difficult time taking its only famous native son to its bosom. After his first novels, which were pretty much ignored, the good people of Monterey got upset with the "earthiness" of *Tortilla Flat* (1935), then Salinas Valley farmers with the sympathetic portrayal of union organizers and striking migrant workers in *In Dubious Battle* (1936), then farmers and many other folks with the ugly treatment of organized agriculture in *The Grapes of Wrath* (1939), then Monterey again (even the sardine canners) with *Cannery Row* (1945), and then the provincials again with the violence in *East of Eden* (1952). They willingly ignored Stein-beck's obvious fondness for this area in "The Red Pony" (1937), and the sentimentality expressed in other stories in *Tortilla Flat* (1935), *The Long Valley* (1938), *Of Mice and Men* (1937), *The Wayward Bus* (1947), *Sweet Thursday* (1954), and *Travels with Charley* (1962), the emotional climax of which occurs when Stein-beck stands on Fremont Peak overlooking the Salinas Valley. He was disappointed in the hometown reaction—or, worse, silence—and relations were ambivalent even when he was awarded the No-bel Prize for literature in 1962.

Though he complained of "those people out there," he inscribed a copy of his Nobel acceptance speech with "Not everyone has the good fortune to be born in Salinas," and before he died expressed the desire to be buried here ("No man should be buried in alien soil"). Steinbeck's simple gravesite is in the **Garden of Memories,** 768 Abbott.

Since his death, feelings have changed considerably: the Cham-ber of Commerce brochures are all labeled "Steinbeck Country," like a brag, and the public library, renamed for the author in 1969, has a statue of him (slightly smaller than life-size, however). **Steinbeck Library,** 110 West San Luis, holds an annual Steinbeck Festival in August (information: 408/758-7311) and has manu-scripts and memorabilia on display; it managed to raise $75,000 in Salinas to purchase the manuscript of his popular short story "The Pearl." Open Mon.–Thurs. 10–9, Fri.–Sat. 10–6.

Even Salinas lettuce growers contributed substantially to save from demolition the **Steinbeck House,**** 132 Central at Stone (two blocks west of Main St.). That 1897 structure, a wonderful Victorian frame house with 15 rooms and witch's-hat corner tur-ret, was his birthplace and home until he left for Stanford Univer-sity in 1919. Happily preserved by a volunteer organization, the house is operated as a luncheon place (see Part IV); the basement shop, The Best Cellar, features Steinbeck's works. Though re-stored, the house has little memorabilia displayed and at the mo-ment isn't really open for tours. Information: (408) 757-8741.

Salinas, established in 1856, got a railroad station in 1868 and four years later took the county courthouse from Monterey. Small in Steinbeck's youth, Salinas now has a population of 81,000. There are, in the Steinbeck House area, some other Victorians of the 1880s, while downtown, within two or three blocks (around West Alisal and Church), are some good 1930s buildings, among them the **Monterey County Courthouse*** (Robert Stanton, 1937), described by Gebhard's architectural guide as "really a perfect example, inside and outside, of the WPA Moderne style." The numerous allegorical bas-reliefs of Monterey historical figures are by Jo Mora; the interior courtyard is a garden. Two blocks away, at Cayuga and San Luis, is an intricate **Queen Anne mansion.***

A block east, opposite the Steinbeck Library, is a **six-gabled Queen Anne,** 328 Church. At 327 Pajaro near San Luis, the **old Presbyterian Church,*** which figured in *East of Eden,* has been remodeled into a restaurant (open daily, lunch and dinner—see Part IV), named for the novel. Further south, at 238 E. Romie Lane off Pajaro Street, the **Harvey-Baker House**** (1868), a redwood house built for Isaac J. Harvey, first mayor of Salinas, and occupied by his family until 1967, has been restored, with period furnishings, as headquarters of the Monterey County Historical Society. Tours first Sun. of the month, 1-4. Information: (408) 757-8085.

Salinas caught the attention of the art world in 1982 when it unveiled a spectacular Claes Oldenburg sculpture, **Hat in Three Stages of Landing,**** on the long lawn outside the Salinas Community Center, 940 N. Main Street. Three 10-foot-high, 18-foot-in-diameter metal hats are landing at intervals, 20, 15, and 10 feet, respectively; they're held off the ground on slender black posts. The hats were modeled after the straw hats worn by anglos and braceros in the fields, but Oldenburg tilted the brims and added a crease in the crowns, to turn sombrero into Stetson. Salinas commissioned the sculpture in 1978 and raised $56,000 to match a federal grant of $50,000.

Northeast of Salinas, about half a mile from Highway 101 at Boronda and West Laurel, stands, in some solitude, the **José Eusebio Boronda Adobe**** (1844–48), an unaltered one-story rancho home restored by the Historical Society to include a museum; many furnishings are original. The state historic landmark is open, free, Sat.-Sun. 1-4, otherwise by appointment. Information: (408) 757-8085.

Salinas's big event is the **California Rodeo**—the state's largest—in mid-July. Information: Box 1170, Salinas 93902; (408)

424-7611. A new annual event is the **California International Airshow,** held at Salinas Airport on an October weekend.

Salinas Valley: Wine Country

Highway 101 shoots southeast from Salinas with hardly a jog or a stop for anything interesting. Most of the acreage is in lettuce, beans, celery, and carrots, but much (more than 40,000 acres) has now been planted in **wine grapes,** primarily premium varietals. The vineyards are owned by San Martin, Paul Masson, Mirassou, Wente, Monterey Vineyard, and giant Almadén (which is California's largest producer of premium wines). Though this area was long ago put in the same growing category as Napa, Sonoma, Bordeaux, and Burgundy, there wasn't much winery development until urbanization in the Santa Clara Valley pushed out Paul Masson and Mirassou, and dams were built in the Santa Lucia Mountains to hold winter rains for summer use.

The Napa, Sonoma, and Mendocino wine districts draw millions more visitors than the wineries down here. The initiated who collect wine can of course call for appointments at the smaller, quality establishments like Chalone Vineyard. Otherwise there are only three wineries that draw tourists. **Monterey Vineyard,** 800 S. Alta, Gonzales (next to Highway 101, but take the main Gonzales exit), (408) 675-2481, is an operation owned by Coca-Cola that offers a nice tour, nice tasting, and 70 degrees of coolness for 100-degree visitors. Open daily 10-5. **Jekel Vineyard,** 40155 Walnut Ave., Greenfield, (408) 674-5524, is a much smaller operation, offering tours 10-5 Thurs.-Mon. Between Salinas and Monterey off Highway 68, the **Monterey Peninsula Winery,** (408) 372-4949, offers tours 10 A.M. till it's dark.

Local vintages are in the limelight every December at the **California Wine Festival** in Monterey. The three-day Festival, at $250 per person, is for the serious wine drinker, collector, restaurateur, or grower. Information: P.O. Box WINE, Carmel 93921; (408) 64-WINES.

Halfway down the valley is the oldest settlement, **Soledad,** location of the thirteenth of the Franciscan missions but probably faintly familiar to newspaper readers as "home," in the **Soledad Correctional Training Facility,** of the "Soledad Brothers" (George Jackson and others).

The site of **Soledad Mission*** (Misión de María Santisima Nuestra Señora de la Soledad—"Holy Mary, Our Lady of the Solitude") was chosen by Father Serra in 1771 but the mission was not established for another 20 years (on October 9, 1791), helping to close the 78-mile gap between the Carmel and San Antonio missions. It wasn't the most successful of missions. At its peak, in 1805, it was one of the smallest physically and had only 688 Indian neophytes. The 1797 adobe church was badly damaged in a flood in 1828, after which a small chapel was built—just three years before the last padre died and the mission was secularized. Though it was regranted to the Church in 1859, the buildings fell into ruins. When the Native Daughters of the Golden West began restoration in 1954, only a few eroded adobe walls rose above a plowed field. The small chapel and the west wing have both been restored and a garden planted, but little remains of the church besides the graves of a mission father and of José Joaquin de Arrillaga, who as governor from 1800 to 1814 presided over the "golden age" of the missions. The Soledad Mission, a cool spot on a hot Salinas Valley day, is open free Tues.-Sun. 10-4. Picnicking.

Highway 146 from Soledad goes to the West Pinnacles area of Pinnacles National Monument (see p. 53 for more information).

To the south of Soledad is a state landmark, the **Richardson Adobe** at **Los Coches Rancho Wayside Campground.*** Behind a screen of closely planted locust trees, the adobe, dating back to 1843, has been, among other things, a stagecoach station and post office. Frémont camped here twice in 1846–47, and you may, too.

King City, described as the "most metropolitan cow town in the West," frequently figures in Steinbeck's novels, particularly *East of Eden*. Steinbeck's maternal grandparents had a ranch nearby, in Hamilton Canyon, that was probably the model for the Trask property in that novel. Steinbeck's father was the Southern Pacific's first agent in King City and also a milling company superintendent; his uncle was a businessman who was smart enough to turn a harness and saddlery business into a Model-T Ford dealership (he was later a judge).

From this market town, take the county road G14 south to **Jolon** in the San Antonio River or Los Robles ("the oaks") Valley. Although on El Camino Real, connecting San Miguel and San Antonio Missions, Jolon was bypassed by the railroad, later by

Highway 101, but that makes it extra quiet around here.

Northwest of Jolon are two similar-looking historical and architectural attractions. First is **The Hacienda**** a Mission Revival building designed in the early 1900s either as a ranch house or hunting lodge by Julia Morgan for the Hearsts, who owned 164,000 acres hereabouts (remember that Hearst Castle, itself on a large ranch, is just across the Santa Lucia Mountains from here). The federal government bought this holding in 1940 for military purposes. **Fort Hunter Liggett** is mainly used by the Combat Developments Experimentation Command as a field laboratory for testing various high-technology developments for the modern battlefield, with emphasis on antiarmor devices and aircraft operations. Local headquarters is in The Hacienda.

San Antonio Mission

At the end of the road, 24 miles from King City, is the building The Hacienda was modeled on, the **Mission San Antonio de Padua,***** third of the missions founded by Father Serra. Portolá camped on the San Antonio on September 24, 1769, after a strenuous time crossing the Santa Lucia Mountains to the west, then continued north in search of Monterey Bay. After that was finally located and Serra had established the Carmel Mission, in mid-1770, he began the effort to close the gap to San Diego. Coming to this oak-dotted valley the next year, Serra hung a church bell from a tree and rang it loudly, shouting (according to one account), "Hear, O Gentiles! Come! Oh come to the holy Church of God! Come, oh come, and receive the Faith of Christ!" That pealing brought one Indian to the dedication of the mission, on July 14, 1771. More showed up later and the local Indians got on well with the padres. San Antonio had a population of 1,296 at its peak in 1805.

One church was completed in 1772 but another was built 1779–80 at the present site, nearer a dependable source of water. The present structure, built 1810–13 on a sturdy rock foundation, is a simple rectangular church with a pitched tile roof, surmounted by a plain cross, that rises just a bit higher than a more elaborate façade, which has two small bell towers on either side of a stepped gable, in the center of which is an arch and another bell. The three entry arches on the ground floor of the façade are continued in the arcaded wing to the left. There is also an interior patio. Restoration of the mission was begun in 1903, ruined in the 1906 earthquake, and picked up again in 1948 through a grant by the William Randolph Hearst Foundation. In the grounds of the mission, which is now a parish church and Franciscan retreat, are a unique water-powered flour mill (1806), aqueduct, wine vat, tannery, barracks, and rose garden. Open daily 9:30-5 for a small donation. Information: (408) 385-4478.

Rising north of San Antonio Mission is the highest peak of the Central Coastal Range, **Junipero Serra Peak,** 5,862 feet. (Hiking in the Los Padres National Forest is discussed in Chapter 12.)

If you're basically heading south, you can take either G14 or G18 to Highway 101. G14 goes between two artificial lakes, **San Antonio Reservoir** and **Nacimiento Reservoir,** water from which feeds the Salinas Valley. There's picnicking, boating, fishing.

Taking a local road due east of Jolon past the San Antonio Union School, then jogging a bit south, then north, takes you to Pine Canyon Road, which zigzags up 3,000 feet to **La Cueva Pintada** ("the painted cave"), a cave 16 feet high, about 45 feet wide, and 15 to 20 feet deep. The floor has been worn smooth by bare feet and the walls covered with pictographs several centuries old.

If you're on Highway 101 as it crosses the San Luis Obispo County line, you can stop at yet one more mission, **San Miguel Archangel**—but that, arbitrarily, is in Southern California, and you'll have to look at another guidebook.

PRACTICAL INFORMATION

Getting There, Getting Around

Nearly everybody arrives by car, gets around by car, and leaves by car. But dedicated users of public transportation need not surrender completely. For one thing, Amtrak's daily Coast Starlight stops at Salinas on its run from Seattle via Davis (bus from Sacramento), Oakland (bus from San Francisco), and San Jose (connecting SP trains from San Francisco and Peninsula stops), to San Luis Obispo, Santa Barbara, Los Angeles, and San Diego. In addition, there's frequent Greyhound service to Salinas from San Francisco via San Jose and Gilroy and from Los Angeles via Santa Barbara,

San Luis Obispo, San Miguel, King City, and Soledad. Greyhound runs three times a day from Santa Cruz and Watsonville to Salinas, seven or eight times from Pacific Grove and Monterey. For the Monterey Bay Shore, the Santa Cruz–Salinas and San Francisco–Salinas buses stop at Castroville and Moss Landing. San Juan Bautista is served once a day from San Francisco via San Jose, Gilroy, and Hollister, and once a day from Salinas.

Gray Line has a day tour from San Francisco to Santa Cruz and San Juan Bautista.

Monterey-Salinas Transit's #20 Salinas bus runs hourly Mon.-Sat. from downtown Monterey to the Amtrak depot in Salinas. See Chapter 10.

For air service to Monterey Peninsula Airport, see Chapter 10.

Where to Stay and Eat

Accommodations (including camping) and restaurants are discussed in Part IV under the heading Salinas/Inland Monterey County and San Juan Bautista (for restaurants) and all Monterey Peninsula headings.

 *Part II*

Monterey Peninsula –
Monterey, Carmel,
Pebble Beach, and
Pacific Grove

CHAPTER 5:

Monterey Peninsula —An Introduction

Many there are who visit the Monterey Peninsula and are tempted to stay, for they feel they have discovered Lotus Land, a place of palmy days, a voluptuous civilization populated by a happy, not to mention prosperous folk. One would like to take a very long lease on a gracious two-story Monterey adobe, one whose long second-floor balcony looks to be ideal for spending a quiet day composing a sonnet, inspired by a wall of climbing bougainvillea or the eerie far-off boom of Pacific waves on a foggy day. If during timeless days one feels inclined, one can ramble through the Del Monte pine forest to the shore to see what's new at the tide pools. A round of golf at Pebble Beach or tennis in Carmel Valley might be nice tomorrow, but right now a little window-shopping in Carmel and an idle hour over tea and scones seems better. If no one is coming to dinner, a meal at L'Escargot or Chez Felix might be just the thing.

The Monterey Peninsula is indeed one of those places like Palm Springs, West Palm Beach, and the south of France where contemporary ideas of the good life have been consummated. The danger is that one could confuse life in such an elysian place with reality. Well, it isn't impossible to build castles in Spain with capital gains from IBM shares and a fat pension. And cloisters for the rich and the retired can be dandy escape hatches for the rest of us.

The Monterey Peninsula fully deserves the attention (and money) paid by the three to four million visitors it gets each year. The Peninsula, hooking out from the coast opposite Santa Cruz across Monterey Bay, was superbly endowed by nature with a large pine and cypress forest that is mostly intact, a rocky coast that, yard for yard, is about the most photogenic in the world, and beginning here and running south, hills that turn into the rugged Santa Lucia Mountains. The remarkably different communities—Monterey, Carmel, Pacific Grove, Pebble Beach, Carmel Valley, and some lesser-known towns—have made the most of this setting, to the point where, in Carmel, cars have to go around trees in the middle of the road.

The attractions include a visible history unusually long for California (the story takes up most of this chapter), evident in the old Spanish capital, Monterey (Chapter 6); outstanding shopping and strolling in the well-organized small town of Carmel (Chapter 9); the landscaped park that Pacific Grove has created along its section of shore, not to mention the millions of monarch butterflies in residence from November to March (Chapter 7); the famous 17-Mile Drive through the Del Monte Forest and the wealthy Pebble Beach community (Chapter 8); six to a dozen outstanding golf courses, scores of tennis courts, and deep-sea fishing opportunities; annual events such as the Monterey Jazz Festival, Carmel Bach Festival, Bing Crosby golf tournament, Monterey Adobe Tour, Laguna Seca races, and the Concours d'Elegance vintage automobiles show (recreational opportunities are summarized in Chapter 10); commercialized attractions such as Monterey's Fisherman's Wharf and Cannery Row; and, as spice, dozens of fine restaurants.

The Monterey Peninsula is not just a stopping place on a long drive; it is a destination; plan to spend at least three days on the Peninsula. It is a very good base for an excursion down the Big Sur coast (Chapter 11) perhaps as far as Hearst Castle (Chapter 12), and to inland destinations (covered in Chapter 4), such as Salinas and other points in "Steinbeck Country," the historic town of San Juan Bautista, and a number of the old Franciscan missions where California history began.

MONTEREY AND CALIFORNIA HISTORY

Monterey, a quiet city of less than 30,000 people, has a long and rich history considering that California was barely settled 200 years ago. The old Spanish capital of California, Monterey for nearly half of the last 380 years existed only as an idea—not just any idea, but a powerful one that led to the launching of expeditions in search of it, with subsequent death in stormy seas or in waterless mountains. The idea of Monterey was a product of imperialism, inspired by Spain's desire to locate and transport great riches, to plant the flag of the king in terra incognita, and to carry the cross to heathen peoples.

Why Monterey was talked about but undiscovered for 168 years, from 1602 to 1770, can be attributed to a prototypical piece of exaggerated publicity about California. The Spanish had established themselves in New Spain—that is, Mexico—by 1522 and began explorations to expand both to the south and the north. In 1532 the bloody conquistador Cortés dispatched expeditions that found what is today called Baja California, the slender peninsula that runs parallel to Mexico's coast, and 10 years later Viceroy Mendoza sent Cabrillo north along the coast as far as present-day Oregon. Strangely, he did not discover the relatively narrow mouth of the great San Francisco Bay, and if he noticed the shallow scallop in the coast called Monterey Bay, he did not describe it. While he probably anchored off Pacific Grove's Point Pinos on November 18, 1542, it was not a momentous event.

Vizcaíno Expedition

The authorities of New Spain took no further notice of the California coast until later in the century, when King Phillip III, concerned about English pirates like Sir Francis Drake and the vulnerability of the Manila Galleon, the vessel that annually transported riches of the East to New Spain, ordered that a harbor of refuge be found on the coast of what was believed to be the island of California. (The Spanish explorers often ignored the results of each other's explorations, for Ulloa in 1539, by reaching the head of the Gulf of California, had proved California was no island.) The Spanish viceroy sent Sebastián Vizcaíno north with three ships to find such a harbor.

Vizcaíno became the fourth explorer not to find San Francisco Bay, but for the benefit of future tourism he found the Point Reyes peninsula and, on December 15 (date variously given), 1602, anchored near what is today Fisherman's Wharf in Monterey. Looking around, his pilot hyperbolized the anchorage or the bay itself—which is 23 miles across—into a wonderful 0, while Vizcaíno aggrandized it as "the best port that could be desired, for, besides being sheltered from all the winds, it has many pines for masts and yards, and oaks of prodigious size proper for building ships, and water in great quantity, all near the shore." The reader might suspect that these early explorers were paid by the superlative, for Vizcaíno went on to say that the area had a climate like Castile, abounded in game, had fertile soil and good pasture lands, and—this must have been catnip for the Catholic Church—Indians amenable to being converted.

Naming the harbor El Puerto de Monterrey in honor of the viceroy, the count of Monterrey (Mexico), Vizcaíno traveled inland and named El Rio del Carmelo in recognition of the three Carmelite friars along on his expedition.

Losing only 40 men on the way back, Vizcaíno sailed away from California, having invented the myth of the great harbor of Monterey. But the Spanish government did nothing, the maps and reports were put in the archives, and Vizcaíno himself was sent off to discover some mythical islands in the Pacific.

The generations succeeded each other, and each ignored California until, more than 160 years later, the moldering Spanish empire mustered the energy for one last expansion: soldiers and Franciscan missionaries would settle Alta California, beginning with Monterey and San Diego, in order to secure New Spain's northern frontier. Gaspar de Portolá would lead a land expedition up the coast from central Baja while three ships carried supplies and other expedition members. The parts of the expedition—minus half the land party, who died, and one ship, which disappeared—straggled into San Diego in the spring of 1769.

Portolá–Serra Expedition

The 56-year-old father-president of the Baja missions, Fray Junipero Serra—a hero whose statue is one of California's two in the U.S. Capitol—remained in San Diego to establish the first mission and European settlement in California while Portolá continued north to find Monterey harbor. Portolá found lots of things, including San Francisco Bay—accidentally but finally—but couldn't identify Vizcaíno's "best port that could be desired" at Monterey either time he came to it. Mystified and discouraged, he went to San Diego, finding the outpost there on the brink of disappearing.

A resupply ship fortuitously arrived with letters encouraging Portolá to try again.

Portolá trudged back north in mid-1770, while Serra went north by ship. The 78-day march was accomplished in only 37 this time. The day being clear when they returned to Portolá's campsite near Point Pinos on May 27, 1770, some members of the expedition finally recognized what Vizcaíno had been describing. Father Font, who came by with Anza six years later, wrote disgustedly that "what is called a harbor has little shelter, and almost none against the northwest wind, which blows there a great deal of the time, aside from the fact that it is so small that with two barks, it is filled up, and likewise very shallow."

A few days later Serra arrived by sea, landed at about the same spot as publicist Vizcaíno (suitably marked by monuments today), hung some bells in a giant oak (now deceased), and celebrated mass. California's second Franciscan mission was officially established on June 3 at the site of the present Royal Presidio Chapel, and Portolá's successor as *comandante* began building the presidio nearby. The next year Serra, to put some distance between his mission and the military and to find water and farmland, moved the mission to a site about five miles across the Peninsula, amending the name to Misión San Carlos de Borromeo del Rio Carmelo, which is customarily referred to as Carmel Mission.

The basic task of the Portolá-Serra expedition was achieved. Serra in his lifetime founded several more missions to shorten the distances between Carmel (where he died in 1784 and was buried, at the foot of the altar) and San Diego, and supported Juan Bautista de Anza's plan for a party of settlers to blaze a trail from central Mexico to Alta California. Anza arrived at Monterey in March 1776 with 247 settlers, more than he had started with, for several women had given birth along the trail. Anza marched on to found San Francisco in June. These settlers doubled California's non-Indian population.

Anza's expedition was perhaps the last tiny triumph for imperial Spain. In 40 years, sapped by the costs of empire and torn apart during the Napoleonic wars and internal troubles that led to the 1820 revolution, Spain could do little to keep its New World possessions, which one by one seized their independence. Not surprisingly, the few unimportant colonial outposts in the frontier province of Alta California were left to survive if they could (soldiers at the presidio sometimes went unpaid for years) and as they would. When the royal arms of the king of Spain were replaced with the eagle-and-snake flag of independent Mexico in 1822 (the flag going up not over the Presidio of Monterey but the Custom House), it made no substantial difference to a people who were thinking of themselves as Californios; by the 1830s they were impertinent enough to send three governors packing back to Mexico City.

Mission, Presidio, Pueblo, Rancho

California in the decades from the 1770s to the 1840s was a simple society. There were only four institutions: missions, presidios, pueblos, and ranchos. The chain of missions, numbering 21 by 1823, were 30 miles apart (a day's ride) on the dusty trail grandly called El Camino Real ("the king's highway," now mostly Highway 101). The mission padres proselytized a substantial part of the California Indian population. Under the powerful protection and the tuteluge of the padres, the neophytes—numbering 15,000 at the mission system's peak—built most of the picturesque mission buildings, learned the rudiments of skilled trades, labored in the fields (pioneering the wine-making industry) and herded the mission cattle—and also were flogged for transgressions and died easily and young of the white man's diseases. All in all, the missions were successful in quickly civilizing the land along the coast, and for 50 years they dominated California.

The four presidios, at San Francisco, Monterey, Santa Barbara, and San Diego, were in actuality scruffy, undermanned barracks, and the few available soldiers were more skilled at causing trouble for the missions than in defending frontier California: the Presidio of Monterey couldn't even keep an Argentine pirate named Hippolyte de Bouchard from sacking and burning the town in 1818.

Along with the military towns around the presidios and four mission pueblos, three civil pueblos were officially established, at San Jose, Santa Cruz (it was named Branciforte), and Los Angeles. Branciforte was a complete failure and the other towns, including infant San Francisco—Yerba Buena—were sleepy villages until a few nomadic English and Yankee merchants injected some vitality into them. Monterey, always the most important town, was capital of Alta California from 1777 and residence of the governor of the two Californias, but its status meant only occasional excitement as foreign ships came into port or during the comic-opera changes of government in the 1830s.

Those were the three institutions until Mexico became independent in 1821. Until then most of the desirable coastal land in California (which had no northern or eastern border) was mission land; smaller pieces were held by the pueblos and only 30 grants were provisionally held by individuals. The first rancho was granted near the Carmel Mission, to one Manuel Butron, a soldier who married a baptized Indian girl. By 1795 there were half a dozen provisional ranchos in the Monterey area. With Mexican independence, California governors began granting land by the square league. Typically a single Californio was entitled to two leagues but often got up to 11 leagues—more than 48,000 acres; foreigners who became citizens received up to the same amount beginning 30 miles inland (Johann Augustus Sutter, Swiss, got 11 leagues around what is today Sacramento). By 1830 there were 50 private ranchos, 14 of them around Monterey and the Salinas Valley—and there was demand for more. (The U.S. government eventually confirmed 79 grants in Monterey County.)

Not surprisingly, the most rambunctious institution came into conflict with the most conservative, and beginning in 1833 the rancheros who ran the government began secularizing the missions, taking back the choice mission lands and distributing them, some to Indians, most to Californios. The ranchos succeeded the missions as producers of California's only exportable commodities, hides and tallow, serving a trade begun only in 1822 by two English settlers in Monterey. (Incidentally, once the cattle were stripped, the meat was left to rot, except for that used in the festive picnics called *meriendas*.) Their owners being wealthy and the same people who administered the province—one American drew up a list of the 46 men who ruled California—the ranchos became the dominant social and economic institution in California until the Americans came with banks, the mining industry, the Southern Pacific Railroad, real estate, machine politics, and gambling and prostitution on the Barbary Coast.

That brief 20 years or so of California history is a reverie. The decades were quickly mythologized into a golden age, a "true Arcadia," by the first generation of California writers. They were Americans who looked for a life and a time and a people that were simple, honest, good, and authentic—and noble—to compare to their own age. The ruins of the missions, summoning images of a past civilization that may have been artless but had great spirituality, added to the rosy picture those writers produced.

The Americans Arrive

That was later. The first Americans who came to California were not very impressed. They universally praised the area's climate and soil and beauty but tended to excoriate the Californios. For example, a lieutenant with the U.S. Exploring Expedition of 1841 wrote: "Descended from the old Spaniards, they are found to have all their vices and scarcely any of their virtues; they are cowardly, ignorant, lazy, and addicted to gambling and drinking; very few of them are able to read and write, and know nothing of science or literature, nothing of government but its brutal force, nothing of religion but ceremonies of the national ritual."

Richard Henry Dana, who had a kinder pen than many contemporaries, visited Monterey and other points on the coast in 1836 as a crewman on the brig *Pilgrim* out of Boston. Like many, he admired the old capital: "Monterey is decidedly the pleasantest and most civilized-looking place in California," he wrote in *Two Years Before the Mast* (1840). "The town lay directly before us, making a very pretty appearance, its houses being of white-washed adobe. . . . The red tiles, too, on the roofs, contrasted well with the white sides and with the extreme greenness of the lawn upon which the houses—about a hundred in number—were dotted about, here and there, irregularly. . . . In the centre of it is an open square, surrounded by four lines of one-story buildings, with half a dozen cannon in the centre. . . . This is the Presidio, or fort."

The shores of the Monterey Peninsula were "extremely well-wooded (the pine abounding them upon), and everything was as green as nature could make it—the grass, the leaves, and all; the birds were singing in the woods."

Dana admired the Californios for their horsemanship and elegance of manner, speech, and dress: "Every rich man looks like a grandee, and every poor scamp like a broken-down gentleman." But he observed that there were several Americans and Englishmen who, "having more industry, frugality, and enterprise than the natives, . . . soon get nearly all the trade into their hands." So the Californios were "an idle, thriftless people, who could make nothing of themselves." "In the hands of an enterprising people," he concluded, "what a country this might be!"

Not only Americans but the European powers coveted portions of Spain's old empire. President Monroe in 1823 tried to warn foreigners off South America, but the Russians, through the Russian-American Fur Company, were already installed in Northern California, at Fort Ross in Sonoma County, and the British, operating through the Hudson's Bay Company, eyed California from their trading posts in Oregon.

But it was the Americans who began to fulfill the dream of extending the United States from the Atlantic to the Pacific, doing so in such a gradual fashion that only historians recognized the process: the Californios fought actively only when it was too late. Every year from the 1820s more Yankee trading ships came into Monterey harbor to pay duty at the Custom House (still standing). Some Americans, as allowed by Mexican law, became permanent settlers, marrying into prominent rancho families, receiving land grants, and, as Dana saw, taking over commerce.

The fur trade brought foreigners not only by ship but also overland: Jedediah Smith and other mountain men forced several passages across the southern California desert and the Sierra Nevada between 1826 and 1828. Only 13 years later John Bidwell led the first party of settlers across the Sierra. Soon there were so many Americans in California that, in 1843, a consul was appointed. Thomas O. Larkin had been a merchant in Monterey since 1832 and was unofficial banker for the California government. His prototypical Monterey adobe residence is now an outstanding attraction along the Path of History.

The Californios were ambivalent about this American creep west into what was still a Mexican province. They welcomed men like Larkin but arrested Jedediah Smith on his second expedition in 1827, turning him loose only when a naturalized Californio, Juan Bautista Roger Cooper, posted a bond of $30,000 for him. (Cooper, half-brother of Larkin, arrived earlier and built a large adobe house, still standing, at Munras and Polk.)

On occasion, however, Californios used the more unruly Americans to their own advantage. In 1836 Juan Bautista Alvarado, a Monterey native, was aided by a Kentucky scoundrel named Isaac Graham, proprietor of an illegal distillery outside town, in getting rid of Governor Nicholas Gutiérrez. The governor had not only tried to stop customs officers like Alvarado (two of whose houses may be seen in Monterey) from accepting bribes but had stirred the natural rivalry between *abajeños* (southern Californians) and *arribeños* (northerners) by moving the capital from Monterey to Los Angeles. Alvarado led Graham and 50 of his cohorts—who were given promises of land—into Monterey and fired their ángle cannon ball through the roof of Gutiérrez's house while he was eating dinner. He surrendered, the capital returned to Monterey, and Alvarado became governor. This, by the way, resulted in self-government under the Mexican flag for California.

In 1840 Alvarado broke his promise of land for the Americans and arrested and shipped them off to Mexico in chains. The U.S. government was incensed; Mexico released and compensated Graham and the roughnecks, who returned to California all too ready to see it become a part of the United States.

The Stars and Stripes Over California

They got their wish in 1842, but only for a day. Fearful that California was to be used to pay Mexico's debt to Britain, and hearing a false report that war had broken out between the United States and Mexico, Commodore Thomas ap Catesby Jones set sail from Callao, Peru, arriving off Monterey on October 20. He found the Presidio almost empty of its garrison and otherwise "quiet, peaceful, and normally dilapidated." He hoisted the American colors—then hauled them down the next day upon learning the two countries were still at peace. Mortified, he sailed south to call upon Governor Micheltorena in Los Angeles; the Californio graciously held a ball in the commodore's honor, but Jones's superiors relieved him of command.

From 1844 the drama involving California was played on a larger stage. "Manifest Destiny" was causing conflict with Britain over what would become Oregon and Washington, and with Mexico over Texas. President Polk wanted California, peacefully if possible, by war if necessary. When he failed to gain California by acquisition for $25 million, he commissioned Thomas Larkin as a secret agent, at $6 a day, to gain the support of such Californio weathervane watchers as Mariano Vallejo and José Castro. (They were a tight bunch: Montereños all, Vallejo was Alvarado's uncle, and both were cousins of Castro; they also had land and power, for Vallejo owned most of the area around Sonoma, and Castro was *comandante* of California and a Monterey ranchero.)

Larkin, operating out of his house and consulate on Calle Principal, spent the winter of 1845–46 in diplomatic efforts that seemed to be leading toward a Californio declaration of independence and a U.S. protectorate, but other Americans in the area seized the initiative.

First, that rash Pathfinder, Capt. John C. Frémont, in March 1846 drew near Monterey leading a party of armed surveyors, irritating General Castro, who had told them to stay away from the coast. Frémont and his men built a little fort at the top of Gabilan Peak, not far from Salinas, and raised the U.S. flag. Though encouraged by Larkin to depart quickly for Oregon, Frémont dallied for three days while Castro rallied the militia. Frémont decamped, heading for Oregon.

There is much controversy about what next happened, but Frémont claimed he received secret instructions to return to California, where he mixed in with impatient Americans—who were, significantly, landless—in the area around Sonoma and Sacramento, and helped foment the famous Bear Flag Republic, which was declared on June 14, 1846. Word having been received that the United States and Mexico were finally at war, Commodore John D. Sloat sailed into Monterey harbor, hovered indecisively for five days, then on July 7 sent marines ashore to raise the Stars and Stripes over the Custom House (there was much flag-raising in those days). The "one-town, one-month" Bear Flag Republic thus ended (though it is honored on the state flag).

Annexation should have been peaceful, for Mexico was not only incapable of defending its province but two years before had left the Californios on their own. Thanks to the vainglory of Frémont, the incompetence of one Captain Archibald Gillespie, who was put in charge of the unruly town of Los Angeles, the general tactlessness of the Americans, and the Californios' uncertainty about their future, there was fighting—a few pitched battles—with one outside Monterey at Natividad (see p. 54), the rest in Southern California. The Californios capitulated in January 1847 and the U.S.-Mexico Treaty of Guadalupe Hidalgo in February 1848 ended all hostilities and ceded California, among other things, to the United States.

Monterey Under the Americans

It took a while for California to get organized. Monterey remained capital, as the headquarters of the military governor. A pushy Frémont claimed the governorship for 50 days before General Stephen D. Kearny arrested him for disobeying orders and sent him to Washington. A court-martial found him guilty and, though Polk countermanded his dismissal from the army, Frémont resigned.

The chaplain of Sloat's squadron, Reverend Walter Colton, was appointed *alcalde* of Monterey in September 1846. That was a job that involved being mayor, sheriff, justice of the peace, and public works superintendent. Using money seized from illegal gambling, Colton put convict labor to work building what is now named Colton Hall, a combination town hall, school, and jail. He also issued an order with unforeseen consequences for the future of Monterey: "To prevent the ruin and destruction of the Pine Forest in the neighborhood of Monterey, it is hereby ordered that no person whatsoever shall cut down any green pine trees in the said Forest without permission from this office." American soldiers about the same time introduced theater to California, putting on *Putnam, the Iron Son of 1776* at Jack Swan's boardinghouse; such plays are still presented at today's First Theater.

Monterey, like most coastal towns, was virtually emptied by mid-1848 with the stampede to find gold in the Sierra foothills; Lieutenant William T. Sherman, stationed in Monterey, had to track down deserting soldiers. One will never know what would have happened if, instead of James Marshall, some early Californian, perhaps Captain Gabriel Moraga, who made some 46 expeditions into the interior of California while chasing Indians, had discovered that gold. The Spanish empire might have been reborn, Mexico's interest in its province rekindled sufficiently to keep its presidios properly manned.

Despite the Gold Rush, Congress made no provision to make California a territory or admit it as a state either in 1848 or 1849 because the Missouri Compromise free state–slave state line bisected California. The last military governor, General Bennet H. Riley, bent to pressure by those anxious for statehood and forced the issue by calling a constitutional convention in Monterey.

The delegates were elected from the Gold-Rush-swelled population of 100,000 (by then only 13 percent were native-born Californios). Of the 48 delegates who gathered at Colton Hall on September 3, 1849, only eight were Californios and only a dozen were Forty-niners; among the mostly young delegates—their average age was 36—were some well known figures such as Vallejo, Sutter, and Larkin. Another was William Hartnell, one of the Englishmen who had gotten the hide and tallow trade started, became a naturalized Californio, collector of revenue at the Custom House, and ranchero, and now served as interpreter for the Spanish-speaking delegates. President was Robert Semple, "Long Bob" for his six-foot eight-inch frame, co-founder with Colton in 1846 of California's first newspaper, and more recently a leader of the Bear Flag Rebellion. Official reporter was a wandering author, J. Ross Browne. Delegates of future importance were Peter H. Burnett, soon to be elected first governor, and William M. Gwin, later one of California's senators and builder of the state's first Democratic machine. (The other U.S. senator California sent to Washington was John C. Frémont, doubly rewarded by having recently become a millionaire as owner of certain Sierra foothill property that yielded $10 million in gold. Larkin had played middleman in forcing poor Alvarado to give up the land for $3,000.)

The delegates formulated a state constitution based on Iowa's and New York's—but written in both English and Spanish. They unanimously decided that California should be a free state, drew the boundaries approximately along their present lines (they could have been extended east to Utah), withheld the right to vote from Californios—not to mention Indians—until they became American citizens, and adjourned October 13. American males in the territory ratified the constitution in November 1849. The next year, under the Compromise of 1850, California was admitted to the Union as a free state.

Monterey Falls Asleep

Thus California became American. The constitutional convention was, meanwhile, Monterey's swan song. Though Monterey was admittedly a pleasant place, the locus of power had moved to where the gold was or where it was traded. The capital was shifted to San Jose at the end of 1849 and eventually wound up at Sacramento. Monterey in 1872 even lost the county seat to Salinas when the railroad was built.

So Monterey went into suspended animation, which was probably a lucky event from the point of view of historical preservation and tourism. The hinterland continued to raise cattle—100,000 head were in the county in 1860—to feed the men at the mines and in the cities. But after two years of drought killed thousands of cattle, many of the ranch owners started planting grain, which has led to the present agricultural bounty in the Salinas and Pajaro Valleys.

But Monterey itself went to sleep and, in fact, almost went bankrupt: it had to sell off most of its public lands—30,000 acres for a pittance—to David Jacks, a Scot who became well hated for having robbed Monterey of its heritage. By 1863 a San Francisco newspaper called Monterey "last in the fierce race of competition which is ever ranging among the towns of California." "Where are the people?" a reporter wondered. "Certainly not in the streets, for there cows and geese hold uninterrupted procession, with the exception of a very occasional lounger at the door of a store. The homes seem as if the shadow of a centennial sleep had fallen over them, and Monterey is inhabited by some hundred Rip van Winkles." A San Jose newspaper later claimed that one-third of the buildings were abandoned and that "lazy vultures" roosted on the roofs. And while the new towns of Salinas and Hollister became quite American and had modern Victorian houses, adobe Monterey remained capital for the substantially dispossessed Californios.

1880: The First Tourists

Collectors of ironies will appreciate what followed. Charles Crocker of the Southern Pacific, the very same railroad that had bypassed Monterey in the first place, was attracted to the neglected beauties of the Monterey Peninsula, seeing the possibilities in the development of a resort. This not only would result in passenger traffic on tracks now carrying agricultural produce, but also would be a tasteful, European-style watering place for the nouveaux riches of San Francisco and the old money back East, whose social approval such former storekeepers as Crocker, Huntington, Stanford, and Hopkins wanted.

The Big Four set up the Pacific Improvement Company in 1878 to buy—from David Jacks, who made a 3,000 percent profit— 7,100 acres on the neck of the Monterey Peninsula. "Crocker's Folly," the old Hotel Del Monte, opened in June 1880, a rambling but palatial, Swiss chalet–English Gothic–California Victorian hotel with phones in every room (though at the time there were few phones anywhere else in the world) and, outside, 126 acres of garden, a polo field, and a race course. From the hotel, a mile east of the old Custom House, a wonderful drive some 17 miles long went through Monterey, through pine forest and along Pacific shore, ending in Carmel. About the same time Mrs. Leland Stanford led in the efforts to restore the romantic ruins of Carmel Mission.

Robert Louis Stevenson, who had spent a relaxing few months in Monterey in 1879, was distressed: "A huge hotel has sprung up and Monterey is advertised in the newspapers, and posted in the waiting-rooms of railway stations, as a resort for wealth and fashion. Alas for the little town! It is not strong enough to resist the influence of the flaunting caravanserai, and the poor, quaint, penniless native gentlemen of Monterey must perish, like a lower race, before the millionaire vulgarians of the Big Bonanza."

And indeed, from the point of view of someone down looking up, that is what happened. All the best people came to the Hotel Del Monte—presidents like Benjamin Harrison and Theodore Roosevelt, millionaires like William K. Vanderbilt and Andrew Carnegie. "Monte Carlo," said Wall Street millionaire Chauncey M. Depew, "cannot compare with it." The old hotel burned in 1887 and again in 1924, to be replaced by a splendid oversize Mediterranean villa (which after World War II became the Naval Postgraduate School).

Meanwhile, a real-estate genius named Samuel F. B. Morse (grandnephew of the painter and inventor) took over the entire property, by then 20,000 acres, and laid the basis for the Monterey Peninsula's modern role as a Palm Springs on the coast. Rerouting the 17-Mile Drive, Morse planned four golf courses that are now world famous, put in trails, bridle paths, and roads in the Del Monte Forest, dedicated large parts as conservation areas, built another Del Monte Hotel—now called the Lodge at Pebble

Beach—and, finally, invited the rich to build grand seaside homes, which they did in profusion.

The New Old Spanish Capital

Simultaneously the old Spanish capital was rediscovered and those adobes that had not dissolved in the rain or been pushed down were restored and, in at least three cases, moved brick by brick. The influential Monterey Art and History Association, founded at the old Custom House in 1931, drew the Path of History. And who should donate money, land (two parks to the city of Monterey), buildings (the Pacific Building and the Casa del Oro to the state historic park), and collections of Californiana but the family of David Jacks.

So, while one generation of Americans, scorning the unambitious Californios, had taken over California and shouldered past Monterey, a later generation took a second look at Monterey's location, style, and Spanish-Mexican heritage—and took it over. What they have wrought has earned huzzahs and some ridicule—from John Steinbeck, for instance, who was born in Salinas and in the 1930s was living in Pacific Grove. In his *Tortilla Flat* (1935), a picaresque novel about Danny and his friends, the poor, carefree *paisanos* who were authentic heirs of the old Spanish capital but were, significantly, living "on the hills where the forest and the town intermingle," Steinbeck allowed a Bronx cheer: "Through the streets of Monterey, fat ladies, in whose eyes lay the weariness and the wisdom one sees so often in the eyes of pigs, were trundled in overpowered motorcars toward tea and gin fizzes at the Hotel Del Monte." It is, appropriately, the hotel's vegetable garden Danny and his friends raid for food to give Teresina Cortez and her eight children—who actually can survive nicely on tortillas and beans.

The last chapter in the Americanization of Monterey was unwittingly written by—Steinbeck. About 1900 it was discovered that enormous shoals of pilchards (young pilchards are called sardines) had come into Monterey Bay and could be caught easily off the Custom House beach with a couple of rowboats and a net. The first cannery was opened in 1902 not far away on Ocean View Boulevard. Soon Sicilian immigrants had built a huge fishing fleet using efficient lampara nets and the street became lined with canneries, packing $7 million in sardines a year. During its World

War II peak, Steinbeck wrote an affectionate, fictional portrait called *Cannery Row* (1945), the story of Mack and the boys (of the Palace Flophouse and Grill) and their riotous efforts to throw a party for Doc, a marine biologist whose lab was sandwiched between two canneries, opposite Lee Chong's grocery and Dora Flood's Bear Flag Restaurant. As it turned out, the book memorialized Cannery Row, for in 1945–46 the fish largely disappeared from the bay, mostly as a result of overfishing during the war. The canneries lay vacant until the 1950s when a former cannery manager saw a commercial opportunity in the literary connections. The street, officially renamed Cannery Row, has gradually developed into a linear Ghirardelli Square, with mostly touristy restaurants and shops. Steinbeck hated it but saw the irony. "When I wrote *Tortilla Flat* . . . the Monterey Chamber of Commerce issued a statement that it was a damned lie and that no such place or people existed. Later, they began running buses to the place where they thought it might be," the novelist wrote to a friend. "When I did *Cannery Row*, I had not only a charge from the Monterey Chamber of Commerce, but from the Fish Canners Association which came to the defense of Cannery Row people with a knightly intensity. They later reversed themselves, too."

So Monterey has come full circle, from a place too difficult to discover to a place that has been discovered time and again. Today's visitor, too, should find something to discover, not only in Monterey but the three Peninsula communities—Carmel, Pebble Beach, and Pacific Grove—that subsequently developed.

CHAPTER 6:

Monterey

HIGHLIGHTS

The reader who scans the history of Monterey in Chapter 5 will see how inextricably its history is bound up with that of California until the Gold Rush. And that history is quite visible. While the barracks of the old Spanish presidio cannot be found, the Royal Presidio Chapel (1795) still stands, as do many adobe houses once enclosed by the presidio walls. In fact, so many buildings remain that Monterey, as the setting of historical drama (as well as melo-dramatics), must be compared to Virginia's Colonial Williams-burg, which suffered a like decline when the seat of government was moved to Richmond after less than a century.

Of course, there are differences. Williamsburg was and is larger and was an ambitious and very costly reconstruction effort that has resulted in a kind of suspiciously real—or embalmed—museum town, while Monterey is a living, breathing city (except in the redevelopment area, of course) that has managed to preserve rather more of its original structures than is usually possible in an American city—not to mention one in a go-go state like California.

WHAT TO SEE

Path of History

Nearly all the best historical buildings are along the three-mile **Path of History,***** first marked with an orange line and plaques on poles in 1938. The narrative below follows the whole path, and includes some nonhistorical sites nearby. Since the path is a bit long, we'll tell you where to turn back, if you're so inclined. Driving the Path of History is not advised.

Start at the waterfront where, near Fisherman's Wharf (we'll mention that later), there's lots of parking.

In the northeast corner of **Custom House Plaza,*** the central public open space of the city's redevelopment area, is the original **Custom House,***** appropriately designated State Historic Landmark No. 1. Here the American flag was first officially raised by Commodore Sloat on July 7, 1846, when he proclaimed (somewhat mildly to avoid great offense to Montereños) that "henceforth California will be a portion of the United States."

The oldest public building in California, a stone and adobe structure shaded by a couple of large cypresses, the Custom House may date back to 1814, though the province wasn't really opened to foreign trade until the early 1820s. One authority says the low middle section of the building was constructed first, on foundations laid by the Spanish in 1814, while the walls and roof were completed by the Mexican regime in 1822, and the two-story north and south towers were added later. State historians, more cautiously, say the north end dates to 1827, the middle and south to 1841–46. In any case, building ownership passed to the third government in three decades, the U.S. government, which continued collecting duty here until 1868, although San Francisco had become the main port of entry for foreign cargo. The Native Sons of the Golden West took it over from squatters and horses and restored it in 1901; custody then passed to the state, which purchased it from the federal government in 1938.

The Custom House has been a museum since 1929, with displays of harpoon guns, Spanish costumes, an old official-seal press, and barrels and boxes to recall the days when duty was collected and mundane and exotic goods exchanged for hides and tallow.

The Custom House and a dozen other buildings are part of **Monterey State Historic Park.***** Except for one house that is commercially leased (Casa Gutiérrez) and three that are being restored (including the Cooper-Molera Adobe), all the state park buildings are open 9-5 daily (closed Jan. 1, Thanksgiving, and Dec. 25), with general admittance on one 50-cent ticket; several house tours require prior sign-up. Park information: (408) 373-2103. Many of the privately owned Monterey adobes are open during the annual Adobe Tour; see Chapter 10.

Pacific House

Across the plaza is the state park building with the best historical exhibits, **Pacific House.***** It is a long two-story adobe with the distinctive Monterey balcony around the entire second floor. Once thought to have dated to 1835 as a hotel and saloon, it is now considered to have been built in 1847 by a Scot, David Wight, for Thomas O. Larkin but first rented to the U.S. quartermaster for offices and storage. By 1850 it became the Pacific House tavern, scene of the farewell dinner for General Bennet Riley, the military governor who called the constitutional convention. The county took it over for a courtroom and offices; later the building housed stores, a newspaper, and law offices, and was the scene of Presbyterian services and dances given by a temperance society named the Dashaways. The local ogre, landlord David Jacks, bought it in 1880, but his daughter, Margaret Jacks, donated it to the state in 1954.

The ground-floor museum has displays of the making of adobe bricks, a painting of a bull-and-bear fight held in the now peaceful courtyard (called the Memory Garden), and numerous items from the Spanish, Mexican, and early American periods. Upstairs is a special museum of American and Mexican Indian and Eskimo artifacts donated by the Holman family, Pacific Grove department-store owners, in 1961.

At 10 Custom House Plaza is **California Heritage Guides,** a guide service (see Chapter 10—"Getting Around" section) that sells books and postcards.

Step through the Pacific House courtyard and across tiny Olivier Street to another state property given by the Jacks family, **Casa del Oro,**** a small, two-story, chalk-rock and adobe building put up by Larkin in the 1840s. It was the Joseph Boston & Co. general store in the 1850s, and its iron safe (the only one in town) protected county tax receipts and gold dust (in condor quills) and flakes (in bags), whence derived the name "house of gold." The safe and other artifacts, such as a coffee grinder and a flour sifter, re-create the original Boston store atmosphere.

Leave Olivier Street and cross Pacific into a modern shopping plaza opened in 1980 as **Old Monterey Heritage Harbor.** The shops that located here all regretted it; in summer 1982 there remained only a bookstore and one restaurant. The concept and name may well change by the time you visit.

Amid the modern buildings are two historic houses of interest, both under restoration. The **First Brick House*** was built by a Virginian, Gallant Duncan Dickenson, who came across the plains and bought $29 worth of land here in 1848, built his own kiln, fired his own bricks, and built this house, then went off to mine gold and settled in Stockton, returning to Monterey as a delegate to the constitutional convention. In 1851, however, the house was abandoned and was sold at sheriff's auction for $1,091—along with 60,000 spare bricks. It is somewhat plain, with only three rooms on each floor, but it was planned to have wings on either side.

Next door is the **Whaling Station,*** a two-story adobe with cantilevered second-floor balcony. Built by David Wight in the 1840s, it was later a boardinghouse for Portuguese whalers employed on the Custom House beach, where whales were sliced up and oil rendered, which activity fairly reeked. It is all very respectable today.

Across Pacific a bit farther along, outside the Presidio gate, is the **Vizcaíno–Serro Landing Site,*** the approximate place where

Vizcaíno landed on December 17, 1602, from his flagship *San Diego*, and Father Serra landed on June 3, 1770, from the *San Antonio*, meeting Portolá and Father Crespi, who came by land a week earlier. The three Carmelite friars accompanying Vizcaíno said the mass under a giant live oak just up the hill and so, 167 years later, did Serra. The oak died in 1905, and the trunk was placed in the garden of the Royal Presidio Chapel (see p. 98). The **Junipero Serra Cross** marks the site while a monument honors Portolá, who founded the stockaded Spanish presidio on an estuary to the southeast.

Presidio of Monterey

Detour into the **Presidio of Monterey*** an open army post. Here on Presidio Hill the Spanish in 1792 built a second fort, **El Castillo,** that served through the Mexican era (it was here that Commodore Catesby Jones mistakenly raised the American flag in 1842) until the Americans came and started a new post, **Fort Mervine,** a thousand feet inland. El Castillo, between Lighthouse Avenue and Corporal Ewing Road, was excavated in 1967 but recovered to await further funds. Adjacent are the **Indian Cross,** marking the 2,000-year-old Indian village the Spanish covered with their fort, and the **Father Serra Monument*** (1890), commissioned by Mrs. Stanford, showing Serra stepping from a replica of a small rowboat.

Across Corporal Ewing Road is the **U.S. Army Museum,**** a 1909 structure remodeled in the Monterey adobe style and housing historical exhibits. Open, free, Thurs.-Mon. 9-12:30, 1:30-4. Information: (408) 242-8414. Above the museum a large granite eagle, the **Sloat Monument,** commemorates the American seizure of California. Close by are the remaining earthworks and cannon of old Fort Mervine, which was closed in 1852 but opened briefly in 1865-66. After the Civil War the army had men at this location from time to time, but the present Presidio and its buildings date from the reactivation of 1902.

The main activity at the Presidio, as at the old Hotel Del Monte, is education: here is the armed forces' consolidated **Defense Language Institute Foreign Language Center,** where a staff that includes 700 foreign-born language instructors teaches 39 languages and many dialects (the capability extends to 20 more languages) to some 4,200 students in demanding 24- to 47-week courses. A unique facility at the Presidio is the Realia Building, where scale models of airfields, a military situation table, a terrain study room, and so forth aid in applying foreign military terminology. This language school had its origin just before the attack on Pearl Harbor in 1941 when the army realized it had practically no Japanese-language speakers. "Largest language school in the free world," the DLI was established in 1963 and centralized here in 1974, though there is an English Language Center for allied military students in Texas. Army Museum and Presidio information: (408) 242-8547.

First Theater

Retrace your steps back to the Presidio gate and walk south on Pacific one block to Scott, rejoining the Path of History. The first time past here we didn't tell you about the interesting old one-story wood and adobe building on the southwest corner. It's **California's First Theater,***** whose life started about 1844 when a sailor from Scotland, Jack Swan, put up the adobe section as a saloon and, in time, the long section of the building as a boardinghouse (it had four two-room units, each with outside doors east and west, the units separated by partitions that could be raised and lowered). In the fall of 1847, when Colonel J. D. Stevenson's regiment of Mexican War volunteers from New York was disbanding in California, four soldiers convinced Swan to let them use the long portion for minstrel shows. Lit by candlelight and whale-oil lamps, with curtains made from red and blue blankets, the Union Theater opened with something on the order of *Putnam, the Iron Son of 1776, Box and Cox, Nan, the Good-for-Nothing*—or possibly scenes from *Romeo and Juliet*—but in any case seats sold for $5 and the place was packed.

The Gold Rush soon reduced the cast and audience to zero. Montereyans bought it in 1906 and gave it to the state, which restored it in 1917. Twenty years later, on June 3, 1937, the new Troupers of the Gold Coast raised the curtain on *Tatters, the Pet of Squatters Gulch,* and have since performed more than 150 old-time melodramas. During the day you can see the theater and theatrical memorabilia, and wander the usual pleasant Monterey walled garden. Open: Tues.-Sun. 9-5; performances Wed.-Sat.

8:30, Sun. 7:30, May–Labor Day; only Fri.-Sat. 8:30 the rest of year. Box office open Wed.-Sat. at 1. Performances: adult—$3.50; child—$2.50 or $1.50.

Continue on Scott and, at the bright yellow Victorian **Perry House** (1860), a restaurant, go right on Van Buren. On the right are the **Francis Doud House** (1860s), a New England–style wooden house (white with green shutters), rented out as shops by the Monterey History and Art Association; and **Old St. James Church*** (1876), first Protestant church built in Monterey (by Episcopalians), moved from the urban renewal area by the History and Art folks, housing the **Mayo Hayes O'Donnell Library** of Californiana. Open Wed. and Fri.-Sun. 1-4. Information: (408) 372-1838.

Backtrack on Van Buren to Jackson, turn left one block, and turn right on Pacific. Try to ignore the Convention Center; we'll return to this area. At #336 is the "House of the Blue Gate," **Casa Soberanes,**** donated to the state historic park by the aforementioned Mrs. O'Donnell. It was built about 1830 by the Presidio *comandante*, José Estrada. Quite impressive, with a large front garden, the two-story adobe has a cantilevered balcony and a roof that slopes to one story in the rear—a common practice at the time. None of the furnishings is original. Open Fri.-Wed.; hourly tours 9-4 except 1p.m.; admission by state park ticket.

Merritt House (1830), 386 Pacific, is an adobe with a two-story Greek Revival porch, lending a southern air to the building. It was built by a Vallejo but bought by Josiah Merritt, an American who became Monterey County's first judge. It now houses a few rooms of the Merritt House inn-motel. A block to the east, at Franklin and Alvarado, **Casa Sanchez** (ca. 1829) has a remodeled first floor (commercial) but an original second-floor cantilevered balcony. Continuing south on Pacific, **Capitular Hall,** at Franklin, has an adobe first floor dating to 1834. Close by, **Casa Serrano** (ca. 1845), 412 Pacific, was home of Florencio Serrano, a teacher who continued teaching, with the help of his daughter, after he went blind. It was in his family until bought by the History and Art Association. Open Sat.-Sun. 1-4. Information: (408) 372-2311. End gables project to close off the long front porch at either end.

At 559 Pacific is the more contemporary building (also housing the Allen Knight Maritime Museum; see below) of the **Monterey**

Peninsula Museum of Art,* which has a permanent collection (including folk art and the work of early Monterey artists) and temporary exhibitions. Open, free, Tues.-Fri. 10-4, Sat.-Sun. 1-4; closed Mon., hols. Information: (408) 372-5477.

Turn right off Pacific into Jefferson and walk a few steps to Pierce. Right on Pierce at #460 is the **Lara Adobe*** (ca. 1849), long associated with the name Jesús Soto but actually with an unclear history until 1919, when purchased and restored by the director of the Hotel Del Monte art gallery. In 1944 she sold it to John Steinbeck, who lived in it a year before he left Monterey, feeling rejected by the town. It features deep-set windows and has a magnificent cypress in front.

From Jefferson walk left on Pierce. You are now in Monterey's civic-center area, called **Friendly Plaza,** a collection of old and new, compatible small buildings. At 502 Pierce the **José de la Torre Adobe** (1852) has several attached lean-tos and one artist-owner cut a large window in the north wall to get more light. At the end of the block at King is the wooden **Gordon House** (ca. 1849–50), a Yankee-looking house of lumber milled in Australia, shipped to England, and transshipped around the Horn to Monterey. It was built by a constitutional convention interpreter and state senator, but named for a later owner.

Colton Hall

The good-looking, imposing but actually somewhat small building in front of you in Friendly Plaza, with a Pacific Street address, is **Colton Hall,***** the first public building of American California and scene of the constitutional convention of 1849. It was built and later named for the Reverend Walter Colton, a New Englander who was chaplain of the *Congress* in Sloat's fleet until appointed first American *alcalde* of Monterey. Two months later, to restore the "civil character" of the office, Colton called an election, which he won. An active man who had written two books and was later to write the valuable *Three Years in California* (1850), Colton exercised all the office's executive, legislative, and judicial functions. He empaneled California's first jury, banned woodcutting in the Del Monte forest, co-founded California's first newspaper, the *Californian*, and in 1847 put convicts and idlers from Colonel Stevenson's regiment to work on a town hall and public school.

Colton ignored Thomas O. Larkin's Monterey style of architecture and put up a good solid New England building of limestone shale and adobe mortar. The rectangular two-story structure is distinguished mainly by a two-story classical portico, with stairways left and right to the second floor. "It is not," Colton admitted, "an edifice that would attract much attention among public buildings in the United States, but in California it is without rival."

Reverend Samuel Willey (later co-founder of the University of California) opened school in the new building in 1849 but took time out six months later to provide spiritual guidance to the men drawing up the constitution. The convention held its official sessions, September 1 to October 13, on the second floor here, but liquid sessions, at which business was also transacted, were held in the upstairs "tea room" called My Attic, at 414 Alvarado. William Hartnell translated for the Californios, who had several delegates, including General Vallejo.

On October 2 the convention adopted the Great Seal, a compact masterpiece of symbolism designed by Major Robert S. Garnett. With the motto "Eureka" ("I have found it!" as Archimedes is said to have shouted upon discovering a way to determine the purity of gold), the seal in its small area shows the goddess Minerva holding a spear, with a sheaf of wheat, a tiny California grizzly bear, a man digging a rectangular hole for what looks like a coffin (actually, he's a miner and that's a placer-mining rocker), no fewer than five ships on San Francisco Bay, an island, and what are alleged to be the Sierras in the background.

When more serious things were decided and voted on, a Lieutenant Hamilton penned the constitution on parchment in both English and Spanish, then everyone signed it and went back to mining gold. A copy of the constitution and other things from long ago are on display upstairs in what is the city of Monterey's museum. Open, free, Tues.-Sun. 10-12, 1-5; closed Mon., hols. Information: (408) 646-3851, 375-9944.

Adjoining Colton Hall on the north, the **Old Jail*** (1854-55), built of Monterey granite with ironwork from San Francisco, served until 1959 and is now city offices.

Across Dutra Street the city has offices in the **Vasquez Adobe,** once home of the Vasquez family, possibly including the *bandido* Tiburcio Vasquez, the coast's own Joaquin Murieta. The second floor was added by a later owner. North of it is one-story **Casa Alvarado,** with a long, low verandah. This was apparently built by Governor Alvarado in the 1830s, but sold in 1842 to the Dutra family, who occupied it until 1946. The adobe walls are faced with clapboard. Look up Jefferson to Van Buren to see a pair of handsome old Monterey Victorian houses. Walk south on Dutra to Madison, where, at the south end of Friendly Plaza, the **Underwood-Brown Adobe** (1843) has been incorporated into a city office building.

Go left on Madison to Pacific and then veer left into Calle Principal ("main street"), where some of the best old houses are. The streets are charmingly crooked around this part of the walking tour, with some awkward intersections and diagonally placed blocks.

At the intersection of Madison, Polk, and Hartnell is the fine, large, two-story **Stokes Adobe**** occupied by offices. An Englishman, James Stokes was a ship's pharmacist's assistant who came ashore and somehow became consulting physician to Governor José Figueroa in the mid-1830s, married a widow with a family, and built this house of stone and adobe, with four rooms on the bottom, three on the top, plus assorted lean-tos and outbuildings, one of which still stands in the rear with part of the wall. There is a large front garden.

Walk down the left side of Calle Principal. This block looks prototypically Monterey. **Casa Gutiérrez,*** at #580 and #590, is an adjoining pair of two-story adobes, one of which is private, the other owned by the state but leased to the Sancho Panza Mexican restaurant. They were built about 1841 by a cavalryman who married here and had 15 children (very large families were the norm among Californios). The house is said to be typical of those belonging to the more ordinary citizens of town. Next door, at #550, in a contemporary structure, is the **Allen Knight Maritime Museum,**** named for the Carmel man who amassed the collection of sailing-ship models, steering wheels, bells, blocks, compasses, lanterns, scrimshaw, navigation instruments, ship nameboards, paintings, books, and such shipping records as volumes of the Lloyd's Register. Of particular interest is a large model of Commodore Sloat's flagship *Savannah*. The museum, sponsored by the Monterey History and Art Association, is open, free, Tues.-Fri. 10-12, 1-

4, Sat.-Sun. 2-4 (afternoon hours only in winter); closed Mon., hols. Information: (408) 375-2553. The association has its offices here.

Adjacent, at #540, the **House of Four Winds*** (1842), was so named as the only town building to have a weathervane on the roof. Under Larkin's ownership, it was a house and a store and, in the 1850s, the residence and office of the county recorder. Taking a lead in adobe preservation, the Monterey (women's) Civic Club purchased it in 1914, restored it and added in the rear, and has occupied it ever since. Oddly shaped, with a hipped roof and a large lean-to addition on the left, the building is still topped by a rooster weathervane.

Further along the block is the **Sherman-Halleck Adobe*** (ca. 1834), a small, one-room structure built by Larkin behind his house, and accessible through the Larkin House garden. The adobe was quarters in 1847–49 of then Lieutenant William T. Sherman, who was adjutant to the military governor, and Captain Henry W. Halleck, of the engineers, who was secretary of state and custodian of the state archives, preparing in that capacity an influential early report on Spanish land titles. Sherman spent some time in 1848 chasing down soldiers whose attraction to gold was stronger than their sense of duty, and also romanced a señorita (see Casa Bonifacio, p. 99). Both Halleck and Sherman left the army and went to booming San Francisco, Sherman to become a banker, Halleck a lawyer and builder. During the Civil War Halleck became general-in-chief of the Union armies, Sherman a victor in many campaigns.

Larkin House

The architecture of that little adobe is, needless to say, far less grand than the **Larkin House***** itself, the gracious two-story adobe with hipped roof, first-floor verandah, and second-floor balcony that Larkin built for himself in 1834. In introducing the New England Greek Revival to California but accommodating it to the long, low architecture of the Spanish Mexicans, Larkin built the prototype of the Monterey Colonial style—distinguished by its proportions and second-floor balcony—imitated in Monterey and since spread to other parts of California.

Larkin came to Monterey from Boston in 1832 and put his Yan-

kee-merchant talents to work in general merchandise, flour milling, trading in lumber, hides, and horses, building, banking (in
willingly lending to prominent Californios, he gained much personal influence), and, eventually, politics. He married the American widow of a sea captain, but unlike many other Americans did
not become a naturalized Mexican citizen. In 1843, with the
American population swelling, Larkin was appointed U.S. consul,
and in 1845 was made President Polk's secret diplomatic agent to
swing California to the United States peacefully, if possible. He
was later the navy's agent and in 1849 an influential delegate at
the constitutional convention.

Larkin's store and office as consul were originally on the ground
floor, the living quarters upstairs. The house was later used as
Alcalde Colton's office and military government headquarters by
Kearny and Mason. Remaining in the Larkin family, it was occupied by his granddaughter, Alice Larkin Toulmin, from 1922 until
1957, when she gave it, fully furnished, to the state. Now shown
by guided 35-minute tour only, the interior features polished redwood floors, early American and Chinese furniture, and a Hepple-
white dining room; Larkin's desk and office safe are on view, and
there are portraits of Larkin and his wife. Open: Wed-Mon.;
house by tour hourly 9-4 except noon; sign up beforehand. Admission to house with state-park ticket; to garden and Sherman-Halleck Adobe, free.

From Calle Principal make a sharp right into Jefferson, then at
a five-way intersection, another sharp right into Polk. On the
northwest corner of Alvarado and Pearl, at that intersection, is another **House of Governor Alvarado,** a wooden building somewhat remodeled and now a bank.

The southwest corner of Munras and Polk is occupied by another state park building, the barnlike **Cooper-Molera Adobe,*** being restored and developed as a major museum, with two and a
half acres of gardens. One of the largest Monterey adobes, it started about 1829 as a long one-story structure with the second story
and balcony added in the 1850s. John Roger Cooper, a native of
the Channel Islands, arrived in Monterey in 1826 as master of his
own ship, the *Rover,* married into the Vallejo family, Hispanicized
his name, and, as the elder half-brother of Thomas Larkin, persuaded Larkin to come to California also. A dealer in hides, tallow,

sea-otter pelts, and general goods, Cooper prospered considerably and received several land grants, including a chunk of the Big Sur (see Chapter 11). His granddaughter, Frances Molera, bequeathed the house to the National Trust for Historic Preservation, which has leased it to the state.

Opposite at 526 Polk, is another good example of the Monterey Colonial style, the **Casa Amesti,**** another National Trust property that is leased to the Old Capital (men's) Club but open for a small fee Sat.-Sun. 2-4 p.m., through the cooperation of the Monterey History and Art Association. A Spanish Basque, José Amesti arrived in 1824 and, like many others, married a Vallejo. He started building the house in 1833, grew wealthy with the years, and added to the house into the 1850s. The long, two-story, balconied adobe has a walled garden. Information: (408) 372-2608.

At this point, the exhausted may want to take a shortcut two blocks to the Stevenson House (see below), at which point the Custom House Plaza is about five blocks away. Otherwise, the Path of History continues as follows.

On Polk at Hartnell, the **Gabriel de la Torre Adobe** (ca. 1836) was occupied by a justice of the peace and became misnamed for years as "the first federal court," which is unsubstantiated, but it is, appropriately, a law office. Passing the Stokes Abode again, continue on Hartnell to another abode, the similarly misnamed **General Frémont Headquarters,** a two-story building dating to before 1850. Available evidence is that Frémont had his headquarters in a tent up the hill. The building is owned by the History and Art Association but leased out to an attorney. At the handsome **Post Office,** Hartnell and Webster, are tile murals (1933) of historical interest. Turn left on Webster, cross Munras, and go left into Houston. The **Casa Munras,** which was opposite the southwest corner of the old presidio, has been considerably remodeled and incorporated into the Casa Munras Garden Hotel as the lobby.

Stevenson House

At 530 Houston, on a quiet side street between Pearl and Webster, is the literary-landmark **Stevenson House,***** a two-story building known as Girardin's French Hotel at the time Robert Louis Stevenson lived here for four months in late 1879.

Stevenson was 28 and had two books behind him but was not yet widely known. He was in Scotland when he received a cable from California from his beloved, Fanny Osbourne, a married American woman he had met at a French art colony in 1876. Casting everything aside, and declaring that "no man is of any use until he has dared everything," the frail Stevenson shipped steerage to New York (a journey described in the first half of *The Amateur Emigrant*, 1895), then took the cheap, uncomfortable immigrant-class accommodations on the transcontinental train to San Francisco (described in the second half of the book), transferred to Salinas and then to Monterey, completing the journey in only three weeks but arriving totally exhausted. After nearly dying during a lone camping trip into the Santa Lucia Mountains, he settled in at the French Hotel, taking meals at Jules Simoneau's restaurant or with Fanny—who was staying at the Casa Bonifacio (see p. 99)—or with the local doctor, a Luxembourger who was concerned about Stevenson's poor health. The local newspaper editor paid him for some articles using money contributed by admirers; even Stevenson's 25-cent meals at Simoneau's were secretly subsidized.

When not sick or writing (he wrote the first section of *The Amateur Emigrant*, finished the novel *The Pavilion on the Links*, wrote several essays, and started a never-finished, now-lost story entitled "A Vendetta in the West"), Stevenson took walks through the pine woods and along the shore, where the ocean fascinated him. "The one common note of all this country is the haunting presence of the ocean," he wrote in the essay "Monterey" (1880).

A great faint sound of breakers follows you high up into the inland cañons; the roar of water dwells in the clean, empty rooms of Monterey as in a shell upon the chimney; go where you will, you have but to pause and listen to hear the voice of the Pacific. You pass out of the town to the south-west, and mount the hill among pine woods. Glade, thicket, and grove surround you. You follow winding sandy tracks that lead nowhither. You see a deer; a multitude of quail arises. But the sound of the sea still follows you as you advance, like that of wind among the trees, only harsher and stranger to the ear; and when at length you gain the summit, out breaks on every hand and with freshened vigour that same unending, distant, whispering rumble of the ocean.

He found on the Monterey Peninsula, according to historian George R. Stewart, some of the geography he used in *Treasure*

Island two years later: the description of the island's shores and the lower elevation of Spyglass Hill was based on the Monterey Peninsula (a Pebble Beach golf course is named Spyglass Hill), the higher elevation on Mt. St. Helena in the Napa Valley, where he and Fanny spent a honeymoon summer in 1880.

Meanwhile, he loved Monterey, which at that time had "two or three streets, economically paved with sea-sand," and two or three lanes well eroded by the rain. He admired the adobe architecture except that the thick walls kept in the rainy-season chill. He found Monterey's native folk, "in that world of absolutely mannerless Americans," to be "a people full of deportment, solemnly courteous, and doing all things with grace and decorum." During the day "there was no activity but in and around the saloons," and evening serenaders went about playing the guitar and singing "old, heart-breaking Spanish love-songs" beneath various windows. He commented that Americans seemed to run everything and own all the land, the Mexicans having been "greedy like children" in selling it for ready money, the Americans with their "Yankee craft" on the other hand having been "greedy like designing men."

Fanny had to go back to her husband in October, and the town gossip became unpleasant, and the fog made his health worse—and so, in December, Stevenson left for San Francisco.

The Stevenson House is now one of two RLS museums in California, the other being the Silverado Museum in St. Helena. The building dates to the 1830s, when it was constructed by the first administrator of customs. Jean Girardin, who married locally and became Juan, converted it into a hotel in 1856, adding to the Houston Street side. After a number of uses over the years, it was purchased when threatened with demolition and given to the state to be preserved as a home of the period (among the period rooms are the kitchen, sewing room, family parlor, children's room with toys, and master bedroom with a four-poster said to have floated ashore from a ship in 1852) and Stevenson museum.

Among the Stevensoniana, some of which was obtained from his stepdaughter, Isobel Field, are his sea chest, addressed to himself in Samoa (where he died in 1894), his 14-foot mahogany dining-room table, several portraits and sketches, and first editions and manuscripts. His "great airy room" is upstairs in the L-shaped annex, behind the back parlor. There are five windows to let in light and a door to a private balcony over the garden. Although there is a desk in the room, Stevenson habitually wrote sitting up in bed. Open daily for tours hourly 9-4 except noon; admission with state park ticket.

Outside the Stevenson House, walk left on Houston, turn left on Pearl, then go right on Tyler to the tree-shaded **Estrada Adobe,*** built as a two-story house about 1823, later made into the St. Charles Hotel with a third story, then expanded as the Mission Inn. The Monterey Savings and Loan Association bought it in 1961, intending to put up a new bank, but decided to restore it (1964) for community use.

Go right on Bonifacio then jog into Abrego for three short blocks, passing the long, low **Casa Abrego** (ca. 1834), partially constructed, tradition has it, with some timbers from the ship on which Napoleon escaped from Elba and wrecked, years later, off Monterey. It is a women's club. Opposite is the interesting **Clock Garden** restaurant (see Part IV). Close by, also at Webster, the large, 25-room **Casa Pacheco*** (1840), is handsome but somewhat remodeled (1929) as a men's club. Like Casa Amesti, both the Abrego and Pacheco houses were occupied by Californios of substance who gave big parties, and Francisco Pacheco was rich enough (he owned 90,000 acres of ranches) and influential enough to be buried in front of the altar of the nearby Royal Presidio Chapel. Also on Abrego is the **Casa Madariaga** (ca. 1848), a typical one-story adobe with rooms opening onto the street.

Royal Presidio Chapel

Turn left into Church Street, to the **Royal Presidio Chapel,*** also known as the Cathedral of San Carlos de Borromeo de Monterey. This is, basically, the first Carmel Mission, the one founded by Father Serra in 1770 within the old presidio. He moved to the Carmel River the next year but the church remained as the presidio chapel, given a permanent building in 1775. Damaged by fire in 1789, it was completely rebuilt in 1795 by workmen from Mexico, essentially as it appears today. Various sources identify Manuel Ruiz as the designer, Antonio Valesquez as sculptor of the chalk-rock figure of the Virgin of Guadalupe near the top of the rounded façade, below the cross. In 1835, after secularization of the missions, it became a parish church, and furnishings from Carmel Mission were transferred to it. Becoming dilapidated, it was reconstructed in 1858 with funds from Romualdo Pacheco, who was later (1871–75) the only Californio governor of the American state.

Now the only remaining presidio chapel, it is distinguished by one of the most ornate façades of all the old Spanish churches. Inside are a Mater Dolorosa brought from Mexico by Serra and old statues of the Madonna and St. John. (You won't find the gold candlestick that the Pirate, in *Tortilla Flat,* bought for the cathedral in memory of his dog.) In the garden is the trunk of the Vizcaíno-Serra oak, from their landing site. Open, free, 8-7 daily.

Bear right on Church Street to Fremont. From here the energetic walker can detour a couple of blocks to **Casa Boronda,** end of Boronda Lane off Major Sherman Lane. Perhaps the oldest adobe residence in Monterey, the house was built by Manuel Boronda about 1817. Born in Spain, Corporal Boronda taught school in San Francisco about 1796, then moved to Monterey, retired from soldiering, and opened a school for boys in this adobe. He was also sacristan at the Royal Presidio Chapel. It is said that Alvarado conspired here with the Kentucky scoundrel Isaac Graham before the coup against Gutiérrez in 1836. The adobe, which is unusual in following a sloping contour, was built with three rooms, with food prepared in a lean-to and cooked outdoors in an oven, as was customary then.

A longer detour down Mesa Road goes to two more adobe houses, **Casa Buelna** (ca. 1818–21), one of the first houses outside the Presidio, and operated as a girls' school, and the **Casa Bonifacio,**** a sentimental favorite among adobes. Originally located on Alvarado at Bonifacio Place, this adobe is where Fanny Osbourne stayed while Stevenson lodged two blocks away. While on the surface very proper ("my literary friend from Scotland has accepted an engagement to come to America and lecture," Fanny wrote primly), in fact their association was the subject of much gossip in the small town.

An earlier romantic story has led to the Bonifacio adobe's other name, "House of the Sherman Rose." One account is that Maria Ygnacio Bonifacio, daughter of an Italian who came to Monterey in 1822, planted a cloth-of-gold rose given to her by young Lieutenant Sherman about 1847. The story has been embellished with the legend that when Sherman left in 1849 he promised to return when the rose bloomed; it did but he didn't. The rose, in any case, adorns the arbor in front, and part was transplanted to the city rose garden. The adobe dates to 1835. It was dismantled and reconstructed here on Mesa Road in 1922.

Back on Fremont, go left immediately on Camino del Estero. At the corner is the **G. T. Marsh store,** Monterey branch of the old San Francisco oriental goods store. It is an interesting Mission Revival building with oriental features. Three and a half blocks along Camino del Estero is the last adobe on the Path of History proper, the **French Consulate,** occupied by the French consul about 1845–48 but dating perhaps to 1830 at its original location at Fremont and Abrego, from which it was moved in 1832. The Girl Scouts have their office here. Behind the building is **El Estero,** part of a tidal estuary since cut off. In the city park here is the **Dennis the Menace Playground*** designed by cartoonist Hank Ketcham (other cartoonists who live here are Marty Links of "Bobby Sox" and Gus Arriola of "Gordo"). The playground does not have an extraordinary design.

Waterfront

Another block brings you to Del Monte Avenue, the main drag. The Path of History carries on along the waterfront to the Custom House Plaza. Dodge right on Figueroa to **Municipal Wharf No. 2,*** a large wharf with a road and parking, commercial fishing berths, fish-packing facilities, a couple of seafood restaurants, places for pipe-smoking pier fishermen to stand, and, at the end, a vista point. The finger piers of the yacht harbor occupy the space between here and **Fisherman's Wharf.***

A smaller version of the San Francisco attraction, this one is not so sickeningly touristy, but all the same has tourist-trap restaurants and sticky-candy shops. (See Part IV for advice). There's a viewing deck above Rappa's at the end of the wharf. From the wharf you can take a 45-minute bay cruise—watch for seals, sea lions, and otters—or take a diving bell down 30 feet under the surface to the kelp beds. Fishing-party boats leave about 7:30 most mornings (see Chapter 10). Fisherman's Wharf dates to 1846 at this location—in fact, the rock on which Commodore Sloat supposedly landed that year is under the shore end of the wharf.

Redevelopment

Fisherman's Wharf has a lot of activity and people, but here and there in your adobe tour you probably heard your footsteps echoing. That was when you passed by or through Monterey's **redevelopment area,** bounded by Franklin, Washington, Van Buren, and the waterfront. The centerpiece, a rambling complex that blends into Custom House Plaza, is **Portolá Plaza,** containing the **Monterey Conference Center** and main downtown hotel, the Doubletree Inn. Robinson Jeffers and John Steinbeck suffer portions of the convention center to be named for them, and a statue of **Portolá** (by Fausto Blazquel) stands at the carriage–tour bus entrance at Del Monte and Calle Principal. The floor plan and interior walkway-stairway system of this blocky center would baffle Rubik, but you may be helped by a scale model of downtown Monterey in the hotel lobby. The Alvarado lobby has changing exhibits sponsored by the Monterey Peninsula Museum of Art.

The city's business center, **Alvarado Street,** which heads south from Portolá Plaza, has some new savings-and-loan and office buildings, all reflecting the adobe style; and the old Hotel San Carlos, Franklin and Calle Principal, is being replaced with something very exciting, we're sure. On the other side of the convention center, redevelopment created Custom House Plaza, in which the two big landmark buildings were given spacious but empty environs, and the disastrously vacant "Old Monterey Heritage Harbor" shopping plaza. The result of all this wonderful development is that whatever downtown commerce hasn't gone bankrupt has largely fled to the suburban Del Monte Center (Macy's et al.) and to Cannery Row (antique shops, galleries, and tourist haunts). What's left are abstractly historical new buildings that lack the human scale and urban warmth of the old adobes, and anyone's choice of derelict or abandoned structures. With friends like the Redevelopment Agency, what city needs enemies? Redevelopment just might have been the worst thing to happen to Monterey since the Argentine pirate Hippolyte de Bouchard sacked and burned the town in 1818.

We hope, at least, that the State Department of Parks and Recreation, which has done terrific things all around California, will survive its years of thin budgets and fill up its bare spaces with such human activities as produce markets and costume pageants.

Naval Postgraduate School

About a mile east of the Custom House is the old Hotel Del Monte and its 600 acres, now occupied by the **U.S. Naval Postgraduate School***.

Charles Crocker of the Big Four must have had a meteorological instinct, for in 1880 he placed "The Most Elegant Seaside Establishment in the World" at a place not quite as foggy as elsewhere on the peninsula—though this is not the Bahamas by any definition. His first hotel, a splendid Gothic palace, was an immediate success (17,000 guests per year), and "the millionaire vulgarians of the Big Bonanza" (as Stevenson termed them) could step off the special trains from San Francisco on the grounds of the hotel. There were carriage drives on the 17-Mile Drive or riding in the forest that at that time covered most of the peninsula; there was hunting and fishing at the Rancho Del Monte in Carmel Valley; sportsmen could play polo and tennis; there was racing; one could use the swimming pool or go down to the hotel's beach, change in the cabanas, and plunge into the chillier Pacific. And there were *two* golf courses, both still in use. Seven years later the hotel was razed in a fire, but was rebuilt on an even more lavish scale—with a grand ballroom and even a billiard room for the ladies—for the next generation of the rich and influential.

After another fire in 1924, the hotel was rebuilt as an opulent neo-Spanish villa, with comfortable tile-roofed cottages scattered on the grounds for those who desired privacy. A Hearst Castle–like Roman Plunge was put in, and by this time the Pebble Beach golf courses and another lodge were under development. When World War II came, the 60-year-old resort was leased by the navy as a preflight school, and at war's end was purchased. The Naval Postgraduate School moved here from Annapolis in 1951.

The school, with 2,000 students (officers of all five U.S. Services and 25 allied countries), is a fully accredited graduate school offering degrees up to doctorates in mainly technical subjects, including aeronautics, oceanography, mechanical and electrical engineering, physics and chemistry, and computer science. The resort grounds have been maintained—the Roman Plunge beckons naval students instead of millionaires now—but facilities have been added that Charles Crocker might have a hard time identifying: a linear accelerator, flight simulators, wave tanks, a smoke tunnel, and an anechoic chamber (it completely absorbs sound waves and radar signals). A research vessel, the *Acania,* bobs in Monterey Bay. The main hotel building, now called **Herrmann Hall,**** is the administration building. To visit, ring the Public Affairs Office, (408) 646-2023. You can glimpse the former grandeur of the resort in the pillared reception rooms, highly polished floors, high ceilings, tall windows, tiled stairways, the ballroom, the carved wood, murals, and paintings. There are views all round from the 120-foot tower.

As a symbol of the navy's involvement in Monterey since the days of Commodores Catesby Jones and Sloat, the school's superintendent reads out Sloat's proclamation at the Presidio every July 4.

Cannery Row

The other principal attraction away from the downtown area is **Cannery Row,*** whose far end is only about a mile from the Custom House. If driving, take the Del Monte Avenue–Lighthouse Avenue tunnel under the Custom House Plaza, bend along the foot of Presidio Hill, veer off Lighthouse onto Foam for one block, then turn right into Cannery Row.

Oh, oh, what's this?

Cannery Row, no matter what it once was, or how it was transformed by one man's imagination and subsequent readers, or how the commercial world interpreted it and exploited it, is at the moment an amazing blend of literary landmark and amusement park, with a dollop of historical preservation. Historical preservationists might be appalled and literary pilgrims incredulous, but people with a carful of kids might positively welcome Cannery Row. It might be said to have something for everybody: a thrill ride, a wax museum, a bust of a Famous Author, gaudy as well as decent restaurants, antique and junque shoppes, balloon races, façades of (possibly) historic buildings, bronze plaques, a scenic location, seals and seagulls, and acres of parking.

Here are three possible perspectives, itineraries, and pertinent facts:

Historical Preservation: Cannery Row is, basically, a former industrial area of no great antiquity or architectural charm. Here there are no New England mills with water wheels or San Francisco chocolate factories or Midwest water towers or New York working wharves. No, here were boxy sheet-metal buildings with a few overhead walkways or conveyors. The sardine-catching and -canning industry lasted barely three decades, died abruptly. The shoreline was wrecked by the ugly development, and the weeds aren't even photogenic. What can one do with such an area? Historic preservation had answers in other industrial areas, but had none here.

The usual thing is for the government or a well-endowed semi-public or private group to preserve a building as a museum. But can there be a Cannery Row sardine-fishing museum of 200,000 square feet spread over several buildings? No, and it's not feasible even if there were exhibits of all of Monterey's history. The next usual thing is to install some comparable activities. But can there be enough deep-sea-diving schools, fishery research laboratories, and maritime history libraries to occupy all this space? Again, no.

Well, the next feasible thing is to allow leasing to some activities that may not be *like* sardine canning but at least don't demand great architectural changes and do allow some degree of public access. That is, law offices and community spaces and antique shops and little theaters and the odd government institution. Even private clubs. You know, *nice* things, *middle-class* activities. Unfortunately, adobe Monterey already had the law offices and other safe tenants. And no one was in charge of Cannery Row, anyway.

So Cannery Row is home of the "world's fastest carousel" and "Al Capone's spaghetti house," and the **Historical Wax Museum of Old Monterey** displays Doc, Hazel, and Mac next to Father Serra, Joaquin Murieta next to Cabrillo and Vizcaíno; for real history buffs, there's the Count of Monterrey. History has become hysteria, façade veneer, facts fiction and fiction facts.

The irony is that the crowds on Cannery Row, so absent from adobe Monterey, would positively shrink from the Ocean View Street of 1945: 19 smelly canneries running 24 hours a day, some 4,000 honest, sweaty workers packing 235,000 tons of—yech! for crying out loud, Linda, this place *stinks,* let's get the kids out of here.

Literary Associations: One is now challenged to identify the

1930s scene that Steinbeck describes in his *Cannery Row* (1945) and sequel *Sweet Thursday* (1954):

Cannery Row in Monterey in California is a poem, a stink, a grating noise, a quality of light, a tone, a habit, a nostalgia, a dream. Cannery Row is the gathered and scattered, tin and iron and rust and splintered wood, chipped pavement and weedy lots and junk heaps, sardine canneries of corrugated iron, honky tonks, restaurants and whore houses, and little crowded groceries and flophouses. . . .

In the morning when the sardine fleet has made a catch, the purse-seiners waddle heavily into the bay blowing whistles. . . . Then cannery whistles scream and all over the town men and women scramble into their clothes and come running down to the Row to go to work. . . . The whole street rumbles and groans and screams and rattles while the silver rivers of fish pour in and out of the boats. . . . The canneries rumble and rattle and squeak until the last fish is cleaned and cut and cooked and canned and then the whistles scream again and dripping, smelly, tired Wops and Chinamen and Polaks, men and women, straggle out and droop their ways up the hill into the town and Cannery Row becomes itself again—quiet and magical. Its normal life returns. The bums who retired in disgust under the black cypress tree come out to sit on the rusty pipes in the vacant lot. The girls from Dora's emerge for a bit of sun if there is any. Doc strolls from the Western Biological Laboratory and crosses the street to Lee Chong's grocery for two quarts of beer. . . .

Steinbeck perhaps knew he was writing a fable. His sentimental myth-making was apparent in *Tortilla Flat* (1935), in which Danny and his fellow wine-drinking *paisanos* are transmuted into Arthur and the Knights of the Round Table. (Indeed, Steinbeck's major posthumous work was a rendering of Malory's *Morte d'Arthur*.) So he populated Ocean View Street with the wise, generous philosopher-king and marine biologist Doc, whores-with-hearts-of-gold like Dora Flood and her girls at the Bear Flag Restaurant, and good-natured, harmless, lovable bums like Mack and the boys of the Palace Flophouse and Grill. No crime, no ungenerous impulses—not even any rats.

In real life, Doc was Edward F. Ricketts, coauthor of *Between Pacific Tides*, one of California's first dropouts, and proponent of the inelegant "phalanx" idea—people as herd—to which Steinbeck was drawn. Ricketts ran the Pacific Biological Laboratories, a lab and supply house at 800 Cannery Row (now a private club) in which Steinbeck had a part-interest. Ricketts was killed in 1948 in a collision close by between train, car, and bottle.

Next door to Doc's lab was the Hediondo cannery, and in between, the path the old Chinaman took to the edge of the water. Across the street, in the books, was Dora Flood's Bear Flag, "a decent, clean, honest, old-fashioned sporting house," taken over by her sister Flora (or Fauna) in *Sweet Thursday*. In real life, Flora Wood's Lone Star Café, somewhat respectable, was in the 600 block.

Opposite the lab, the famous vacant lot and its rusty boilers and pipes was home for Mr. and Mrs. Sam Malloy in *Cannery Row* and Suzy in *Sweet Thursday* (the Rodgers and Hammerstein musical was called *Pipe Dream*). The site is very much occupied today, but scarcely by ne'er-do-wells. On the right, in the books, was Lee Chong's remarkably well-stocked Heavenly Flower Grocery, bought in the sequel by a gent named Joseph and Mary Rivas. In real life, that was the Wing Chong Market, now the Old General Store (antiques), 835 Cannery Row.

To get to the Palace Flophouse, you would cross the vacant lot, walking diagonally left, past the black cypress tree, across the Southern Pacific tracks, "up a chicken walk with cleats," and there it was: "a long low building" with "a good roof, a good floor, two windows and a door." Look in vain for it; the closest you'll come is the "Steinbeck tree" at the foot of Irving Street.

The La Ida Bar, run by Wide Ida, was given no fictional location but could be seen from Doc's lab. Kalisa's restaurant, a homey, international-vegetarian eating place at 851 Cannery Row, has been identified as La Ida's.

Literary pilgrims can safely ignore the crassly named "The Original" Steinbeck Lobster House, Doc Ricketts Lab, a place for "libations and entertainment," Floras Elegant Saloon (modern-day commerce has no need for apostrophes), and Grapes of Wrath Antiques.

Tourists: At last we come to the opinion of real people. They'll like Cannery Row, because it doesn't have any of the dusty musty air of the Monterey adobes or the alienating public plazas and blockbusting buildings of redeveloped Monterey. Here, if a place wants to impress upon you the fact that it's historic and fun, it'll throw six ceiling fans and sixteen stained-glass windows at you, and won't spare the catsup and onion slices. It has many restaurants known for their lush decor: red velvet and gold brocade for steak houses, a Hollywood Hong Kong set for a Chinese restaurant, and portholes, anchors, and nets for seafood restaurants. Cannery Row has a hundred shops, and most of Monterey's art galleries; many are open in the evening.

So you may enjoy Cannery Row or prefer to spend the evening in your hotel room rereading the book to see what it was perhaps really like. By 1980 Steinbeck's reinvented Cannery Row had changed so much, with the leveling (often by arson) of canneries and the installation of parking meters and building of highrise motels (a $24 million, 160,000-square-foot **aquarium** will open in 1984), that when Hollywood went to film the novel, they couldn't do it on location: Ocean View Street had to be re-created inside an MGM sound stage for another transformation of a myth. Crazy.

PRACTICAL INFORMATION

Information on Getting There, Getting Around, and What to Do is in Chapter 10. Accommodations (including camping) and restaurants are discussed in Part IV under the heading Monterey Peninsula and listed under Monterey, Pacific Grove, Pebble Beach, Carmel, Carmel Highlands and Highway, and Carmel Valley; see also Big Sur Coast and Salinas/Inland Monterey County.

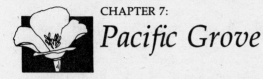

CHAPTER 7:

Pacific Grove

HIGHLIGHTS

Occupying the northern tip of the Monterey Peninsula, Pacific Grove is a small city—only 1,700 acres and 18,000 people—that has preserved almost every inch of its remarkably scenic shoreline and made it accessible to visitors. What the resort prides itself on, however, is millions of orange and black insects—monarch butterflies—that spend the winter here, clustering on favored trees in groves of pine, cypress, and eucalyptus. Understandably, the city slogan is "Butterfly Town U.S.A."

As with the metamorphosis that produces monarchs, the history of Pacific Grove is one of transformation, and can be illustrated in the change of name of two of the points of land that stick out into Monterey Bay between Point Pinos, the landmark that Cabrillo named in 1542, and Cannery Row, which John Steinbeck, who lived in Pacific Grove in the 1930s, named in 1945.

One of the points was once Point Aulon. The Costanoan Indians who lived here—they're all gone now—dived off this shore for the large mollusks with the mother-of-pearl shells that they named *aulun,* the Spanish called *aulone* or *avalone,* and we call abalone.

That was when the city was entirely rocky shore and pine forest.

In 1875 a group of Methodist Episcopal ministers, seeking a place "not merely to hold religious meetings but to afford a summer resort for Christian people . . . as free as possible from the follies and vices of the fashionable watering places," founded the Pacific Grove Retreat Association. Beneath the pines they pitched neat rows of tents that could be rented for $2.25 to $5.50 a week. The ministers ordained some pretty Victorian, almost Puritan, blue laws, prohibiting liquor, waltzing, and other things, demanding the most modest swimming costumes, and requiring that lights go out at 9 P.M.—later advanced to the licentious hour of 10. In 1879, Robert Louis Stevenson, wandering down the hill into the campground, closed for the season, thought that he had "never been in any place that seemed so dream-like." Here, "in the warm season, crowds come to enjoy a life of teetotalism, religion, and flirtation, which I am willing to think blameless and agreeable."

In line with their aims, the ministers fenced off Point Aulon and renamed it Lovers of Jesus Point.

But in time people stayed all year, cottages and some Victorian mansions replaced the tents, a grid-iron street plan was developed (unlike the higgledy-piggledy growth of Monterey), and the city of Pacific Grove incorporated in 1889. It was the home of the Chautauqua of the West from 1879 and kept up its moral standards for several decades ("Carmel-by-the-Sea, Monterey-by-the-Smell, and Pacific Grove-by-God" was the saying). Steinbeck took a satirical swipe in *Tortilla Flat:* "The W.C.T.U. met for tea and discussion, listened while a little lady described the vice and prostitution of Monterey with energy and color. She thought a committee should visit these resorts to see exactly how terrible conditions really were. They had gone over the situation so often, and they needed new facts." But in time there were enough people who wanted more fun in Pacific Grove, and the last of the blue laws, prohibition, was voted out in 1969.

And sometime back the name of the point of land was shortened to Lover's Point, certified in 1961 by the U.S. Geographic Board. One can eat, drink, and be merry, and swim with brief costume there now.

The other point of land used to be called China Point, as the location of the local population of Chinese. Steinbeck, who lived a few blocks away in a cottage his father built at 147 11 St. (*Pastures of Heaven, To a God Unknown,* "The Red Pony," *Tortilla Flat, In Dubious Battle,* and *Of Mice and Men* were written there), set Chin Kee's squid yard—the last resort of the unemployed—at China Point, and complained when the Geographic Board renamed it Point Cabrillo: "Phooey—any fool knows it was China Point until certain foreigners became enamored of our almost non-existent history." The Chinatown mostly burned down in 1920—the residents scattered—and the site is now occupied by Stanford University's Hopkins Marine Station. Ironically, that is where Steinbeck picked up his lifelong interest in marine biology.

WHAT TO SEE

Butterflies

Pacific Grove may be the only city in the world to have erected a **statue to a butterfly*** (by Gordon Newell, it's at Lover's Point). In fact, every October a thousand schoolchildren with orange and black wings parade to honor the insect that festoons their trees and attracts tourists.

The monarchs, *Danaus plexippus,* congregate at several points on the central California coast, flying at most about 200 miles in order to regenerate the species and otherwise spend the winter in congenial surroundings. A few arrive in October as the vanguard for the millions who glide in (monarchs do not fly by continuous fluttering) by the November migration peak. They settle in branches or the hanging moss in selected pine, oak, cypress, and eucalyptus, clinging even to each other in clusters of as many as 1,000 on a three-foot branch. Visitors to the butterfly groves (see below) come with binoculars for the morning stirring: unless disturbed by the unruly (under Ordinance No. 11.48.010, the city imposes a $500 fine for molesting or interfering with the monarchs), the butterflies, with wings folded to look like dead leaves, are quiet until shafts of sunlight hit their cluster. At that moment the wings come open and quiver and soon the butterflies launch themselves in search of garden flowers—especially the purple, blue, and pink blossoms of the jeweltree shrub—and each other. They are inactive on dull, overcast, cool days.

In March they leave their wintering quarters and scatter to localities where milkweed grows; monarchs lay on that plant because the larvae feed only on milkweed, whose taste renders the butterfly unpalatable to predators. The eggs hatch soon into black and white caterpillars that after two weeks go into the chrysalis or pupa stage—the chrysalis is light green, dotted with gold—and in a month the winged orange and black butterfly emerges.

The **butterfly trees*** are here and there but the **butterfly groves***** that are best for watching can be found on the west side of George Washington Park (along Melrose Street) south of Pine Avenue, and behind the Milar Butterfly Grove Motel, Lighthouse Avenue and Ridge Road, whose office has information and souvenirs.

If you want to know more, or are having difficulty finding the best butterfly trees, stop in at the **Pacific Grove Museum of Natural History,***** Central and Forest Avenues. Founded in 1881 and opened in 1900, the fine small museum has exhibits of a butterfly tree, local sea otters and birds, Indian artifacts, and a relief map of Monterey Bay, showing the gigantic subsea canyon. Open, free, Tues.-Sun. 10-5. Information: (408) 372-4212.

Along the Shore

The best way to see most of Pacific Grove's scenic shore is to leave Monterey on Cannery Row or Lighthouse Avenue, jogging down to **Ocean View Boulevard.***** This follows the landscaped paths and sidewalks past **Hopkins Marine Station** (closed to the public), **Lover's Point**** and **Pacific Grove Marine Gardens Park**** (glass-bottom boat trips in the summer, a "magic carpet" of pink-blossomed ice plants, beach, playground, snackbar, picnicking), to **Point Pinos,**** most of which is a U.S. Lighthouse Reservation but open to the public for picnicking. (Another entrance is off Asilomar Avenue near the golf clubhouse.)

Built of granite quarried here, the **Point Pinos Lighthouse**** has been in operation since 1855, the only one of the first six on the California coast still in its original form. Sperm oil was first used to produce light, then kerosene, then in 1915 electricity. The lighthouse building was modified after being damaged in the 1906 earthquake, but the mechanism, lenses, and prisms are all original equipment. Open, free, 1-4 on weekends (except holidays). The

Great Tide Pool of *Cannery Row* where Doc collected specimens is here at Point Pinos.

The shoreline road follows the Point Pinos shore, then goes past **Asilomar State Beach.*** The beach is white sand with scattered ice plant, and a fringe of pines seems, wrote Steinbeck, "to hold a piece of night throughout the day." Under these trees is the **Asilomar Conference Grounds,*** a state-owned facility on 60 acres that has been the scene of many social, ethical, religious, scientific, educational, and governmental conferences: the old Chautauqua of the West transformed to meet today's needs. The buildings date to 1913, several of them (administration building, chapel, Crocker, Scripps, and Merrill Halls) and the stone entrance gates being representative of Julia Morgan's Craftsman style. Wood and stone are used in a more contemporary but appropriate way in the later buildings by John C. Warnecke & Assoc.—whose Surf and Sand hotel complex (1959) won an AIA award—and Smith, Barker, Hanssen. When conferences do not need the space, ordinary visitors can rent rooms (see Part IV).

Victorian Houses

Most of Pacific Grove is residential, primarily small vacation or retirement cottages but with excellent Victorian houses here and there. On Ocean View Boulevard at 5th Street you passed one of the best, **Green Gables**** (1878), which has four rooms for visitors (see Part IV). The house has a corner tower facing diagonally. David Gebhard's architectural guide remarks that the inn reflects the English Queen Anne style, with half-timbering. A block or so away, at 230 6th St., the **Trummer House*** (ca. 1889), with more American Queen Anne elements—shingles, spindle-work—provides a contrast. Further from the shore are the **LaPorte Mansion**** (1880s), 1030 Lighthouse Ave., **Gosby House*** (an inn), 643 Lighthouse Ave., and next door, **Hart Mansion*** (Maison Bergerac restaurant), and **Langford House,*** 225 Central at Evans, which was owned by the judge who had the gate between Pacific Grove and Monterey removed in 1880. **Holman's Department Store,** Lighthouse Avenue, isn't historic but is where the flagpole skater in *Cannery Row* drew crowds from miles around ("since there weren't many flagpole skaters and since this one was by far the best, he had for the last year gone about breaking his own world's record," which was 127 hours). The Eureka Federal Savings office at 599 Lighthouse houses the small **Bear Flag Museum,** exhibiting Monterey Peninsula memorabilia and California art. Open Mon.-Thurs. 9-4:30, Fri. 9-6.

PRACTICAL INFORMATION

Information on Getting There, Getting Around, and What to Do is in Chapter 10. Accommodations (including camping) and restaurants are discussed in Part IV under the heading Monterey Peninsula and listed under Pacific Grove, Pebble Beach, Monterey, and Carmel, Carmel Highlands and Highway, and Carmel Valley.

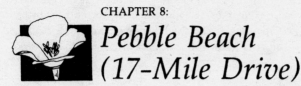

Pebble Beach (17-Mile Drive)

HIGHLIGHTS

The very rich, being different from you and me, not only have more money, they live at Pebble Beach. The wonder is that they allow us to come in and look at their million-dollar digs and divots and their priceless stretch of Pacific shoreline.

For Pebble Beach is basically a private, fenced-in residential playground, admission by privilege of home ownership or by $4. It may be the only town in the United States where you have to pay at the gate to reach the U.S. Post Office.

"Town" actually stretches things, for the thousand or so residences are scattered in sometimes splendidly secluded locations at the edges of *six* golf courses or within the whack of a tennis ball of the rocky shore. The less well-to-do have houses here and there in the **Del Monte Forest,** the woods that still cover most of the Monterey Peninsula. And our remark about paying admission stretches the truth, for walkers and bicyclists can enter free (8-11 A.M. only!). The $4 in any case can be knocked off the tab at the Lodge at Pebble Beach, the successor of the old Hotel Del Monte. Furthermore, you can probably argue us into defending the gate fee because of the costs of maintaining the private 17-Mile Drive as a turnpike for rubberneckers and shutterbugs as well as to hold down the crowds at the annual Bing Crosby National Pro-Am Golf Championship (or the U.S. Open—held here in 1972 and 1982—or the PGA—held in 1977) or the yacht regattas in Stillwater Cove or the horse shows or the annual Concours d'Elegance, which has a pre-1914 vintage car, two Ferrari, and three Rolls-Royce categories; Bugattis have won the most often.

WHAT TO SEE

Well, one's experience is enriched, not impoverished, by visiting Pebble Beach, if only to drive or pedal the **17-Mile Drive.***** If you're touring the Peninsula from north to south, you've driven through Monterey and Pacific Grove and rounded the Peninsula at Point Pinos to the Pacific Grove gate of the 17-Mile Drive. Don't try to clock the distance, for the shoreside road is only about 12.8 miles, and the inland loop through the forest back to Pacific Grove takes it up to 18.6. (There are also entrances in Monterey off Forest Lodge Road; off Highway 1 on Carmel Hill; and in Carmel on North San Antonio Avenue.) A route map is available at the gate, and the main drive is marked. If you get lost on the smaller roads while looking at the houses, you can, as another guidebook puts it so well, "knock on a door and the butler will gladly direct you."

Points of interest: **Spanish Bay**** and **Moss Beach**** are straight ahead when the 17-Mile Drive dips toward the sea. Portolá camped here in 1769 while trying to find Monterey Bay, but it may have been too foggy to recognize Vizcaíno's O-shaped bay. Picnicking. A new resort hotel is proposed for this area. **Point Joe,**** perhaps named for an old Japanese squatter amid the links and mansions who had to be bought off before he'd leave, has been the scene of three shipwrecks in what is nicknamed "The Restless Sea," the conflux of several ocean currents. You're passing the two golf courses—Dunes Course (1925) and Shore Course (1963)—of the **Monterey Peninsula Country Club** (clubhouse by Clarence A. Tantau, 1925), members only. You can sometimes spot blacktail deer on or near the edges of the greens of these and other courses. Between the fairways of the Shore Course and across the network of bridle paths are the jumps of the **Bird Rock Hunter–Steeple-**

chase Course, used for hunter trials and other equestrian events. The 11th Cavalry used to gallop here before World War II.

Seal and Bird Rocks

Past the two courses is a pulloff for the **Seal and Bird Rocks,**** where you can likely see hundreds of barking California and stellar sea lions sunning or swimming (anything smaller than a sea lion may be a leopard seal or a harbor seal), and maybe spot some sea otters, who were once on the way to extinction but now number up to 1,500. Look for the otters in kelp beds, where they'll be feeding on abalone, sleeping, or grooming, which is a constant process to keep their insulating fur from matting. You'll probably see more sea gulls, nearly black cormorants standing vigil for their next meal (though they may be dozing in overstuffed satiety), and sea ducks. Picnicking is allowed.

The next two golf courses are **Spyglass Hill Course** (Robert Trent Jones, 1966), ranked in the top 40 nationally and open to the public, and the 6,500-yard **Cypress Point Course** (Alister McKenzie, 1928; clubhouse by George Washington Smith), in the top 20 but private. Part of the 16th fairway is over the Pacific Ocean. From the **Cypress Point Lookout**** on a clear day you can see the Point Sur Lighthouse 20 miles to the south.

On the inland side of the road at Cypress Point is the **Crocker Monterey Cypress Grove,***** 13 acres of the rare, photographically dramatic cypress, the oldest and biggest of which is named for railroad builder Charles Crocker, who was the founder in 1880 of the whole Pebble Beach–Del Monte Forest playground.

Fancy Houses

Between Cypress Point and the Lodge at Pebble Beach are some of the most visible of the expensive homes, beginning with what appears to be a castle in the cypress, the **Fagan** (or **Helen Crocker) House**** (George Washington Smith, 1927–28), a stone "Byzantine palace." Many of the others along here date to the late teens and 20s when the developer of the Del Monte Properties (now Pebble Beach Company—owned by 20th Century–Fox), Samuel F. B. Morse, deliberately set out to create an American Riviera for the wealthy. There are houses by Willis Polk, Julia Morgan, Bernard Maybeck, Lewis P. Hobart, Bakewell and Brown, and other major California architects—but most can't be seen unless you happen to know the owner. Jack Morse kept things here well under control until his death in 1969. On the coast road here you can look for the **Ford House** (1924), a Maybeck Spanish Colonial; **Chase House** (1924), a somewhat Romanesque stone residence by Addison Mizner; and the Spanish Colonial Revival **Vincent House** (1924) and **Hatley House** (1926), both by G. W. Smith. More obvious are some striking modern houses with large windows to bring the view into the living rooms.

Passing **Sunset Point** you come to a tree you've seen on a million postcards and every tour brochure: the **Lone Cypress,***** standing in isolated splendor at the end of a little point of land. Pity the poor rich who live in the house next door. Before you get to **Pescadero** ("fisherman") **Point,** the southern tip of the Monterey Peninsula, on the inland side is the **Ghost Tree,*** a wind-and-spray-bleached cypress of unusual bleakness that gives you an idea why Robert Louis Stevenson called the cypresses "ghosts fleeing before the wind."

Pebble Beach Lodge and Links

Around Pescadero Point is the center of local activity, the Spanish Colonial Revival **Lodge at Pebble Beach**** (Lewis P. Hobart, 1915), in front of which is the famous 18th green of the **Pebble Beach Golf Links** (John F. Neville and Douglas Grant, 1919), one of the top 10 golf courses in the country, home of the Crosby "clambake," and open by reservation to the public (green fee is $50 unless you're staying at the lodge). The 6,815-yard course is one of the world's most challenging. Laid out as a figure-eight on the edge of three coves and out along two points on Carmel Bay, the course has nonparallel fairways; out-of-bounds, high roughs; one green (the seventh) the size of a postage stamp; one (the eighth) in which you hit across the water; many deviously placed, deep bunkers; lots of traps; also rocks and trees, culminating in the beautiful shore-side 18th green, in which once again you shoot over the water. "Beauty and the beast," one sportswriter called the Pebble Beach Golf Links.

The Lodge at Pebble Beach is pretty expensive, also pretty comfortable, but it's worth a few bucks to stop for lunch and get the gate charge rebated. (See also Part IV.) **Stillwater Cove*** is a safe anchorage if you've come by yacht, the **Collins Polo Field** just dandy if you've brought your polo pony.

The Carmel gate is a mile from the lodge, but you can also loop back to Pacific Grove, with stops at **Shepherd's Knoll*** and **Huckleberry Hill*** for views from the top of Carmel Hill.

PRACTICAL INFORMATION

Even Elysian Fields need a guidebook. Information on Getting There, Getting Around, and What to Do is in Chapter 10. Accommodations and restaurants—the small range there is—are listed in Part IV under Pebble Beach, but see also Carmel, Carmel Highlands and Highway, Carmel Valley, Pacific Grove, and Monterey.

CHAPTER 9:

Carmel
and Carmel Valley

HIGHLIGHTS

Carmel attracts, yet once you get there you may want to flee to some large place like the beach to breathe deeply. On the one hand Carmel has some unpretentious little inns that are antidotes to a month of Holiday Inns, some awfully good restaurants, and dozens of worthwhile shops. On the other hand the village downtown is so self-consciously cute, over-refined, and controlled that it cloys— and you look forward to doing something muscular and sweaty, or maybe vulgar, like jamming a hot dog in your mouth and cheering loudly at a football game. In short, Carmel is too dainty.

Though the town extends north and east of Father Serra's Carmel Mission, and is suburbanizing rural Carmel Valley, the settlement did not follow until long after the mission's roof had collapsed in neglect and then been restored. In fact it was the ruined mission, located 17 miles by carriage-and-four from Monterey's old Hotel Del Monte, that attracted the post–Gold Rush genera-

tion, including the writers and artists who created Carmel's lingering reputation as an art colony, "the seacoast of Bohemia," as it
was termed by one literary historian.

Carmel missed becoming the Catholic equivalent of Pacific
Grove when an effort toward that end failed in the 1890s. In 1903
a couple of high-minded developers, Devendorf and Powers, obtained most of the Peninsula's south shore from ranchers and offered lots to poets and painters and professors from Stanford and
Berkeley for as little as $50 (houses now start at $250,000). Two
years later the poet George Sterling and the photograper Arnold
Genthe built rustic houses, followed the next year by novelist
Mary Austin. They in turn attracted cronies and hangers-on, as-
piring writers and established figures. There were visitors like
Jack London, Joaquin Miller, and Ambrose Bierce; Charles Warren Stoddard and painter Charles Rollo Peters would visit from
their homes in Monterey; there were short-term settlers like Upton
Sinclair (who wasn't very popular but added political dash), William Rose Benét, Van Wyck Brooks (who got married here), and
young Harry S. Lewis (better known later as Sinclair, "Red"
Lewis wasn't much liked, either, during his six months in a shack
at the beach, but he came back the next year and sold 15 story
plots to Jack London).

With Sterling as their cynosure, the Bohemians talked incessant-
ly and had wild beach parties, took walks on the shore and in the
pines, did a little writing now and then—nothing of any great importance, as it turned out, but their presence in a scenic place attracted the nation's attention.

Austin and Sterling both left about 1913–14, approximately the
time Carmel started building up, and things weren't the same after
that. Harry Leon Wilson, who was once well known as author of
Ruggles of Red Gap, was resident after 1912, Lincoln Steffens
from the late 1920s (photographers Edward Weston and Ansel Adams came later); the most illustrious second-generation Carmel artistic figure, and its most solitary, Robinson Jeffers, came in 1914.

Jeffers arrived in August that year, already depressed by the
outbreak of war in Europe. "When the stage-coach topped the hill
from Monterey," he later wrote on the dustjacket of *Roan Stallion*
(1925), "and we looked down through the pines and sea-fogs on

Carmel Bay, it was evident that we had come without knowing it to our inevitable place." The town was small but tidy-looking. The main street, Ocean Avenue, hadn't been paved yet, so it was dusty and muddy in turn; trees had been planted down the middle to anchor the surface. Houses looked like rural retreats, and often occupied dozens of acres. But the Arts and Crafts Club was eight years old, the outdoor Forest Theater (the only Carmel leader in any cultural movement) was putting on a Mary Austin play, and William Chase was conducting summer art classes for vacationing teachers. The unknown Jeffers built his then-isolated Tor House and Hawk Tower, achieved fame for his misanthropic epics set on the Big Sur Coast, and kept to himself. Increasingly he felt hemmed in by development and even had to sell off some of his property because of high taxes. He died, aged 75, in 1962.

Just about the same time John Steinbeck, who lived in Pacific Grove in the thirties, visited Carmel with his poodle Charley and commented sardonically: "If Carmel's founders should return, they could not afford to live there, but it wouldn't go that far. They would instantly be picked up as suspicious characters and deported over the city line."

Carmel's residents long ago passed the ordinances necessary to protect this wooded Arcadia, measures "by which Carmel's greatness in simplicity might be preserved," said the 1929 city code. It became a town where traffic is routed around trees in the middle of the street, where there's hardly a sidewalk or streetlight outside the commercial area, where commercial signs are kept small and unobtrusive: a place with no traffic lights, parking meters or garages, buildings more than three stories high, neon signs, juke boxes, wax museums, courthouse, jail, mortuary, cemetery—not even a school (they're outside village limits) nor any mail delivery, because the houses do not have numbers (many people bestow names on their houses, everybody goes to the 6,649-box post office to collect mail and pass the time of day on the several benches with those recognizable as residents). There's no nightlife to speak of and those under 18 have to be in by 10:30.

As the real artists left, their places were taken by the affluent and the retired, whose Sunday paintings fill the local art galleries and whose screeches against tourist buses and commercialization fill the local columns. Today's square-mile Carmel-by-the-Sea (the long-standing but pretentious official name) is a rich plot of land, with an assessed valuation of something like $125,000 per quarter-acre. It has rather more than 5,000 residents (mostly old, mostly conservative) and, daily, four times that many visitors (amazingly, all kinds). There are 50 little motels and inns that are booked up long ahead of time for such events as the Carmel Bach Festival, about 70 restaurants, 70 art galleries, and well over 150 shops. It has, by its computerized city inventory, 10,555 trees, all protected by a fierce ordinance ($500, a year in jail) and a five-man forestry department.

Carmel has in the past exuded so much sweet charm that tourists have swarmed in like honeybees, riling the residents and threatening to make Carmel the chief victim of its own appeal. Tourists as well as guidebook writers might feel a bit awkward coming to a place that has an organization like SCAT (Sensible Citizens Against Tourists). Carmelites aren't the only ones to wave cudgels at outlanders; they're doing it up and down the coast: in Bolinas, Mendocino, Big Sur—even in San Francisco. We are the first to agree about some of the evil effects of mass tourism. For example, higher rents have driven out many of the mundane little shops and services—like dry-cleaners—that even rich folks need. There is too much traffic congestion. Carmel has to fight to keep out standardized American tourist facilities, like fast-food franchises, and to prevent too much buildup of freeways and motor lodges outside the city limits. Yet much as Carmelites might favor keeping the tourists out and re-creating the quiet, artsy village of yore (we are told it once existed), we believe Carmel is dependent on the tourist trade and must cope creatively, as the National Park Service is doing in Yosemite Valley.

The individual traveler (i.e., the reader of this book) can play a part in keeping Carmel in equilibrium by planning ahead (reading up, sketching an itinerary, making reservations), parking well away from Ocean Avenue (there's free parking at the Sunset Center, 8th and San Carlos, for example), and walking as much as possible.

What are Carmel's attractions? In ascending order, gallery-hopping, shopping, architectural and literary landmarks, the Pacific shore, and Carmel Mission.

WHAT TO SEE

The mission first because it was first, in 1771, after Serra left the mud-and-stick church in Monterey's presidio. The **Mission San Carlos Borromeo de Carmelo,***** Rio Road just off Highway 1, but less than a mile south of Ocean Avenue, is, with Santa Barbara Mission, the most beautiful of the California missions, mostly as a result of the landscaping vegetation and accessories in front and in the courtyard (trees, fountains, vines, flowers, memorials) and that particular mellowness that comes to Spanish-style masonry when the weather has been at it awhile.

This building is in fact the seventh since the mission was established: the first was a log shelter; the present 1793–97 structure of stone was designed by Manuel Ruiz, a master mason brought from Mexico for the job, and built under the supervision of Serra's successor as father-president of the California missions, Fermín Francisco de Lasuén. The church, which has been designated a basilica (one of 11 Catholic basilicas in the United States), has two unequal bell towers, the left-hand one being larger and more Moorish-looking, and a distinctive star-shaped (quatrefoil) window above the portal. The chapel has a vaulted ceiling.

What still stands today, extensively but carefully restored, is only part of what existed in the missions' heyday, when there was a large quadrangle with many quarters for the padres and the Indians, soldiers' barracks, and workshops, not to mention outbuildings and corrals (one of the most complete and authentic re-creations of an entire mission, still in its rural setting, is Mission San Antonio de Padua, in southern Monterey County; see Chapter 4).

We should, however, be grateful for what somehow survived the secularization of the missions and the three or four decades of neglect. When Robert Louis Stevenson was here in 1879, he found the church "roofless and ruinous, sea-breezes and sea-fogs, and the alternation of the rain and sunshine, daily widening the breaches." Private ranchland extended right up to the church walls. He may not have even known that rubble covered the under-floor graves of Fathers Serra (d. 1784) and Lasuén (d. 1803), who between them had founded 18 of the 21 missions. (Their graves were discovered in 1882.) Stevenson visited the mission on the feast day of St.

Charles of Borromeo, November 4, when the padre from Monterey
rode across the hill to celebrate mass with the few Indians left in
the neighborhood: "You may hear God served with perhaps more
touching circumstances than in any other temple under heaven,"
Stevenson wrote after hearing a blind, 80-year-old Indian conducting an Indian choir that sang, to Gregorian music, correctly pronounced but odd, nasal Latin.

The church got a steeply pitched roof in 1884 but careful restoration wasn't undertaken until 1936–40, when the church was restored to its 1797 appearance. Today's visitor will be quite impressed. The **Serra Museum** has a large collection of Serra
artifacts, including his small, cell-like room and his elaborate sar-
cophagus (by Jo Mora), and the original silver altar pieces Serra
brought from Mexico. You can also see the original mission kitch-
en, a re-created version of the mission library of 1,500 volumes—
the first library in California—and the old cemetery, including the
grave of "Old Gabriel," an Indian baptized by Serra who died in
1890, at the age of 140 (the inscription says 151). The **Harry
Downey Museum** at the mission shows the reconstruction of this
and six other California missions by Downey. The mission is open,
free (donations requested), Mon.-Sat. 9-4:30, Sun. 10:30-4:30. Information: (408) 624-3600; check the Yellow Pages for times of
masses.

Carmel's Coast

"Praise the sea," wrote the English lexicographer John Florio; "on
shore remain." The communities on the Monterey Peninsula face
the sea in different ways. For Monterey the Pacific Ocean was
basically functional: it provided a relatively quick but not undan-
gerous form of transportation from New Spain or anywhere else,
and the ocean itself had created at least the semblance of a harbor.
There were sea lanes before land roads.

So Monterey oriented itself toward the water: the Custom
House, whose foundation was near the lapping waves, Fisherman's
Wharf and later wharves, the marina, Cannery Row, and even the
Naval Postgraduate School (since the navy likes to be near the
water). Pacific Grove, Pebble Beach, and Carmel were founded
well over a century later, in more affluent times, perhaps, but in
any case after vacationing-away-from-home had become something

the less affluent could participate in. And the founders and settlers came by land, sometimes from back East, sometimes by train from San Francisco: no one had to sail into Carmel Bay and establish a beachhead. So the newer settlements had a different attitude toward the ocean: it was mostly scenery, nature's decoration outside windows and at the edge of yards and golf links, a playground to the extent the water temperature allowed.

The **Carmel Coast*****—which by some definitions extends far south toward Big Sur—is a good one, as poets like Jeffers, photographers like Weston and Adams, and painters by the dozens have discovered. The town fronts on a broad white strand on Carmel Bay, the **City Beach**** where Ocean Avenue ends. It is, as we suggested above, a good place to go if you feel claustrophobic inland, but it is a dangerous place to swim. The sand is of the variety good for burying toes and building sandcastles—in fact, it is so good that Carmel puts on the Great Sandcastle Contest here every year, on a weekend afternoon in September or October. The sand sculptures are splendid if unfortunately transient. Sand dunes stretch north to the Pebble Beach Golf Links. Visitors with cars or bicycles can take **Scenic Road***** south past some expensive but generally unpretentious homes around Carmel Point to **Carmel River State Beach**** at the rivermouth; this includes a lagoon and nature reserve. For **Point Lobos State Reserve***** and other points just south of Carmel, see p. 164.

Architecture

We are quite sure you won't quickly forget some of the architecture you find in Carmel. Most appropriate for a town that accentuates the small, controlled, and picturesque, there are a large number of houses called, variously, fairy-tale, Hansel and Gretel, or Comstock dollhouse. The archetype is the **Tuck Box** (ca. 1925), the well-known breakfast and tea shop (one is tempted to write "shoppe") on Dolores between Ocean and 7th (remember, no house numbers in Carmel). This style originated with a rancher named Hugh Comstock. His wife Mayotta once made a rag doll for a friend's child and then found herself in the doll business. She asked her husband to build a full-fledged **dollhouse,** which still stands on the east side of Torres between 5th and 6th. Comstock became a self-trained architect and builder, going on to build more dollhouses but also innovating in adobe ranch styles (Isabella and Inspiration; Ocean View and Stewart) and otherwise being quite original, as for example the **Butterfly House** on Carmel Point.

On the oceanside of Scenic Road is Frank Lloyd Wright's classic thin-stone **Walker House**** (1952), with a porcelain enamel roof; it's located on a rocky point. Between Ocean View and Stewart, look uphill for Robinson Jeffers's eucalyptus-obscured **Tor House** and **Hawk Tower,***** built of stone with his own hands and still occupied by members of his family.

Jeffers bought what was once a much larger piece of land in some isolation here in 1919, hired a contractor and a stonemason, then hired himself as mortar mixer and hod carrier so he could learn the stonemason's art. Granite boulders were lifted from the beach to construct a small house modeled on a Tudor barn in Surrey that Una Jeffers had liked, with a single large room upstairs for beds and Jeffers's desk, a redwood-paneled living room, and three other rooms downstairs (he died in "The Bed by the Window" with its inspiring view).

The next year Jeffers alone was able to start building walls, a garage, and the square, three-story Hawk Tower (finished 1924), the latter designed after the ancient Irish towers, with the fireplace appropriately inscribed in Latin with a quotation from Virgil: "They make their own dreams for themselves." Other rooms and an annex were added to Tor House in time, and the eucalyptus have grown high on three sides. Here, there, and everywhere are embedded stones from around the world. In "Tor House," one of several poems he wrote about his home, Jeffers predicted that

> . . . if you should look for this place after a handful of lifetimes
> Perhaps of my planted forest a few
> May stand yet . . .
> . . . fire and the axe are devils.
> Look for the foundations of sea-worn granite,
>   my fingers had the art to make stone love stone,
>   you will find some remnant.
> But if you should look in your idleness after ten thousand years:
> It is the granite knoll on the granite
> And lava tongue in the midst of the bay,
>   by the mouth of the Carmel
> River-valley, these four will remain. . . .

You will know it by the wild sea fragrance of wind
Though the ocean may have climbed or retired a little; . . .
My ghost you needn't look for; it is probably
Here, but a dark one, deep in the granite. . . .

The poet's son Donnan had to sell all but a half-acre because of high taxes, but otherwise preserved Jeffers's furniture, paintings and objects, and entire library until 1979, when the Tor House Foundation purchased the property for $250,000; Donnan's widow has life estate in part of the house, but visitors (six at a time), can tour Fri.-Sat., on an hour-long visit. The English cottage garden alone is worth a tour, and the extremely personal, hand-crafted house and tower are well worth the $5 tour charge. Information and reservations, which are a must: Robinson Jeffers Tor House Foundation, Box 1887, Carmel 93921, (408) 624-1813. Bring film and wear sturdy shoes.

Curiously, Carmel takes no interest in the **Lincoln Steffens Home** at Ocean and San Antonio, where the muckraking journalist (1866–1936) wrote his well-known *Autobiography* (1931). "I have been over into the Future, and it works," he wrote there of his visit to Russia in 1919. Strange that he chose to live in a place so purposefully archaic.

Among other buildings of note are the **Harrison Memorial Library*** (1927), on which Bernard Maybeck consulted but which has been expanded since; **Cypress Inn** (ca. 1920), Lincoln and 7th, with a wonderful Spanish Mission-style portal; **Charles Greene Studio*** (ca. 1918), west side of Lincoln between 13th and 14th, designed by one of the Greene brothers for himself (two of his houses for other people are in Carmel Highlands); and the **Converse House** (William W. Wurster, 1933), west side of Santa Rosa Street between Ocean and Mountain View.

Devendorf Park on Ocean between Junipero and Mission is a convenient place for a picnic lunch (no tables); you can get the fixings at the famous **Mediterranean Market,** opposite at Ocean and Mission. The park has a statue of Father Serra.

The big cultural event is the July-August **Carmel Bach Festival** (founded in 1937). Festival performances take place at the mission and 730-seat **Sunset Center,** San Carlos and 8th. The center, occupying the largest plot of land in Carmel, also has a gallery with changing exhibits. The old open-air **Forest Theater** (1910), Mountain View and Santa Rita, is frequently in use in summer, and has free summer Sunday programs.

Shopping

Shopping is a little more exciting in Carmel than in most places because it is accompanied by a feeling of discovery. The feeling is akin to the delight Americans who are used to efficient, stream-lined, but bland shopping centers and city shopping districts experience when they explore the twisty streets and alleys of medieval European towns or the chaotic bazaars and souks of the East. For Carmel's 150 shops are not neatly lined up for efficient browsing, instead are more likely to be tucked away in courtyards and lanes and rambling shopping-gallery buildings. Some are out of Hansel and Gretel, like Tuck Box Court (Dolores near 7th) and the El Matador shops (Ocean near Lincoln), while others are in 1920s or modern Spanish Colonial Revival, like Las Tiendas Court (Ocean near Dolores), La Rambla Court (Lincoln near Ocean), and Mission Patio (Mission between 5th and 6th).

The shopping district takes up about 20 small blocks on and off Ocean Avenue, on Junipero, Mission, San Carlos, Dolores, Lincoln, and Monte Verde, and including the cross streets, 4th, 5th, 6th, and 7th avenues. You can find nearly anything you desire, especially the higher-priced things. Shopping here being such a serious matter, we've described it in more detail in Chapter 10.

Art

There is art and there is . . . art. Carmel's **art galleries** display rather more of the latter than the former. Indeed, some of the art-gallery owners are artists—or perhaps it is the other way around. The painters seem excessively fond of crashing waves and wind-bowed cypresses, perhaps even more than the photographers, and we would say that some sculptors are positively transported by the sight of driftwood.

Well, by our definition we are forced to recognize that there are seascapes and there are . . . seascapes, so if you've got several hours you might look into some of the 70-odd galleries in Carmel (God help us, there are more in Carmel Valley, Monterey, and Pacific

Grove) to see what you might find. The free *Monterey Peninsula Review,* for one, has a complete list, but if you merely want to browse for an hour, circle the block bounded by 5th, 6th, San Carlos, and Dolores, where there are about 27 galleries.

Otherwise, here is a selection of galleries of note:

Arts & Designs of Japan (by appointment, 408/624-0822): wood-block prints, textiles

Carmel Art Association: exhibition of local artists

Casa Dolores Gallery: Western art

Connoisseur Gallery: Sixteenth- to twentieth-century art

Josephus Daniels: photography

Davis-Holdship: traditional American, early Carmel

Bill Dodge: primitives

Galerie de France: French impressionist, post-impressionist

Galerie de Tours: Nineteenth- and twentieth-century European, American

Pasquale Iannetti: Sixteenth- to twentieth-century European prints

Seals & Owls: Canadian Eskimo

Southwestern Arts: American Indian

Weston Photography Gallery: photographs

Zantman Art Galleries: American, European art, sculpture

Carmel Valley

Carmel Valley** is so different that it might be wise to think of it as named for the Carmel River that meanders through it rather than for small, cute Carmel-by-the-Sea. This is a sweet valley where once the mission's cattle and sheep grazed, where life on the Mexican ranchos must have been as idyllic as portrayed by Gertrude Atherton and Mary Austin, and where now the affluent live and anyone can play.

The play includes **golf** (the several courses are very visible), **tennis** (John Gardiner's Tennis Ranch is discreetly signposted T. R. Gardiner's), **riding** and **polo,** all as described in Chapter 10 under "What to Do." The **Hidden Valley Music Seminars Institute for**

the Arts, Carmel Valley Road and Ford Road, has a heavy summer schedule of opera, recitals, and special events.

The scenic valley begins at Highway 1 not far from Carmel Mission. The intersection of Carmel Valley Road and Highway 1 is where nearly all the commercial development is, but this area is really the suburb of Carmel-by-the-Sea. The **Barnyard** and **Carmel Crossroads** are two collections of shops, mostly oriented to the visitor.

The valley road runs languorously in the sun (there's far more here than on the Peninsula) for 14 miles to **Carmel Valley Village,** the only real town to serve the ranchers, rock stars, and resorts. The road then winds, and winds, into the lower parts of the Santa Lucia Mountains before emerging some 40 miles later in the Salinas Valley at Greenfield. Unless you're staying at one of the several resorts, we'd recommend at least a short drive to Carmel Valley Village.

There are a couple of intermediate destinations. The first is **Garland Ranch Regional Park,**** eight miles from Highway 1. Hikers and riders can enjoy wildflowers and birdwatching along seven miles of trails, which include a 1.5-mile loop from the visitor center and a three-mile climb up Snivley's Ridge. There's also picnicking. Information: (408) 659-4488.

The more remote destination, 25 miles off Highway 1, in the Cachagua Valley, is Comsat's **Jamesburg Earth Station,** location of a 97-foot dish antenna 10 stories tall. This is one of a network of 325 antennas in 133 countries (the United States has eight) that, along with five Intelsat satellites, comprise the world's satellite communications system. Calls from the United States to Asia are routed through here and bounce off the satellite high over the Pacific Ocean. Guided tours are possible; call (408) 659-2293 for information, or check with one of the visitors' bureaus.

The next destination, even more remote, is the **Tassajara Zen Center,** but that has more associations with Big Sur and is covered in Chapter 11.

PRACTICAL INFORMATION

Information on Getting There, Getting Around, and What to Do is in Chapter 10. Accommodations (including camping) and restaurants are discussed in Part IV under the heading Monterey Peninsula and listed under Carmel, Carmel Highlands and Highway, and Carmel Valley; see also Pebble Beach, Monterey, and Pacific Grove.

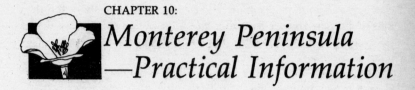

CHAPTER 10:

Monterey Peninsula —Practical Information

HIGHLIGHTS

WHAT TO DO

The people who live on the Monterey Peninsula spend an enormous amount of time not working—that is, playing. From Bach to golf, gray-whale watching to hang gliding, adobe house tours to shopping, fishing to jazz, the visitor, too, will find many ways to spend the time other than driving and eating.

Shopping

To go to the Monterey Peninsula without looking in the window of one Carmel shop is like going to Las Vegas without betting so much as a nickel at a slot machine. Here, instead of shopping to live, you can live to go shopping. The town exists almost exclusively for recreational shopping. Residents long ago filled up their walls and cupboards and shelves and rooms with Eskimo carvings and English wrapped candies, French antiques and California crafts, framed orange-crate labels and potted herbs, down quilts and intelligent toys. From day to day even the well-to-do need Ajax cleanser and four-penny nails and a couple of new shoes for the kids and a new shower curtain. (A plumber's helper? No, we don't have anything like that here, ma'am; did you try the Northridge Mall in Salinas?)

The visitor, on the other hand, will find delight in Carmel, at least for two hours; grit your teeth after that. As described in Chapter 9, most of the shops are located in dozens of courtyards, malls, patios, arcades, and lanes, and along the 10 or 11 shopping streets. There's only one biggish shopping gallery downtown, **Carmel Plaza** (CP in our listings below), Ocean Avenue between Mission and Junipero Serra. At Highway 1 and Carmel Valley Road are two drive-in-and-park shopping centers, both nevertheless devoted to recreational shopping. One is the attractively designed and landscaped but quite meandering complex called the **Barnyard** (BY in the listings). The other, still developing at this writing, is **The Crossroads** (CC).

We don't neglect the Peninsula's other cities. Monterey has most of the functional shops, with big stores (Macy's and Saks—but no Penney's or Sears) and smaller ones mainly located at suburban **Del Monte Center** (DMC in the listings), Highway 1 and Munras Avenue, before Carmel Hill. These stores, significantly, do not advertise in tourist media. **Cannery Row** (CR) has the kind of retailers that serious shoppers tend to avoid. **Pebble Beach** (PB) shops, around the Lodge, have a captive clientele and so do not advertise themselves widely. **Pacific Grove** (PG) and **Carmel Valley Village** (CVV) have some stores of interest, and we identified *one* in Seaside.

Here's our mini–Yellow Pages shopping guide. No parenthetical letter code means it's downtown Carmel.

African imports: Baobab Collection (CC)
Americana: Grapes of Wrath Antiques (CR)
American country: The Plantation Peddler (CC),
    Mum's Place (PG), The Two of Us (PG)

American Indian arts, crafts: Southwestern Arts Ltd. (near BY)

Antiques (see also major categories): Anna Beck (near BY), Antiques & Accents, J. B. Whitney, Aunt Penny's Attic (M), Cannery Row Antique Warehouse (CR), Bower & Bossier, Carmel Antiques, Golden Eagle, Luciano Antiques, Emporium Galorium, Antiques (CR), Royal House Antiques (PG), Sewers of Paris (CR), Clearing House Antiques (PG)

Aquascutum: Rudy-Harris Ltd. (BY)

Art supplies: Artist's Palette (BY)

Balancing, air: Air Balance Engineering

Bath accessories: Pampered Hamper (CP), Port of Carmel, Le Bain (CC)

Brass: Shells of Carmel, Anchor Gallery, Import House (all CP), Brass International, Brass of California (also English; BY), Sweet Thursday (CR)

Brass rubbing: Brass Rubbing Centre Ltd.

Bookbinding, fine: The Book Bindery

Books: Books Inc. (CP), Waldenbooks (DMC), Thunderbird (also restaurant; BY), Old Monterey Book Co. (used, rare; M), Apple Pie (children's; CR), The Book Room, Carmel Bay Co., Carmel Book Shop (used, rare)

Canadian imports: Arctic Bay Trading Co. (has Hudson's Bay blankets; CC)

Candles: Candles of Carmel, Wicks & Wax

Candy: See's (DMC), Godiva Chocolatier (BY), Mrs. M's Fudge, Adams Too/Eden of Flavor (crystalized flowers and seeds), Sweet Temptations (BY), Cottage of Sweets, Barton's

Carpets, oriental: Conway of Asia (also carousel horses)

Cat things: The Cat's Meow (BY)

Cheese: Cheese Shop (CP), California Seasons (CR)

Children's clothes: Mrs. Pussycat's Porch (BY), The Crib Set (infants, toddlers), Rosemary & George, Top Notch, Belles & Beaux (girls' sizes 7–14), Bernadine's Bib 'n Tucker, Deb and Heir (M), Richardson's Strawberry Patch (girls)

Chinese imports: China Art Center, Cathay of Carmel (BY), G. T. Marsh (M)

Chocolate: Godiva (BY), See's (DMC), Grandma Buffalo's Chips (cookies!; CR)

Christmas decor (all year!): Everyday Is Christmas (CP), The Holly Berry (BY), Holiday Hutch (CC)

Clocks: Timepeace (the mouse clock performs at 1 P.M.), Van's Clocks 'n Things, Toc of the Town, Antique Clock Shop (CR)

Coins: Blackburn & Blackburn, Kremer's Serendipity (coins as display; BY), Cannery Row Stamps & Coins (CR)

Cosmetics: Cosmetiques, Merle Norman (DMC)

Crafts: Carmel Work Center Shop, Countrywide Crafts (BY), Carmel Creations (CP), The Red Rooster (BY), The Plantation Peddler (CC)

Cyprus imports: Patrician (BY)

Decoys: Decoy Gallery, House of Steins

Department stores: Macy's (DMC), Holman's (PG), Carmel Bay Co. (specialized)

Dog things: Total Dog (BY)

Dolls: Unicorn (BY), Trotter's London Tower (antiques; PG)

Down: European Down Shop (CP), Down by Bugaboo (BY), Scandia Down (CC)

Ducks, stuffed cloth: Raffles (CP)

English country: The Collection (CC), Carmel Bay Co.

Eskimo crafts, art: Seals & Owls

Fabrics: Old World Cloth (imported), The Cotton Bale (BY), Kazuko's (Asian fabrics, couture), House of Fabrics (DMC), La Fille du Roi (French)

Fudge: Mrs. M's Fudge

Games: Game Gallery, Thinker Toys (CP), Chess Corner (CP)

Gifts or things no one really needs: Something Extra (BY), among others

Golf: Pebble Beach Pro Shop (PB), Village Golf Shop

Gourmet: Mediterranean Market (also DMC), Nielsen Bros. Market, Peter's European Foods

Greek imports: Kolonaki (CP)

Handblown glass: John Calder, Cloud Art Glass (BY)

Hats: High Hatter

Hay, feed: Carmel Valley Market (CVV)

Herbs: Adams Too/Eden of Flavor (live herbs, also tea, perfume)

Housewares, home accessories: Carmel Bay Co., La Porte's (PG), Glass & Brass (M), Byron & Schiller (CP), Allen & Co. (CP), The Collection (CC), Countrywide Crafts (BY)

Irish imports: Country Dublin Ltd.

Iron, hand-forged: Barnyard Village Blacksmith (BY)

Jewelry: Contempo, Jewels by Jeffrey, Sun Studios, Gem Craft (all CP); Jewel Boutique, Jewelry Designs/Michael Sherman, D'Lanor (all BY), Concepts, Jean-Pierre, Henry Corbat, Ladyfingers (art nouveau designs), Tusk Jeweler (CR), B&G Traders, Kocek Jeweler, Jade Dynasty (PB)

Kitchenware: Dansk II (seconds), Collector's Kitchen, Carmel Bay Co., Adams Eden of Flavor/Pot-Bellied Stove, Kitchen Traditions (M), The Peppercorn (also BY), Cheese Shop (CP)

Kites: Come Fly a Kite (CP)

Leather: Leather Bound (CP), Hide Park (BY), Michael's Leather Classics, Skin Fits, Mark Cross (PB), The Book Bindery, King of Hearts, North Country Leather

Lingerie: Bloomers (BY), Intimate Intrigue, Silver Thimble

Marimekko fabric: The Cotton Bale (BY)

Men's wear, accessories: Robert Talbott Shop (also PB), Rudy-Harris Ltd. (BY), Derek Rayne Ltd., Dick Bruhn, Back Pocket, Gentlemen's Quarters (CP), Hastings (DMC), Oxbridge Men's Wear, Leonard's (M)

Metaphysical: The Pilgrim's Way

Mexican crafts: Monterey Mexico (M)

Miniatures: Edgemere Shop, R. E. Smith Ltd., Spencers Carmel, The Wooden Horse

Music boxes: The Music Box

Natural food: Cornucopia (BY), Nature Foods Center (DMC)

Needlework: Carmel Needleworks, Les Nouvelles (BY), R. E. Smith Ltd., Fads & Yarns (DMC)

Norwegian imports: Norway House

Objets: Byron & Schiller (CP), Anderle

Orange crate art: The Fine Print (BY)

Orientalia: G. T. Marsh & Co. (one of the oldest
stores around, 1876; M), Song of the Orient (CP),
Orientique (BY), The Oriental Shop (BY), Conway
of Asia (rugs; CVV)

Pendleton woolens: Nell's Plum Tree

Perfumes: Rainbow Scent Co., Bloomers (BY)

Pewter: The Pewter Shop (BY), Edgemere

Photography gallery: The Weston Gallery, The Print,
Friends of Photography (Sunset Center), California
Views/Pat Hathaway (historical; PG)

Polish imports: Imports from Poland (CP)

Porcelain, antique: Davis-Holdship; Beverly, Keller &
Scott

Posters, prints: Poster Graphics (CP), The Fine Print
(BY), Fads & Frames (DMC), Monterey Bay Co.
(CR)

Preserves, jams, jellies: Tuck Box Gift Shop

Quilts: Wild Goose Chase (PG)

Records: Carmel Music (old, new), Do-Re-Mi (BY)

Religious art, books, gifts: The Hermitage Shop
(including fruitcake and brandied date nut cake
made by Big Sur's Camaldolese monks), Kingdom
Come (near BY)

Running: Carmel Tennis (BY)

Scandinavian imports: Dansk II, House of Sweden,
Norway House

Scottish imports: Scottish Shop, Scotch House (BY)

Sea-otter things: Friends of the Sea Otter (also their
office; BY)

Shells: Shells of Carmel (CP)

Shirts: The T-Shirt Corner (BY), Whale of a Shirt
(silk-screened)

Silk: SamSong (Thai; CP), Taj Gallery (Persian)

Silver, antique: Beverly, Keller & Scott, J. Douglas
Antiques

South Asian imports: India-Burma Imports

Spices: Adams Too/Eden of Flavor

Stained glass: Light Opera (CP), Over the Rainbow

Stamps: Blackburn & Blackburn, Kremer's Serendipity (stamps as display; BY), Cannery Row Stamps & Coins (CR)

Stationery: Mr. Peabody's (BY)

Steins: House of Steins

Stoneware: Frangella Designs (BY)

Straw: Village Straw Shop

Sweaters: Sweater Corner, Sweater Shop, Sweater Connexion (BY), M. Raggett

Swedish imports: House of Sweden

Tea: Adams Too/Eden of Flavor, McNaney Mercantile (BY)

Tennis: Carmel Tennis

Tobacco, pipes: Carmel Pipe Shop

Toys: Thinker Toys and Thinker Trains 'n Things (see $10,000 locomotive; CP), The Wooden Horse, Toys Etc. (DMC), Carmel Bay Co., Grapes of Wrath Antiques (old toys; CR)

Travel accessories: The Village Traveler (CP)

Trays: The Second Look (Couroc factory-store seconds; Seaside)

Velour: Sew Softly

Western gear: Hudson & Co. (also imported saddlery; BY)

Wine: Monterey Peninsula Winery (tasting room; M), Carmel Vintage Shoppe, Gifts from Bacchus, Mediterranean Market, Bargetto Winery (tasting room; CR), Rapazzini Winery (tasting room), Petit Bazaar (accessories), Monterey Wine Market (CR)

Women's fashions, accessories: Saks Fifth Avenue (DMC); I. Magnin, Mark Fenwick, Mayfair, Peck & Peck, Joseph Magnin, Cardinale Shoes, Rose Brown, Nina B., Madrigal (all CP); Pappagallo, Patrician, Top Filly (sportswear), La Boutique (all BY); Ellie's Hayloft, Woolen Mill, Plum Pretty (large sizes), Reincarnation (Victorian; PG), Seasons, M'Lady Bruhn, Ornamentique, JAG/Carmel, Nako's (half sizes; DMC), Lanz of California, La Province de Pierre Deux, Lilli, Rittmaster (furs)

Wood stoves, fireplaces: Schrader (PG)

Picnicking, Beach Play

But wait a minute, how can you go to a beautiful coastal place and spend all your time shopping? Besides, spending several hours in Carmel is somewhat like eating every night at a French restaurant.

The Monterey Peninsula shore, from Monterey State Beach all the way around to Point Lobos State Reserve, is nearly all accessible to the public in one way or another. Casual walkers won't be tolerated at the links-by-the-sea at Pebble Beach, but the shore off the rest of the 17-Mile Drive is open—to those who have paid admission (see Chapter 8). Where there isn't a state or city park, the shore is still pretty public, thanks to the California Coastal Act of 1972 and the watchdog Coastal Commission.

Note that we have used the word *shore*. That's because it's not all continuous beach. Beaches are generally of the pocket variety, here and there in the shoreline of sculpted rock. The photography and tide-pool exploring are terrific everywhere, but picnicking and general beach play are best at big, sandy **Carmel Beach;** long, flat **Monterey State Beach;** safe and shallow **Lover's Point Beach and Playground;** and big **Carmel River State Beach. Asilomar State Beach** is only intermittently sandy. No state beach has lifeguards (except Santa Cruz's Twin Lakes), so watch for all water hazards, including riptides, crosscurrents, and sharks (they're further out, and have attacked surfers).

The inland parks for picnicking include Veterans Memorial Park and Lake El Estero Park, Monterey; George Washington Park, Pacific Grove; and Garland Ranch Regional Park, Carmel Valley.

Watching Sea Otters and Gray Whales

California sea otters are the cuddly little fellows who lie on their backs in the kelp beds and groom themselves. In the same position, using their chest as kitchen table, they'll crack open clams and crabs on a rock perched on their chest. And they'll also carry their young in the same position, paddling from here to there on their backs.

Once hunted to near extinction up and down the coast from Alaska to Baja by Russian and other fur hunters working out of Fort Ross and other California points, the sea otter has managed to maintain a population of 1,800 to 2,000, from Santa Cruz south to Avila Beach, mostly along the Big Sur Coast and Monterey Peninsula shore. Terrific animal, says Friends of the Sea Otter, an organization of influential Peninsulans headquartered at the Barnyard, Carmel (408/625-3290). Sure, terrific at gobbling up clams and abalone at an alarming rate (an otter consumes 25 percent of its body weight each day—fully 2.5 tons per year), say fisherman, divers, and the Department of Fish and Game.

The battle so far favors the sea otter. You may spot them cavorting in the water at numerous points on the Peninsula, including Fisherman's Wharf, Cannery Row, Lover's Point, Point Pinos, four points along the 17-Mile Drive, and Whaler's Cove at Point Lobos State Reserve. The fishing-trip operators (see below) can point them out in kelp beds farther out.

The other wildlife you will want to go out to sea to see is the **California gray whale** during the annual migration between the Arctic and Mexican waters. Gray whales, too, have made a comeback from near extinction—hardly any were seen in 1945 but now there are 10,000 to 17,000 of the 40- to 60-foot, 30-ton creatures. Peaceful, curious, the gray whales swim, heave, leap, cavort, surge, crash, "skyhop," and blow plumes of water, seemingly for the benefit of the tens of thousands of camera- and binocular-wielding observers each year.

The gray whales spend four months gorging themselves on krill and other strainable sealife up around Alaska before, around January, departing south. The largest herd steams south to Baja California, the smaller to Korea. The whales don't eat much during the three months of swimming south, the two months of mating in the warm lagoons, or the three months of returning north. Calving is in the lagoons or on the way back, the gestation period being 13 months.

You can see gray whales in the distance, or sometimes quite close, from rocky promontories such as Pillar Point (Half Moon Bay), Davenport (north of Santa Cruz), and Point Lobos State Reserve (near Carmel). But the best viewing is from the deck of an excursion boat, for which reservations are absolutely necessary. Along with Frank's, Randy's, Sam's, and Monterey Fishing Trips (see below), other trips are offered out of Monterey by Nature Expeditions International, 599 College Ave., Palo Alto 94306

(415/328-6572), and Shearwater Journeys, 362 Lee St., Santa Cruz 95060 (408/425-8111). Sailing out of Half Moon Bay are boats sponsored by the Coyote Point Museum, San Mateo; Marin Adventures, Kentfield; Oceanic Society, San Francisco; Pillar Point, Half Moon Bay; and the Whale Center, Oakland. Ask if there will be a naturalist on board, and bring Dramamine pills if you get queasy easy.

Fishing

Besides pier and surf fishing, there's deep-sea fishing. Party boats go out after salmon, rock cod, red snapper, albacore, and sea bass at 7:30 A.M. daily from Monterey. Charge is $19 or so for adults, $11 or so for children; bait is provided, rods are $2.50. License ($4 or $5) is required in salt water except off piers. These fishing folk are all based at Fisherman's Wharf, and most offer bay excursions, otter- and whale-watching, too (see above): Sam's (408) 372-0577; Chris's, 375-5951; Frank's, 372-2203; Randy's, 372-7440; and Monterey Fishing Trips, 372-3501.

They'll also rent equipment for dangling a line off a pier or rocks, which are good places to catch fish attracted by the upwelling of food from the deep Monterey Bay canyon.

Skin and Scuba Diving

You can dive for fun or for abalone and ling cod off Carmel River State Beach, Pacific Grove Marine Gardens, and elsewhere (license required), for fun only in the marine reserve off Point Lobos. Aquarius Dive Shop, 2240 Del Monte Ave., Monterey, (408) 375-1933, has information, instruction, rentals, etc., and is open seven days.

Surfing

Everybody who goes into local waters more than two feet deep wears a wet suit, and all are savvy to hazards such as sharks and rocks. Some good waves are found north at Santa Cruz and south at Andrew Molera State Park.

Music

The event you definitely have to get tickets for long in advance is the **Carmel Bach Festival,** usually held the last two weeks in

July. Founded in 1937 the festival celebrates Bach but does not ignore Telemann, Vivaldi, Mozart, Handel, Purcell, Haydn, and even later composers like Brahms. The festival includes six concerts with full-length operas and masses (repeated once), at the Sunset Theater, with the festival orchestra, chorus, and chorale conducted by music director Sandor Salgo; a dozen recitals (baritone and piano; organ; violin and harpsichord; etc.) at two local churches; a concert (repeated once) at Carmel Mission; and several symposia and lectures, which are free. Six-concert tickets are $60-$84, singles $10-$12; recital singles are $4. Information: P.O. Box 575, Carmel 93921; (408) 624-1521.

Probably the second most popular event hereabouts is the **Monterey Jazz Festival,** held on a long weekend in mid-September at the 7,000-seat arena at the county fairgrounds. Founded in 1957, the festival includes five concerts by the biggest jazz names. Programming and band choices cannot be called daring or pioneering, however. Season tickets are $28.25-$37.75, singles $6-$10. Information: P.O. Box Jazz, Monterey 93940; (408) 373-3366.

The **Hidden Valley Music Seminars,** Ford Road and Carmel Valley Road, (408) 659-3115, has the most active program of recitals, concerts, and operas, with many international guest artists. The **Monterey County Symphony** has six concerts October-May, and the **Monterey Peninsula Chamber Music Society, Monterey Peninsula Choral Society,** and **Carmel Music Society** have concert series.

Theater

Theater on the Peninsula doesn't attract stars of any brightness, but there's nevertheless likely to be something to attend on a weekend visit.

The **Wharf Theater,** Fisherman's Wharf, Monterey, (408) 372-2882, puts on both serious plays (e.g., *The Little Foxes*) and big musicals (e.g., *Hello Dolly!*). **The First Theater in California,** Scott and Pacific, Monterey, (408) 375-4916, uses its historic stage to do nineteenth-century melodrama; a perpetual second bill is *The Drunkard;* see Chapter 6 for details. Carmel's **Studio Theater Restaurant,** Dolores between Ocean and 7th, (408) 624-1661, lets you eat dinner (see Part IV) while enjoying comedies, light drama, and thrillers. The **Outdoor Forest Theater,** Mountain

View and Santa Rita, (408) 624-1531, has alfresco Shakespeare and other classics on summer Thursday, Friday, and Saturday evenings (dress warmly); box office opens at 7:30 P.M. (no reserved seating). **Hidden Valley Music Seminars** (see above under Music) also mounts stage plays.

The local tourist papers list all current productions at the above and at Monterey Peninsula College and Hartnell College, Salinas.

Entertainment, Nightlife

The big place is **The Club,** Del Monte and Alvarado, Monterey, (408) 646-9244, with dancing daily 8 P.M.-2 A.M. (disco and bands), three bars, backgammon in the library, conversation pits. **The Oz Restaurant,** 724 Abrego St., Monterey, (408) 649-6350, gets name performers, has dancing 9:30 P.M.-1:30 A.M., serves lunch, dinner besides. There's also entertainment at hotel lounges (Holiday Inn–Monterey, Casa Munras, Hilton Inn, Hyatt Del Monte), a few restaurants (Kalisa's, Mark Thomas' Outrigger, The Rogue), and club-bars (Boiler Room, First National Fog Bank, Flora's, Sly McFly's)—all on Cannery Row, and Cuckoo's Nest, Monterey. Downtown Carmel and Pebble Beach are quiet at night. Check the listings in the *Monterey Peninsula Review* and other tourist media.

House Tours

The annual **Adobe Tour** of 15 to 20 of the Monterey adobes is scheduled on a weekend in April, tickets $5 adult, $2.50 child. The tour includes special displays, slide shows, a concert of early mission music, etc. Information: Monterey History and Art Association, P.O. Box 805, Monterey 93940; (408) 372-2608. The **Victorian House Tour** in Pacific Grove also runs for two days in April. Write: Chamber of Commerce, P.O. Box 167, Pacific Grove 93950, (408) 373-3304.

Other Non-Sports Events

The **sand-castle-building contest** in Carmel is sometime in the fall, the Carmel **kite-flying contest** in April. The celebration of Monterey's birthday, the **Merienda,** is in June in the Pacific House Memory Garden, and on July 4th there's a **reenactment of Sloat's landing.** Pacific Grove has a **Feast of Lanterns,** recalling

Chinatown past, for four days in July. Antique-car buffs can't miss the **Concours d'Elegance** at the Lodge at Pebble Beach (and historical auto race at Laguna Seca) in August. The **butterfly parade** in Pacific Grove coincides with the monarchs' return in October.

Golf

Golf is the Monterey Peninsula's best-known spectator and participatory sport. If you could play all 17 or so courses, you would have about 75 miles of driving, fairway shots, pitching, chipping, and putting, and some of the play—as TV viewers of January's **Bing Crosby Pro-Am Championship** at the Pebble Beach Links know—would be amazingly scenic. And at the Cypress Point Course you have to drive the ball more than 220 yards across an ocean inlet on the 16th hole. (See details, Chapter 8.) Here are some of the public courses:

- Old Del Monte Golf Course, Monterey, (408) 373-2436. $15 plus $12 for cart.
- Laguna Seca Golf Club, Hwy 68 outside Monterey, (408) 373-3701. $13 weekdays, $15 weekends.
- Pacific Grove Municipal Golf Course, (408) 375-3456 or 373-3063. $6.50 ($4.50 for 9 holes).
- Peter Hay Par 3 (9 holes), Pebble Beach, (408) 624-3811, x-228. $4.
- Spyglass Hill Golf Course, Pebble Beach, (408) 624-3811, x203. $22 for nonguests, $17 for members, plus $15 cart.
- Rancho Cañada Golf Club (two 18-hole courses), Carmel Valley, (408) 624-0111. $14.50 to $17.50.
- Pebble Beach Golf Links, (408) 625-3811, x-239, is officially semiprivate but open to the public most times—but the fees are stiff: $50 for nonguests, $32 for guests, including cart.

Other courses—Carmel Valley Golf & Country Club, (408) 624-5323; and Corral de Tierra Country Club, Hwy 68 outside Monterey, (408) 484-1112—have reciprocal arrangements with other country clubs. Pebble Beach's Cypress Point Club, (408) 624-6444, is private. It seems, however, that guests at some of the top hotels can make arrangements to play at all of these courses. Finally, if you know someone in the military here, you can golf as a guest at the Fort Ord course or the Naval Postgraduate School Golf Course, which is one of the old Del Monte Hotel links. There are several tournaments in the course of the year.

Note: **Golf Central,** (408) 624-6611, gives reports on waiting times at Pebble Beach, Del Monte, and Spyglass Hill, and will book starting times.

Tennis

A mecca for tennis players with money—lots of it—is **John Gardiner's Tennis Ranch** in Carmel Valley; (408) 659-2207 is the telephone number, but it may not get you in (best write). The **Carmel Valley Racquet Club,** (408) 624-2737, has 18 courts for members (and members of other clubs with reciprocity privileges) and guests, also by reservation. The **Beach/Tennis Club,** Pebble Beach (408) 624-0106, is private except for Lodge guests. **Carmel Valley Inn and Tennis Resort,** (408) 659-3131, and the **Hyatt Del Monte Racquet Club,** (408) 373-0200, are public, by reservation. There are, otherwise, dozens of public tennis courts in city parks and schools. The Peninsula visitors bureau has a full list.

Polo

No kidding. Sundays at 11 at the Carmel Valley Polo Club, at 2 at Pebble Beach's Collins Field. Free admission.

Riding

Pebble Beach Equestrian Center, (408) 624-2756, and Jacks Peak Stables, (408) 375-4232, let horses for cantering in the Del Monte Forest. Carmel Valley Riding Center, (408) 624-4530, and Whiffletree Ranch, (408) 659-2670, have mounts for more open, rural riding out in the Carmel and Cachagua Valleys.

Hang Gliding

Kitty Hawk Kites, billed as the largest hang-gliding school on the East Coast, opened a West Coast school on the dunes east of Monterey (P.O. Box 828, Marina 93933; 408/384-2622). The beginning course for $47 includes classroom instruction and five flights about five feet above the ground; after that, the sky's the limit.

Car Races

The Grand Prix Formula 5000 Races are held at Laguna Seca Raceway on Highway 68 outside Monterey, over a long October weekend. The crowds book all the rooms for miles around.

GETTING THERE

We'd be dishonest if we didn't say it's easier to get to the Monterey Peninsula by **car** than by any other means. The most scenic highway from San Francisco is entirely along Highway 1, but if you're short of time, take Highway 101 or Interstate 280 to San Jose, then Highway 17 through Los Gatos to Santa Cruz, then Highway 1 around Monterey Bay. If you're really in a hurry, take Highway 101 to Prunedale, 156 to Castroville, then 1 into Monterey. From the south, Highway 1 is the scenic route on the Big Sur Coast, but it's long and winding. Highway 101 (to Salinas and Highway 68 into the Peninsula) is faster and generally unscenic, and in the summer very hot.

Bus riders need not despair. Greyhound runs seven or eight times daily from San Francisco via San Jose and Salinas to Fort Ord, Monterey, and Pacific Grove. Local Greyhound numbers: (408) 373-4735, 424-1626.

Amtrak's extremely popular Coast Starlight runs daily Seattle–Oakland–L.A.–San Diego, with a stop in Salinas. From the train depot, Greyhound and Monterey-Salinas Transit provide frequent service to downtown Monterey (see next section), and some hotels will pick you up in Salinas.

Air: AirCal, Golden West Airlines, and United—at the moment—serve the Monterey Peninsula Airport. The airport is a few miles east, off the Monterey-Salinas Highway; not far from Highway 1.

Gray Line has a day-long (11-hour) tour starting at 9 A.M. from San Francisco, daily April-Oct., three times a week Nov.-Mar. The bus takes Highway 17 to Santa Cruz, Highway 1 into Monterey, trundles past some adobes, through Pacific Grove, along the 17-Mile Drive, pretty much avoids Carmel, and returns via Sali-

nas and San Jose. Frankly, we're not sure it's worth the cost—
$38.75 adult, $25.75 child—for this quick look.

GETTING AROUND

It's relatively easy to idle by car along Monterey Peninsula's entire
shoreline, preferably counterclockwise from Monterey around to
Carmel, because of the occasional one-way street, the ease of turning right when necessary, and because you're in the lane closest to
the shore. If you're coming from the Bay Area, exit Highway 1 on
Del Monte Avenue and then hug the coast. A map is useful but if
you don't have one, follow the car in front of you. Don't forget the
$4 gate charge for the 17-Mile Drive.

The main artery on the Peninsula is Highway 1 between Monterey and Carmel. It's a freeway with stoplights. Since Carmel's
Ocean Avenue can be a traffic jam, we'd encourage southbound
motorists to exit Highway 1 at Carpenter Avenue, northbound
drivers at Rio Road, and to approach downtown Carmel from the
side.

There's plenty of pay **parking** down by the waterfront in Monterey. Parking is free in Carmel but there's a limit of one or two
hours, strictly enforced, in the Ocean Avenue area. Best park three
or more blocks away; the Sunset Center, 8th and San Carlos, is
convenient and only two blocks from Ocean. Pacific Grove isn't
fussy but a parking spot along Ocean View Boulevard may be difficult to find on a weekend. Pebble Beach has provided parking on
the 17-Mile Drive wherever they want you to stop.

As we've hinted in sightseeing chapters, you should try to **walk**
around Monterey's Path of History and in downtown Carmel,
though cars and bicycles are more convenient for coastal sightseeing in Pacific Grove and Pebble Beach.

All the major **rent-a-car** firms have offices at the airport, major
hotels, and/or downtown Monterey locations.

Monterey-Salinas Transit operates 16 **bus** routes between Watsonville in the north to Big Sur in the south, with service most
frequent on the Monterey Peninsula. The three big transfer points,
the beginning and end of most routes, are at Munras and Tyler,
Monterey; Salinas and Gabilan Streets, across from Greyhound, in

Salinas; and Beach and Main, Watsonville. Fare is 50 cents per zone, including one-way transfers; Big Sur is the fourth zone from the Peninsula, which means a $2 fare—cheap. Service is 6 A.M.–7 P.M. on most routes. Service along Del Monte Avenue, Monterey, and Monterey–Del Monte Center–Carmel, is about every 15 minutes at peak times and all day Saturday.

Here are the principal routes and destinations; tourists will find the #2, #3, #4, and #22 quite scenic.

- #1–Asilomar: from Monterey along Lighthouse Avenue, near Cannery Row, into Pacific Grove, to Asilomar Conference Center.
- #2–Lover's Point: from Monterey along Lighthouse, near Cannery Row, into Pacific Grove, to Lover's Point and Point Pinos Light Station.
- #3–La Mesa Village: from Monterey to Del Monte Center and neighborhoods.
- #4–Carmel Valley: Monterey to Del Monte Center, then into Carmel along Carpenter, Ocean, San Carlos, and Rio to the Mission, then out Carmel Valley Road to the Village.
- #5–Carmel Point: Monterey to Del Monte Center through downtown Carmel as far as Santa Lucia and Carmelo.
- #14–Presidio: Monterey through the Presidio to Lighthouse and Fountain, Pacific Grove.
- #20–Salinas/Monterey, via Marina.
- #21–Salinas/Monterey, via Highway 68, including Monterey Peninsula Airport.
- #22–Big Sur: Monterey transit plaza to Carmel (Junipero, 6th, San Carlos), the Mission, Point Lobos State Reserve, Bixby Creek Bridge, Andrew Molera State Park, Pfeiffer Big Sur State Park, and Nepenthe restaurant. In summer, you leave Monterey at 10:20 or 2:20, arrive Nepenthe 11:40 or 3:40; leave Nepenthe 12:50 or 3:50, arrive Monterey

2:05 or 5:05. (Other Monterey–Carmel–Big Sur service is via Coastlines, Box 587, Monterey 93940; 408/649-4700.)

Rider's Guide and information from MST, 1 Ryan Ranch Road, Monterey 93940; (408) 899-2555 or 424-7695.

Taxis: Yellow Checker is the largest cab company, 24 hours: (408) 646-1234 (Peninsula), (408) 443-1234 (Salinas).

Sightseeing: Gray Line, operating from the Casa Munras Hotel, Monterey, (408) 373-4989 or 757-5307, has a 2½-hour tour three times a week of Monterey, the 17-Mile Drive, and some of Carmel (tour buses are not popular there), for $11 adult, $7 child. Less superficial bus tours, with or without lunch or coffee stops, are offered by **California Heritage Guides,** 10 Custom House Plaza, Monterey, (408) 373-6454; they also offer custom tours in your car—$7.50 per hour, minimum two hours, maximum five persons—or by foot in historic Monterey—$2 per adult, minimum 6 persons, 1½ hours. **Chartered Limousine Service,** Box 5756, Carmel; (408) 394-6519, has custom tours in small or large limos or buses. **Limousine d'Elegance,** Box W, Carmel, (408) 624-4901, uses a chauffeur-driven 1948 Rolls-Royce "only."

Bay cruises: If you want to see Monterey Bay, including sea lions, sea otters, Cannery Row, and Lover's Point, **Chris's, Randy's, Frank's, Sam's,** and **Monterey Fishing Trips,** all on Fisherman's Wharf, Monterey, will take you out for half-hour cruises for $2 adult, $1 child (under 6, free), while the Lover's Point glass-bottom boat tour, half an hour, costs $2.75 adult, $1.75 child under 14.

Bicycling: The **17-Mile Drive** offers the best cycling, and you can get in free—but only 8-11 A.M. when there's no major event at Pebble Beach; entry only at the Pacific Grove gate. **Ocean View Boulevard** and **Sunset Drive** in Pacific Grove are extremely scenic. Try also the north-south **Scenic Avenue** in Carmel. The only **bicycle path** is along the bayshore from the north end of Seaside (pick the path up at Del Monte Boulevard at Fremont Boulevard) past Fort Ord to Marina. Because there's no alternative route, you *can* ride on the Highway 1 freeway from Munras Avenue south. Bicycle rental (all area code 408): Freewheeling Cycles, 188 Webster, Monterey, 373-3855; Les Joselyn Bicycle, 638 Lighthouse

Ave., Monterey, 649-8520; Valley Cycle Center, 563 Carmel Rancho Center, 624-5107. Oliver Cycle, 270 Cannery Row, 373-2696,
rents mopeds for $20 per day.

WHERE TO STAY AND EAT

Accommodations (including camping) and restaurants are discussed in Part IV under the heading Monterey Peninsula and listed under Monterey, Pacific Grove, Pebble Beach, and Carmel and
Carmel Valley; see also Big Sur Coast and Salinas/Inland Monterey County.

Part III

Big Sur Coast
and Hearst Castle

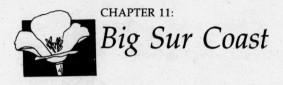

CHAPTER 11:

Big Sur Coast

HIGHLIGHTS

Big Sur happened when the Santa Lucia Mountains were pushed so far westward they practically fell in the Pacific Ocean, leaving barely enough room for a narrow winding road and space for residents and visitors to drink up the intoxicating scenery. There are several hundred of the former, millions of the latter imbibers.

The beauty may be difficult of access—but then it might spring on you like a puma. The elements—waves, wind, thunder, lightning, rain, floods, fire—sometimes clash with ferocity, adding to that beauty a dimension of cruelty and terror. Near this "jagged country which nothing but a falling meteor will ever plow," California's greatest poet, Robinson Jeffers (1887–1962), built his Tor House and Hawk Tower of sea-worn granite on a Carmel headland. On this coast he found the settings and characters, stories, and themes of his tragic narrative poems, *Tamar* (1924), *Roan Stallion* (1925), *The Women at Point Sur* (1927), and *Thurso's Landing* (1932). Here he was inspired by "the great phantoms, the fountains of light, the seed of the sky." Even his characters can be described in terms of the land:

He was like this mountain coast,
All beautiful, with chances of brutal violence; precipitous, dark-natured,
    beautiful; without humor, without ever
A glimmer of gayety; blind gray headland and arid mountain, and trailing
    from his shoulders the infinite ocean.

("Give Your Heart to the Hawks," 1933)

Henry Miller (1891–1980), who was the center of an art colony of sorts on the Big Sur coast during his 20 years here, 1944–64, found Jeffers's voice appropriate for Big Sur's "almost melodramatic" character: "If the soul were to choose an arena in which to stage its agonies, this would be *the* place for it. One feels exposed—not only to the elements, but to the sight of God. Naked, vulnerable, set against an overwhelming backdrop of might and majesty, one's problems become magnified because of the proscenium on which the conflict is staged."

In his *Big Sur and the Oranges of Hieronymus Bosch* (1957), which like Jeffers's poetry can serve as a guide to the area, Miller remarked that "it was here . . . that I first learned to say *Amen!*" But he added mischievously: "And here too that I came to dwell with more than a feeling of mystification on that edifying observation of Céline's: 'I piss on you all from a considerable height!' "

Power and Solitude

It is improbable that many of us are temperamentally suited to living in such a place, any more than we can tune our lives by the primordial violence of Jeffers's tragedies or the Rabelaisian energy of Miller's monologues. But, as the presence of the Esalen Institute (a leader in the "human potential" movement), the Tassajara Zen Center, and both a Carmelite monastery and a Benedictine hermitage indicates, the Big Sur offers spiritual power and solitude to those who want it, not idle Fisherman's Wharf entertainment to gaggles of tourists.

Well, not to enshroud the coast completely in a mythology as chilling as the fog that hangs close in the summer, the experience of Big Sur can be subdivided and the parts defined.

First, you can drive the 93 miles between Carmel and San Simeon on a road that resembles the Riviera's Grande Corniche in precipitousness and splendor of views. Both southbound and northbound travelers have a delight as their destination: the Monterey Peninsula to the north, William Randolph Hearst's Hollywood castle to the south. Between the two is scenery but little in the way of "attractions." Further, the only place actually labeled "Big Sur" doesn't seem to be there. It's a sign on the highway before you get to the edge of a six-mile sprinkle of roadside structures—downtown Big Sur, as it were—in the redwooded Big Sur Valley. Don't look too hard for "Big Sur" or you won't find it, they say.

Besides the rugged, too-often inaccessible shore, the Big Sur in practical terms consists of coastal redwoods, the southernmost of the *Sequoia sempervirens* that, uniquely, thrive in creek canyons along the cool California coast from here to Oregon; chaparral-covered hillsides; three state parks; the Ventana Wilderness of Los Padres National Forest; the two-lane highway, which is mandated to remain so under a 1976 law; a few old ranchos with "No Trespassing" signs and rugged-looking cattle; the several places for deep searching of minds, souls, and bodies; a handful of stores, cafés, and rustic lodges; and in some wide parts of the road, rows of mailboxes, representing the Big Sur's permanent residents, between 1,300 and 1,700 of them on the whole stretch of coast.

The visitor may feel unfocused unless he's determined just to hold the steering wheel tightly until he gets to Hearst Castle, which is the Big Sur's Disneyland. On the other hand, for those who stay a while, at a state park, at Esalen or Tassajara (both have hot springs), or at a rented cabin or hidden hut by a marijuana patch somewhere in the national forest, the activities add up to exploring within and without—"there being nothing to improve on in the surroundings," Henry Miller commented, "the tendency is to set about improving oneself."

The Big Sur doesn't have much of a history. Portolá and Anza found the Santa Lucias an obstacle to cross to the flats of the Salinas Valley. Holding tenuously on to Alta California at the few missions and pueblos, the Spanish weren't ones for idle exploring or vacationing in the coastal mountains. It wasn't until 1834 that the first rancho, Juan Bautista Alvarado's Rancho El Sur ("Sur" meaning south of Monterey), was granted between the Little Sur River and Cooper Point. But the more distant parts of the Big Sur were not really settled until the 1850s and later, and then by only a few people.

For decades the Big Sur was accessible only by a horse trail, not a very good one at that, which followed the first ridge. In time a stage and wagon road went as far as the Big Sur River. Not until 1920 did construction of a regular road begin, using much convict labor, and not until 1937 was it open through San Simeon.

"Herd of Independent Minds"

Meanwhile, the land and the isolation bred a hardy sort of people, bred also a body of story and legend that has clung to the coast like a barnacle. In time, artists came and celebrated the place in verse and prose because of its solitude, privacy, impossible beauty, and other things they found there. "A herd of independent minds," Henry Miller dubbed his crowd. Then art-colony hangers-on, hippies, dope smokers, and assorted transients came because of the artistic coast, the mellow social atmosphere, the relative absence of law and bourgeois thinking. Then, to an area that didn't even get electricity until the 1950s, came people with BMWs and lots of money. They put up pavilions of glass and redwood, installed Jacuzzis.

Actually, all these late-arriving caricatures were just as independent-minded as the earlier pioneers on the Big Sur, but instead of being simple, solid folk who raised cattle in the unwalked hills, they were brittle refugees from the city, fleeing high-pressure careers, smog, divorces, television.

For a time it looked as if the old-timers and newcomers would get along as well as any particular cat and specific dog. The small world developed extremes, demographic stratification. One sort of people would congregate at a rustic place with knotty-pine walls and a smoky-beery air where it was okay to shout across the room. The other would tool up to the mineshaft-modern inn of freshly weatherbeaten cedar, where the alcohol was served in long-stemmed crystal and any red meat had a French name.

Then Ansel Adams had an idea to protect the Big Sur Coast.

The famous photographer, whose stark black-and-white prints of Half Dome and sunrises over Taos would fetch tens of thousands of dollars, looked out his window on Carmel Highlands and saw suburbia creeping across Malpaso Creek.

The facts seemed alarming: the Big Sur's population doubled between 1960 and 1977, the number of residential units tripled (to 850); the trickle of cars on Highway 1 became what sometimes seemed a bumper-to-bumper stream—two million motorists a year—between Carmel and Hearst Castle, San Francisco and L.A.; 800 vacant lots lay open to development; real-estate prices were being bid to impossible levels, partly because of the sheer desirability of living on the Big Sur, partly because lack of water and sewage facilities limited the number of buildable lots—but mostly, some said, because the Coastal Commission, suspicious of any structures larger than trellises and bird feeders, blocked one development after another.

Where was all this leading? Ansel Adams doesn't take trendy pictures of tract houses or carnival freaks or high-fashion models posed with snakes and Pyramids. The space in front of his camera, between his vision and the spray-glistening rock, the moody group of redwoods, must be clear of human detritus, whether Parthenons or McDonald's.

Ordinarily, Ansel Adams should have received a lot of support along the Big Sur. The cars and the outlanders were causing congestion, raising the local anxiety level. But Big Sur isn't ordinary and Ansel Adams and his Big Sur Foundation didn't get a battalion of coastal dwellers to join the campaign. What they got were the outlanders, the Sierra Club (on whose board Adams sat for decades) and the Wilderness Society (headed by his former business manager), environmentally minded congressmen from Ohio and Texas and everywhere else who saw the Big Sur as a national resource, not to mention attraction.

The Big Sur Conservation Battle

A Big Sur National Seashore bill was introduced. The old ranch families and the Jacuzzi set allied against the outsiders. Socialism! Elitism! Federal protection is federal ownership, controls, parking lots at each end of the highway! We'll be bought out! Worse, we'll suffer the fate of the other national park in-holders: nibbled to death by bureaucrats! In the meantime, hordes of tourists to make Big Sur a Coney Island!

No, siree, Bob: don't fence me in.

There were other efforts, attempts to find a middle ground. The Big Sur Land Trust was founded to gather land and preserve it, just preserve it. A campaign got underway to incorporate the entire Big Sur Coast, to maintain as much local control as any city can get. Residents didn't like any of these ideas very much. For one thing, there was already a lot of public land; for another, some of the old ranches were owned by investors, who didn't see much profit in being bought out for parkland. Everybody went to Washington, buttonholed legislators.

In the House the national seashore concept was abandoned and a plan to allow Los Padres National Forest to expand, with mixed federal, state, and local control, was substituted. Ansel Adams thought that was all right but residents didn't like that, either. They were saved by the bell and Sleeping Sam.

What happened was as dramatic as legislating can be. San Francisco's Congressman Phil Burton, who knows more than anybody about how to make a national park (Redwood, Golden Gate, Channel Islands), was carrying the Big Sur Scenic Area bill and got the House to pass it handily in August 1980. The next month, two days before Congress was to recess to campaign, a Senate committee hadn't even scheduled hearings on the stricter Seashore bill.

Burton, past master at parliamentary dodge-and-dart, picked up a ridiculously minor bill that had already cleared the Senate, got a quick House vote to tack on the Scenic Area bill passed by the House, and so sent it directly to a conference committee, thus bypassing the entire Senate. This was done very quietly, but an aide to Senator S. I. "Sleeping Sam" Hayakawa heard about it, and the conference committee blocked Burton. Congress recessed. In November Ronald Reagan and a Republican majority in the Senate were elected. The curtain fell on the Scenic Area.

In their fight the residents had said that the Big Sur was better off left alone. To protect it, you'd have to identify it, name it, buy it, fence it, plan it, control it. And you'd end up destroying it.

But it's a choice of poisons. The cars are more numerous every year; the county's coastal program, approved by the watchdog Coastal Commission, actually allows another 600 residences and

400 tourist units; the Hearst Corporation is building a big tourist complex at San Simeon.

The Big Sur conservation drama is not finished. Jeffers would end it tragically, Miller hilariously in a giant debauch. It might, probably will, end ambiguously, but it couldn't end in a better place.

WHAT TO SEE AND DO

The granite beauty of the Big Sur Coast begins on the Monterey Peninsula, leaving behind the dull Monterey Bay sand dunes fronting Fort Ord. Drive out of Carmel on Highway 1. Rio Road to the right leads to **Carmel Mission** and Robinson Jeffers's **Tor House** (see Chapter 9). The bridge across the Carmel River is the beginning of California's first official **Scenic Highway.*****

To the right, most of the land from Mission Point to the mouth of the river and south almost to Point Lobos is **Carmel River State Beach,** which has no facilities but is good for fishing, poking around on the beach, and birdwatching in the marsh. There in a small area you can see shorebirds and marshbirds (herons, egrets, pelicans, sandpipers, and cormorants you'll recognize; willets, greater yellowlegs, and killdeer perhaps not) and visiting birds from nearby woods and meadows (hawks and kingfishers included) and migrants (ducks, Canadian honking geese, and even snow geese). No dogs, fires, or camping on the beach, which is the last beach that is both sandy and public for many miles.

South of the river mouth (or lagoon), above the beach, is a **replica of Portolá's cross,** the one he left in this vicinity in October 1769 after coming to, but because of the fog failing to recognize, Monterey Bay. When he came a second time, on May 27, 1770, he found the cross still there but decorated by the Indians with arrows, sticks with feathers, a string of small fresh fish, some pieces of meat, and a pile of mussels. (It is said that the Indians later told the padres that the cross had been spotlighted from the sky, so the offerings were left at the cross to appease God.) This time the day was clear and the exploration party finally recognized Monterey Bay.

Opposite the state beach, in an idyllic setting overlooking the peaceful artichoke fields on the floodplain (note the migrant-work-er housing on the south edge), is the white Spanish Colonial **Carmelite Monastery,** built in the 1920s for an order of nuns who practice seclusion; sisters of another order are associated with the Carmel Mission and the parochial schools. Gardens and chapel are open daily 9-5; mass daily at 8 A.M., Sun. 9 A.M. Below is **Monastery Beach,** where swimming is discouraged because of the steep drop-off.

Up **San Jose Creek** Robinson Jeffers and his wife once came upon a vacant cabin with a "desolate, tragic look," empty since its owner had been killed by his stallion. This was the inspiration for *Roan Stallion*, his first popular success.

Point Lobos State Reserve

The next turn to the right is to paradise—that is, to **Point Lobos State Reserve,*** 1,276 acres of the purest natural beauty, a Monterey cypress-fringed promontory described by an oft-quoted phrase, "the greatest meeting of land and water in the world," elsewhere as "the crown jewel of the State Park system." We'd agree with either of those assessments; it is a place to be returned to time and again, in different weather, different times of the day, different seasons, and even after dozens of visits it would be new on the next.

The reason is that Point Lobos is both compact and extraordinarily varied. There are more than 300 plant species, ranging from the springtime show of lupines, poppies, buttercups, and other wildflowers to Monterey cypress, the twisted, distorted trees that are beautiful in adversity and so symbolize the whole stretch of coast. And there are more than 250 species of birds and animals: two species of sea lions (from their Spanish name came the peninsula's name, Punta de los Lobos Marinos, "point of the Sea Wolves"), the harbor seal, the killer whale (occasionally seen around Sea Lion Rock in search of succulent seals), some of the 1,000 California sea otters who thrive in a protected zone along the Big Sur Coast, two species of cormorant, the western gull, and the brown pelican.

Not surprisingly, this was one of Jeffers's favorite spots. He placed the Cauldwell ranch of *Tamar* here and has Tamar ask the ghost of Helen:

> . . . do you remember at all
> The beauty and strangeness of this place? Old cypresses
> The sailor wind works into deep-sea knots
> A thousand years; age-reddened granite
> That was the world's cradle and crumbles apieces . . .

> . . . there is one more beautiful thing,
> Water that owns the north and west and south
> And is all colors and never is all quiet,
> And the fogs are its breath and float along the
>   branches of the cypresses.
> And I forgot the coals of ruby lichen
> That flow in the fog on the old twigs.

It is said that Robert Louis Stevenson, who stayed awhile in Monterey in 1879, was thinking of Point Lobos when he described Spyglass Hill in *Treasure Island* (1883). (Life imitates art, so a hill and golf course at nearby Pebble Beach are named Spyglass Hill.)

Point Lobos somehow survived the urbanization of the Monterey Peninsula. It passed from owner to owner (once even changing hands at a card game), was a whaling station 1861–84, coal-shipping point, and cattle ranch, and was even burned a couple of times. Yet it finally went into the caring hands of a good owner and in 1933, with the help of the Save-the-Redwoods League, into the trusteeship of the state. In 1960 some 750 acres of submerged land was added—the first underwater ecological reserve in the country.

Three Trails at Point Lobos

Point Lobos is not oriented for auto touring: the main road goes along part of the south shore, then stops; a spur goes to Cannery Point. The more satisfactory way to get around is by foot or bicycle—in fact, you can get in free if you leave your car outside the reserve, on Highway 1.

The **North Shore Trail** roughly starts at Granite Point, goes out Coal Shute Point, then runs around Whaler's Cove to Cannery Point, over Vizcaíno Hill and along the edge of Bluefish Cove to East Grove, ending at the junction with the **Cypress Grove**

Trail.*** With a printed guide pamphlet, this trail takes you from a parking area to **Allan Memorial Grove,***** one of only two native groves of Monterey cypress (*Cupressus macrocarpa*), the other being at Cypress Point on 17-Mile Drive. (Monterey pine is everywhere.) The trail heads to the left under trees decorated with lace lichen, which is often mistaken for Spanish moss, to a vista over **Headland Cove,***** where sea otters occasionally anchor themselves to the kelp (giant kelp is the most common seaweed here) and snack on shellfish, crabs, and sea urchins. The trail continues to a vista of **Sea Lion Rocks***** and **Point Lobos***** proper, both habitats of the California sea lion and Steller sea lion. South Point is a good place to watch the California gray-whale migration past the reserve between November and April. (See Chapter 10 for more on otter- and whale-watching.)

Looping around the cypress grove, the trail goes out on North Point, where a litter of shell fragments indicates this was one of the fishing spots used by Indians. Just a few hundred feet north of here is the mouth of the submarine **Carmel Canyon,** which runs northwest 13 miles to join the deepest submarine canyon on the California coast, the **Monterey Canyon,** more than 10,000 feet deep at a point 40 miles out to sea. Upwellings of cold water carrying mineral nutrients from these canyons create the rich intertidal life. Off the shore of this headland are the **Pinnacles,** aptly named creations of wave erosion. Across from North Point you can see **Big Dome,** at 260 feet the highest point in the reserve.

The trail loops back to the parking lot, where it joins **Sea Lion Point Trail**** to a point overlooking **Devil's Cauldron.**** Along the south shore a trail parallels the road to Pebbly Beach, Hidden Beach, and China Cove to Pelican Point, from which you can see **Bird Island,** home of thousands of gulls, cormorants, and other sea birds, including brown pelicans, which are in residence from the end of April to November.

There are guided walks (daily in summer, weekends only in the off-season) to six different areas of the reserve and, when tides and weather permit, tide-pool exploration walks for limited numbers early on summer mornings. The south road has some strategically placed picnic tables, water fountains, and rest rooms. There are some rules: no cooking, no smoking except in cars, no collecting of natural material, no pets on the trails, no fishing. Picnic only at

posted areas, swim only at China Cove, dive only between Guille-
mot Island and Granite Point (free permit required), and stay on
the trails. Hikers and bicyclists enter free; if you want to bring
your car in, there's a charge of $2, and you may have to idle at the
gate. The park closes at sundown. Information: (408) 624-4909.

By the way, the movie *Jonathan Livingston Seagull* was filmed
nearby.

Back on Highway 1 you come to the last residences of the idle
rich, in **Carmel Highlands,** location of the famous **Highlands Inn**
(see Part IV) in **Carmel Riviera,** which appropriately has a Men-
tone Drive and a San Remo Road, and on Yankee Point. Here
begins the Big Sur Coast proper.

Along the Big Sur Coast

Malpaso Creek appears frequently in Jeffers's work. Under "Mal
Paso Bridge" (1925) "the long-maned sea-waves/Beat up into the
stream." Upstream at an abandoned coal mine Barclay died at the
end of *The Women at Point Sur* and at a pool Tamar seduced Lee
(which sounds fine except he was her brother).

With the hills rising higher to the left, the drop-off to the shore-
less sea becomes sheer. At **Granite Creek** the bridge seems to go
over a tongue of the ocean; you can hike down to the water on
either side. Further on, near Doud Creek, is a vista point and just
beyond is **Rocky Point,** location of a restaurant. Offshore is a
lengthy stretch of sea-otter refuge. From the old lumber camp of
Notley's Landing, a paved road goes up **Palo Colorado** ("redwood") **Canyon** to Bottchers Gap, a trailhead (and campground)
for Ventana Wilderness.

Los Padres National Forest and Ventana Wilderness

This seems to be a convenient place to describe the Monterey
County portion of **Los Padres National Forest,** whose second and
larger part is down around Santa Barbara. Most of the Monterey
portion is the 98,000-acre **Ventana Wilderness,** the closest national wilderness to the Bay Area and therefore popular with hikers.
The Ventana spreads over the northern section of the sometimes
rugged, always scenic **Santa Lucia Mountains** of the Coastal
Range. The mountains are ecologically diverse, with some nine
plant communities, mainly coastal woodland, chamise-chaparral,

grass, and foothill oak. In the open areas the spring wildflowers—lupine, poppies, Mariposa lilies, and some 30 rare and endangered species—put on a terrific display.

Nearly the entire wilderness and much of the northern section of Los Padres outside the Ventana were ravaged in August 1977 by California's third worst forest fire. By the time the lightning-caused Marble Cone blaze was controlled, 178,000 acres (278 square miles) had been burned. Many trees—the Santa Lucia or bristlecone fir, which is peculiar to this area, plus ponderosa and Jeffrey pine, coastal oak, and madrone—were lost, but the disastrous impact was to the watershed of the Carmel, Arroyo Seco, and Big Sur Rivers; these are the principal sources of water for the Monterey Peninsula, a stretch of the Big Sur Coast, and part of the Salinas Valley.

In the fall of 1977 the immediate fear was that winter rains in the Santa Lucias, which can be a torrential 70 inches, would cause devastating mudslides and floods, erosion and silting. Without the trees and brush to check the winter rain runoff, sedimentation can increase up to 900 percent. In 1972, after only 4,000 acres of watershed above Big Sur village was burned in the Molera blaze, rains in October started mudslides that wiped out the post office, four businesses, and several homes, and cut Highway 1 for six weeks.

So, after the Marble Cone fire, bridges were purposefully dismantled and trucked away, riverbanks were cropped of brush and trees to create flood channels, the state park was stripped of movables, a 12-foot dike was built to protect a historic cabin, and a large aerial reseeding program—500 tons of fast-growing rye grass—was undertaken. Luckily, as California's long drought came to an end, the first October 1977 rains in Big Sur were light and because of the preparation, there was no repetition of muddy 1972.

Ventana Wilderness has now recovered nicely, from the hiker's point of view. The 200 miles of trails reopened completely in the spring of 1980. Rye grass covered the hills, chamise and chaparral plants such as the manzanita came back quickly, wildflowers flourished, new trees sprouted in enriched soil in spaces newly cleared of underbrush and weak trees. While many tree skeletons will be apparent for a decade or more, the views from the high ridges and peaks (which range from 2,500 to 3,000 feet up to Junipero Serra

Peak, 5,862 feet), especially close to the shore, remain unscathed.

The three heavily used entrance stations on the coastside are Big Sur Station, half a mile south of Pfeiffer–Big Sur State Park; Bottchers Gap Station, eight miles up Palo Colorado Road; and Nacimiento Station, on Nacimiento-Fergusson Road. The three inland are Carmel River Station, Cachagua Road, off Carmel Valley Road (on the way to Tassajara); Arroyo Seco Station, Arroyo Seco Road, west of Greenfield; and Indian Station, Milpitas Road, north of Mission San Antonio. The trailheads usually have car camping, parking, picnic tables.

From Bottchers Gap you can hike an eight-mile round-trip to Devil's Peak, 4,152 feet, taking in some of the best views in the northern Ventana. From Arroyo Seco there's a six-mile round-trip trail up to Black Butte, 4,941 feet. And from Nacimiento Station there's a six-mile circular hike up Kirk Creek to Vincente Flat, with good ridgeline views.

You'll need a campfire permit, if the Forest Service is allowing fires; a wilderness permit, best obtained in advance; a map; and your own water. Information, permits, maps: U.S. Forest Service, Monterey District, 406 S. Mildred Ave., King City 93930, (408) 385-5434; also from the Big Sur Station (open daily 8-5) and Carmel River Station (Wed.-Sun., 8-5).

Campers may wish to sleep with one eye open. Not because of bears but blundering **Santa Lucia wild boars.** These half-American, half-Ukranian pigs were released on the San Carlos Ranch in the 1930s and have spread over three counties. The sharp-tusked boars are commonly 200 to 250 pounds (the record monster was 810 pounds, killed by a hunter in 1979) and have an aversion to people. Unfortunately, they have poor eyesight and, infrequently, may not see you or your sleeping bag.

Despite the cool fog on the shore, the Santa Lucias in the summertime can be ferociously hot; spring and fall are better times to walk a pack.

Tassajara Zen Center

What the Marble Cone fire spared, perhaps through intervention by higher authority, was the **Tassajara Zen Mountain Center,** the largest Zen training center outside Japan. The semimonastic Soto Zen Buddhist community was started in 1966 at **Tassajara**

Hot Springs by the San Francisco Zen Center. The center has several well-known Northern California enterprises, including a farm in Marin County and, in San Francisco, the Tassajara Bakery, Greens Restaurant, and the Whole Earth Bookstore. The training center here has both male and female students, married and single; serious students stay an average of three years, rising at 4 A.M. and undergoing a strict regimen of physical and mental exercise.

We mention Tassajara at length because it is, from May 1 through the summer, a hot-springs resort, though not your everyday resort. In fact, with no telephones, electricity, or air conditioning, no bar, music, dancing, or television, Tassajara is more like a retreat for spartans, ascetics, recluses, and people like Governor Jerry Brown, playwright Michael McClure, and jazz musician Taj Mahal, and others who would find lush Pebble Beach not to their liking.

What Tassajara offers the 55 to 65 guests is lots of peace and quiet, good vegetarian cooking (two Tassajara cookbooks have been best sellers), walking and hiking, and the springs and streams that have drawn visitors since the 1880s.

You need motivation and some tolerance to come here, for the rates are high (day visiting is cheaper) and the 20-mile drive in via the Carmel and Cachagua Valley roads raises hair and, in twists and turns up and down 5,000 feet, burns out brakes and clutches. Novelist Herbert Gold says he ruined his Jaguar on this road, donated it to the Zen Center. Overnighters and day visitors (9 A.M.–8 P.M.) are by reservation only. Information: Zen Center, 300 Page St., San Francisco 94102, (415) 863-3136; and, locally, (408) 659-2229 or Tassajara Springs 1 (via Salinas operator).

Bixby Creek

Back on Highway 1, on the other side of Rocky Creek, another left turn will take you onto a bypassed portion of the old **Coast Road,** a rather more twisty, overgrown, unpaved version of Highway 1, which it rejoins at Molera Park. Actually, unless you're going to be coming back this way, stay on the highway so you won't miss the famous **Bixby Creek Bridge,** a 700-foot concrete-arch span that is 265 feet above the creek. Contrary to what other guidebooks say, this is not the world's longest concrete-arch bridge; it couldn't even make that claim when it was opened in 1932. But it is still one of the world's most photogenic small bridges, visible for miles before you get to it. In the movie *The Graduate* (1967), this was the bridge Dustin Hoffman zipped across in a sports car in a memorable long shot. (Three other Big Sur Highway bridges have the same design, but aren't as large.) Lady Bird Johnson dedicated the scenic highway here on September 21, 1966. Since the plaque has been swiped, we'll quote you the inscribed lines by Jeffers from "Continent's End" (1925):

> I gazing at the boundaries of granite and spray, the
> established sea-marks, felt behind me
> Mountain and plain, the immense breadth of the continent,
> before me the mass and doubled stretch of water.

On Castle Rock, the headland north of the bridge, are the ruins of **Bixby's Landing,** the cliffside terminal of a hoist that was used to bring lime three miles down the steep canyon to be loaded onto a boat by a wire cable. Jeffers called this Thurso's Landing and has his narrative poem of that title come to a wild conclusion here. Just south is appropriately named **Hurricane Point.**

The mouth of the **Little Sur River,** often blocked by a sand bar, has a very attractive beach, but this being private property, it may not be accessible. Some owners turn a blind eye on trespassers, of whom there may be a number; don't ignore the possibilities, for the tideland *is* public property.

Just beyond, on a surprisingly massive 400-foot-high "black lava rock-head" (Jeffers), is the **Point Sur Light Station** (closed to the public), built in 1889 after disastrous wrecks off this foggy point in 1873 and 1879. Now the automated million-candlepower light flashes every 15 seconds (the light can be seen 25 miles out) and sends a radio signal to help navigators find their position. A compressed-air foghorn serves when the fog is thick, as in summer. The navy does some discreet work here, so don't trespass.

Andrew Molera State Park

Below **Pico Blanco** ("white peak"), at 3,710 feet the second highest in the range and near a very large source of aspirin binder, the highway bends inland behind Pfeiffer Ridge and into the Big Sur

River valley, the location of many redwoods and, because it is sheltered, perhaps half of Big Sur's people. Around the mouth of the river, including four miles of shoreline, is the undeveloped **Andrew Molera State Park,**** a 2,100-acre piece of the old Rancho El Sur that was granted to the state in 1965 by Frances Molera in memory of her brother (both were distant cousins of the original grantee, Governor Alvarado). The white-frame rancho headquarters, built of lumber brought around the Horn, is still standing. While the park is closed to cars at the moment (there's a parking area at the entrance), walkers are encouraged to go in and explore the shoulder of Pfeiffer Ridge or walk half a mile through the meadow down to the mile-long sandy beach (swimming is not advised, but surfing can be excellent). The walk-in campground (50 sites) has primitive facilities. Information: see Pfeiffer–Big Sur State Park below.

Big Sur Village

Back on the highway, as you leave Molera Park you'll enter the Big Sur River Valley and come to the first of the scattered establishments that comprise **Big Sur Village;** the remainder are in little clusters under the redwoods over the next six miles ("Getting There, Getting Around" lists exact mileages, to help hikers and others). There are perhaps 10 places to stay, including private campgrounds, and another eight places in which to eat. Although differing in character, all but one are rustic to a degree: the exception, the **Ventana Inn,*** richly built of aged cedar and natural woods, caters to the well-fixed from down Hollywood way. Casual wayfarers will enjoy stopping at the **River Inn** and, particularly, the famous **Nepenthe.***** Located in a striking building (Rowan Maiden, architect) of redwood, adobe, and glass, with casually spectacular views from 808 feet above the shore, the Nepenthe (Greek for "removing sorrow" and a drug to induce same) dates back to 1947, before which time Orson Welles and Rita Hayworth had a honeymoon cabin here. Both the Nepenthe and the River Inn, whose style is more frontier log cabin, serve food all day long, have decks for alfresco nibbling, imbibing, or contemplating, and are Big Sur social centers at night, with frequent entertainment. (See Part IV for more details.)

Local arts and crafts are displayed at **The Phoenix,*** part of

Nepenthe's complex of redwood and glass, and the **Coast Gallery,** ** with showrooms inside two converted redwood water tanks at Lafler Canyon. What is for sale is the best evidence that there are, indeed, artists, sculptors, poets, writers, and various craftspeople living around here; many also sell their works in Carmel and Monterey. Both have good selections of books by Big Sur authors and about the country. The strangest shop—strange because its style and goods are so out of place—is the **Ventana Store,** * at the Inn. Cartier lighters and Mont Blanc pens? Yes, also expensive cutlery, silverware, yardage, kitchen and garden stuff.

Two other points of interest are the **Big Sur Grange Hall,** where residents hold town meetings, square dances, movies, and a big annual theatrical production called the Potluck Revue, and **St. Francis of the Redwoods Chapel,** whose glass wall opens for mass (inquire as to times), enabling one to sit under the redwoods.

Pfeiffer–Big Sur State Park

The destination for most hikers, campers, and picnickers is **Pfeiffer–Big Sur State Park,** *** a small (810 acres) but select park on a stretch of the Big Sur River. In the river bottom and canyon grow some of the most southerly coastal redwoods, but since the weather is comparatively dry, there are intermixed sycamores, black cottonwoods, big-leaf maples, alders, and willows. Above the river, vegetation is more characteristic of the chaparral community: coast live oaks, tan oaks (whose bark was stripped and shipped to Santa Cruz for tanning leather in the early part of the century), California laurel, and brushy shrubs. A self-guided, mile-long **nature trail** ** begins across the river from the Big Sur Lodge. The vegetation species to watch out for, as ever, is poison oak; "leaves three, leave them be" is what to tell the kids.

The Esselens, the local Indian tribe, had left the Big Sur Valley by the time the first settlers came. The pioneer in the park area was a man named Davis, who, about 1860, built the **Homestead Cabin** * near what is today's picnic area. The cabin was later occupied by the family of one of the Rancho El Sur's vaqueros, Emanuel Innocenti (his name is on Manuel Peak north of the park), then in 1884 by John Pfeiffer, who homesteaded 160 acres between the Big Sur River and his father Michael's parcel in Sycamore Canyon. In 1934 John Pfeiffer donated part of his land and sold another part to the state and county as parkland. The U.S. Forest Service meanwhile obtained most of the other Pfeiffer land and acquired the access road down the canyon to **Pfeiffer Beach***** (day use only); the access road, Sycamore Canyon Road, is a mile south of the park entrance, off Highway 1. Jeffers' "Give Your Heart to the Hawks" is set in the canyon, Pfeiffer Point being renamed Fraser's Point; in that brutal narrative, an orgy on Pfeiffer Beach ends in fratricide. Rather more romantic were the scenes filmed here for *The Sandpiper*, with Elizabeth Taylor and Richard Burton.

Pfeiffer–Big Sur, besides being a very popular place to camp, is a principal trailhead into the Ventana Wilderness. Before leaving the park on the **Mt. Manuel Trail** or the **Pine Ridge Trail** (two miles long within the park), obtain a wilderness permit at the ranger station, accessible either from Highway 1 or the park road across from the picnic area. Trails within the park are the **Oak Grove Trail**** (1.5 miles), **Valley View Trail**** (.6 mile)—both of which connect to the **Pfeiffer Falls Trail**** (.4 mile)—and the **Buzzards Loop Trail*** (3.1 miles round trip). There's wading in the Big Sur River and swimming in some of the deeper pools— very sylvan places—plus fishing (trout is planted weekly in the summer). Rangers conduct campfire programs and nature walks in the summer. Information: (408) 667-2315.

Big Sur Lodge, by the way, is located inside the park. Dating back to 1945, it offers full facilities, including a pool (see Part IV).

Past the exclusively primitive **Big Sur Inn** (Deetjen's), some of which is hidden up Castro Canyon, is a vista point at **Grimes Point,** near which the architect Nathaniel Owings (of Skidmore, Owings & Merrill) built a house for himself.

Partington Ridge

Continuing south, one canyon past the picturesquely situated Coast Gallery, is a road up to **Partington Ridge.** Henry Miller lived here 1947–64 in a newly built house on three acres that was simply presented to him by a woman who thought he needed it more than she did. *Big Sur and the Oranges of Hieronymus Bosch* and much of *Sexus* (1945), *Plexus* (1949), and *Nexus* (1960) were written here. After his death (in the plusher environs of Palos Verdes) Miller's painter friend Emil White (to whom he had dedicated *Big Sur*) enlisted the Big Sur Land Trust and converted his house into the **Henry Miller Memorial Library.** You can see the sign east of the highway south of the Nepenthe, but the collection of Milleriana and Big Suriana is open only by appointment, daily 9-noon. Information: Land Trust, Box 1645, Carmel 93921; (408) 667-2574.

Also a longtime resident on Partington Ridge was novelist and songwriter Lillian Bos Ross and her sculptor husband. Her *The Stranger* (1942), which was subtitled "A Novel of the Big Sur," was filmed here in the early 1970s as *Zandy's Bride,* with Gene Hackman and Liv Ullmann. North of the Partington Ridge Road the rugged **de Angulo Trail,**** built by Jaime de Angulo, author of *Indian Tales,* winds it way up to the top of Partington Ridge and then on to the Coast Ridge Road and into the Ventana Wilderness.

Julia Pfeiffer Burns State Park

Further south, another mountain ranch, Saddle Rock Ranch, has become public parkland. **Julia Pfeiffer Burns State Park,***** largely undeveloped, is known particularly for pretty little McWay Cove. The short **Waterfall Trail***** goes there from the picnic ground under the redwoods in McWay Canyon, beneath Highway 1, to an overlook on a steep bluff over the cove. Opposite is an 80-foot waterfall and, to the right, Saddle Rock. You can often spot harbor seals, sea lions, and sea otters, as well as cormorants and other aquatic birds, in the cove. This is a good vantage point in early winter for watching gray whales, which have even been known to come into the cove.

The scenic overlook and retaining wall are all that remain of what must have been a spectacular place to live, Waterfall House, built in the 1920s by Lathrop and Helen Hooper Brown. Brown, a one-term congressman who was Franklin D. Roosevelt's best man when he married Eleanor Roosevelt in 1905, began buying the Saddle Rock Ranch in 1924. In 1962 his widow gave it to the state in memory of "a true pioneer," Julia Pfeiffer Burns, daughter of Michael Pfeiffer. In 1970 almost 1,700 acres of submerged land, remarkable for its underwater canyons, tunnels, caves, and natural bridges, were added to the park, but is open only to experienced diving groups (entry permits from Pfeiffer–Big Sur Park rangers).

At the moment the only other part of the park that is really open is the **Tan Bark Trail,** beginning at Partington Point and running in a series of switchbacks up to the ridge, then down to Highway 1. Information: see Pfeiffer–Big Sur State Park.

One of the next roads that seems to go over the edge into the ocean actually leads to the **Esalen Institute,** one of the originals in the human potential movement back in the 1960s. It started at the old **Slate's Hot Springs,** sulfur baths that are now a center of introspection as perspective on the universe. The public can use the hot springs—from 1:30 to 5:30 *a.m.* Sun.-Thurs.—for $3 per person. The frequent seminars and whatnot are open by reservation only, and it costs; write, or call (408) 667-2335.

Nature Reserves

At the mouth of Lime Creek is **John Little State Reserve,**** an undeveloped 21-acre area open for day use only. Down the road is another preserve, 3,900-acre **Big Creek Ranch,** managed by the University of California as a wilderness laboratory. The Nature Conservancy (156 Second St., San Francisco 94105; 415/777-0718) has hikes in spring and summer for $22, including bus from Carmel Valley.

Up Wildcat Creek, Lillian Bos Ross placed Zande Allan's ranch in *The Stranger,* which, by the way, presents a vivid picture of life hereabouts when it was wild and woolly, in the 1870s.

Lucia is a tiny place that consists mostly of Lucia Lodge, with coffee shop and gas station. Beyond is a road up to the **Immaculate Heart Hermitage** of Camaldolese Hermits at New Camaldoli, (408) 667-2456, the first American branch of this Benedictine order. The 40 monks live secluded lives and visitors are welcome only at the church at Sunday mass and at the guesthouse shop, where carvings, art, and brandied fruitcake are sold (the Hermitage Shop in Carmel is another outlet).

The private campground (60 sites) at **Limekiln Beach Redwoods,** south of Lucia, includes trails to waterfalls and lime kilns used in the last century. Day visitors, $1.50, Information: (408) 667-2403.

Back into Los Padres

The highway now runs through Los Padres National Forest for some 18 miles. The Forest Service has thoughtfully provided a few vista points and coastside picnicking and camping areas along here. You can camp at **Kirk Creek** (33 sites) and **Plaskett Creek** (44 RV sites); picnic at **Mill Creek, Sand Dollar Beach** (where hang gliding is popular above the sandy crescent beach), and **Willow Creek;** fish at all five sites; and hike at all but Willow Creek. Kirk and Willow Creeks have vista points.

From the shoulder north of Willow Creek you can take a steep trail down to **Jade Cove,*** named for the once-rich deposits of nephrite or Pacific blue jade, unique to this site. This seems an unlikely place for arduous adventure, especially involving bureaucracy, but it was in 1971. That was when the world's-record precious stone, a 9,000-pound jade boulder worth $180,000 was "collected." A diver named Don Wobber and three others spent several months diving, tediously worked loose a huge boulder wedged into a crack 35 feet below the surface of the cove, tugged the thing onto a metal sled, floated it to the surface, dragged it up the beach and to the road—and into a 14-month journey through the state bureaucracy before they were able to claim it. The Oakland Museum later purchased the stone for $20,000 and placed it in the central courtyard garden. Wobber described the adventure in *Jade Beneath the Sea: A Diving Adventure.*

The best chance the landlubber has to find more than common green and black serpentine is at low tide or after a winter storm when waves have brought up underwater deposits, which a diver can go after anytime.

As you have noticed from the map, there haven't been any roads across the Santa Lucias, but south of Kirk Creek is a turnoff onto the **Nacimiento-Fergusson Road**** (or Jolon Road), the only feasible lateral road in the whole stretch of coast from Carmel to Cambria. While scarcely a shortcut between Highways 1 and 101, this 29-mile road, paved for all but two miles, goes up to 4,000 feet then down to Jolon and San Antonio Mission (see Chapter 4 on inland Monterey County). From 101 are access roads to the eastern campsites in the forest. The ruggedly picturesque road is best for westbound travelers, who get to enjoy downhill views to the ocean.

Gorda

If you're not careful you might miss **Gorda,** a nine-acre town with a population of 20, named for an offshore rock the Spanish thought curvaceous (*gorda* means "fat lady"). It's one of the metropolitan centers of what some call the South Coast, as opposed to the North Coast of Big Sur. The "Gorda Mountain Boys" are known to be more reclusive than the extroverts to the north. Gorda, which is mostly a gas station, store, and restaurant, was sold in 1979 for $585,000 to a bunch of kids: Kidco Limited Ventures, run by the four youngsters of a money-minded San Diego family. Their town grosses more than half a million a year. Recently they have been getting along with the Gorda Mountain Boys.

South of Willow Creek a terrible road goes up toward the old **Los Burros Mining District,** the only place in these mountains where gold has been mined, starting in the 1870s when Chinese miners were active. Quantities of silver, chromium, platinum, and mercury have been produced, but Acapulco gold is now more common. The mining center of Manchester is a lost ghost town, burned completely before the turn of the century.

After Salmon Creek (up which a trail goes to **Salmon Falls**) is the Monterey–San Luis Obispo County line. This is, arbitrarily, the boundary between Northern and Southern California. The change is not immediately apparent: no plastic palm trees are in sight, and you can't see Hearst Castle from here.

Across the county line is another miniature settlement called **Ragged Point,** south of which **San Carpoforo Creek** enters the sea. Portolá, coming up the coast from San Diego in September 1769, here saw the Santa Lucia Mountains blocking his way, and turned up the creek canyon, eventually coming out of the hills near what became San Antonio Mission.

PRACTICAL INFORMATION

Getting There, Getting Around

Highway 1 is a two-lane scenic road for most of the distance from Carmel to San Simeon. Drive it as such, rather than as a freeway, and you'll like it. While southbound drivers have to drive on the side next to the ocean drop-off, the views are a bit better than for those going north. There are frequent vista points. For bicyclists, this road is part of the Pacific Coast Bicentennial Route, but that unfortunately doesn't increase the width of the shoulders, presently zero to four feet. South of Nepenthe, the traffic is lighter. The section between Big Sur and San Carpoforo Creek has about 17 uphills, four of them bears.

Monterey-Salinas Transit's #22-Big Sur bus runs from Monterey/Carmel all the way to Nepenthe twice a day from the end of May to mid-September, twice on Saturday only the rest of the year. If you take the earliest summer-schedule bus about 10:20 A.M., you'll get to Pfeiffer–Big Sur State Park at about 11:30, which gives you until about 4 P.M. to have a look around. Round-trip from Monterey/Carmel to Point Lobos/Carmel Highlands is only $2, Bixby Creek/Hurricane Point $3, Point Sur/Big Sur/Nepenthe $4. The bus originates in Monterey at Munras and Tyler, stops in Carmel at 6th and San Carlos. Information: (408) 899-2555, 424-7695.

For the convenience of hikers, hitchhikers, bicyclists, and others, here are the mileages from Carmel south: Carmel 0, Point Lobos 4, Rocky Point Restaurant 12.5, Palo Colorado Road 12.8, Bixby Creek Bridge/Old Coast Road 15.1, Little Sur River 18.4, Point Sur 20.5, Molera Park 23.4, Old Coast Road 23.5, River Inn 26, Big Sur Campground 26.2, Riverside Campground 26.3, Glen Oaks Motel/Ripplewood 26.6, Grange Hall 26.8, St. Francis of the Redwoods 26.9, Fernwood 27.2, Pfeiffer–Big Sur Park/Big Sur Lodge 28.1, Forest Service office 28.5, Sycamore Canyon Road (Pfeiffer Beach) 29.1, Ventana Inn etc. 30.3, Nepenthe 31, Big Sur Inn 31.7, Coast Gallery 34.1, Julia Pfeiffer Burns Park 39, Esalen 42, Lucia 52, New Camaldoli 53, Limekiln Campground 54, Nacimiento-Fergusson Road 57, Pacific Valley Center 59, Jade Beach/Willow Creek 61, Gorda 66, Piedras Blancas Light Station 87, San Simeon 93, Cambria 102, Morro Bay 121.

For sightseeing bus tours along the coast and to Hearst Castle, see this section at the end of Chapter 12.

Where to Stay and Eat

Accommodations (including camping) and restaurants are listed in Part IV under the heading Big Sur Coast; see also Hearst Castle/San Simeon and all Monterey Peninsula headings.

CHAPTER 12:

Hearst Castle

HIGHLIGHTS

To go to the San Simeon area without visiting Hearst Castle is like going to Bedloe's Island without touring the Statue of Liberty or Agra without seeing the Taj Mahal. Not only are the places themselves nearly nonexistent outside their only points of interest, but the points of interest themselves are so big, unique, spectacular, that they are symbols of an entire nation or the style of an age.

Hearst Castle is both. The grandiose palace is emblematic of immoderate young America's ambition, extravagance, riches, willingness to express its personality loudly, can-do spirit, overweening self-esteem, belief in living pleasurably or hedonistically, desire to shape reality to fantasy and dream (that Hearst Castle is actually in Southern California is no coincidence), lust for the rich antiquity of Europe with a generous mix of American elements . . . gasp. America is large; it contains multitudes; and here they are.

The castle is also a symbol of a past age. They don't make people like Hearst anymore. Today's millionaires are either poorer or more discreet in setting up their households.

In short, do visit Hearst Castle. But unlike the Statue of Liberty or the Taj Mahal, reservations are a must.

WHAT TO SEE AND DO

Stand on the bank of San Carpoforo Creek and imagine that one man could own all you can see to the south—no fewer than 50 miles south—and far across the hills to the east, a total of 265,000 acres. Imagine this person could also own a chunk of what were once just about the three richest mines in the United States: the Ontario in Arizona, the Anaconda in Montana, and the Homestake in South Dakota. The person you're imagining was real. His name was George Hearst. His only son, William Randolph Hearst, managed to outdo his father in vast accumulation by putting together the world's most powerful press combine—at its peak, 29 newspapers, 15 magazines, 8 radio stations, 4 film companies—and adding to the family landholdings until he owned an area twice the size of Delaware. Since Hearst was a maker of news (his "yellow press" stampeded the United States into the Spanish-American War) as well as the most amazing purveyor of it, it is a pity that he didn't live long enough to see his granddaughter, Patty, become the most headlined kidnapping victim of recent times—and the wealthiest, least likely person ever described by the FBI as "an armed, dangerous fugitive." The presses would probably have never stopped running.

William Randolph Hearst was also a fabulous spendthrift who year to year would buy up a quarter of whatever art was on the market, and nearly bankrupted himself to build a true Xanadu on the California Coast, a fantastical pleasure dome now modestly named **Hearst San Simeon State Historical Monument,***** less reverently called **Hearst Castle.** It rises toward the sky from a foothill of the Santa Lucias to the south, and you may enter.

George Hearst, who would become a senator from California before dying in 1891, began purchasing land here at a price of 50 to 70 cents an acre in 1865. That was two years after the rough-hewn millionaire and his cultured wife produced William. The elder Hearst stocked the land with prize cattle and built a white ranch house (still standing near the Hearst Castle driveway as headquarters of the now-diminished 85,000-acre Hearst ranch). George often brought Willie and his friends camping, hunting, fishing, and riding here. Willie pranked his way out of Harvard (the last joke involved chamberpots engraved with his professors' names) but two years later, in 1887, got George to give him the *San Francisco Examiner.* The razzle-dazzle Hearst empire was thus founded.

Even after leaving San Francisco for New York to play in politics, the press baron continued to visit what he always was to call the "ranch" at San Simeon. His biographer, W. A. Swanberg, says that Hearst was inspired about 1905 to build a castle on "Camp Hill," a 1,465-foot knoll commanding a view of the Pacific and the mountains. In 1919, after his mother, Phoebe Apperson Hearst, who was the major influence on her son's character, bequeathed him the ranch, Hearst began to build his palace on the renamed La Cuesta Encantada—"the enchanted hill."

This isn't one of those castles transported stone by stone from Europe. He had a remarkable architect, Julia Morgan (1872– 1957)—the first woman civil engineering graduate at Berkeley in 1894 and the first female graduate of the École des Beaux-Arts in Paris in 1902—but the signature of William Randolph Hearst is all over the creation.

It was a gigantic building project that employed from 25 to 150 men for more than 20 years. The building site of more than 120 acres on a nearly bare hilltop was cleared: some of the massive oak trees were carefully put in containers and moved (Hearst all his life was protector of trees, toads, mice—fearing their death as well as his own). All the building materials had to be transported at great expense by sea to San Simeon Bay wharf (site of a charming village today), then up the hill on what is now a five-mile driveway. First constructed were the three Spanish-Mediterranean guesthouses ("bungalows" on the blueprints); Hearst temporarily occupied the largest, the 18-room **Casa del Mar,** and the Hearst family today still has the only access.

La Casa Grande

Work then began on **La Casa Grande,** the twin-towered, basically Spanish-Moorish castle, in 1922. Structurally, the 137-foot-high castle is poured reinforced concrete with a facing of Utah limestone; most of the exterior elements—the cornices, balconies, gables, columns, windows, and other ornate features—were designed and crafted here. For a couple of reasons, the castle has never been completed. Hearst was always dissatisfied with something or had a new idea. Julia Morgan was kept busy for almost 20 years (until she retired and her assistant took over), redesigning the original towers, which Hearst thought severe, and replacing them with the present ornate ones, enlarging the astonishing Neptune Pool not once but twice, adding the recreational wing before the main building was complete, adding a clearly Oriental teak gable between the Baroque Spanish towers. At times, the design is byzantine, not to say peculiar: there's a closet with a closet in it, a bathroom that's 35 feet long but only five feet wide. (Morgan's working model is in the San Luis Obispo County Historical Museum.)

Meanwhile, in two five-story warehouses in New York, in a warehouse at the San Simeon Bay wharf, in two acres of vaults beneath the Casa Grande, Hearst's gargantuan collection of art and antiques lay waiting. He bought the contents of Hamilton Castle in Scotland; he bought an entire Spanish cloister, packed up in 10,700 crates; he bought 50 entire Gothic rooms, enormous carved ceilings, paneling by the roomful, staircases, doorways, windows, fireplaces, mantels, and corbels; he bought stained glass, fabrics, mosaics and tilework, Persian carpets by the dozens, antique beds, choir stalls, lecterns, cabinets, tables, chairs, and lamps; he bought statues, busts, paintings, drawings, tapestries, vases, candlesticks, silver table services, icons, urns, ceremonial cups, banners, armor, jewel boxes, and ancient sarcophagi; and in 1932 he bought yet another entire monastery, a Cistercian one.

For 50 years he spent a million dollars a year on art. "Compulsive," "promiscuous," his biographer says; "awful," "grotesque," his critics said; "pushover," thought the art dealers. Julia Morgan had to cope with Hearst's eclectic, predominantly Spanish, Italian, and French tastes, by designing room after room to fit some well-liked piece, like a carved ceiling, using a policy of "mix and match" so that Gothic, Etruscan, and Greek elements would fit in the same room with the overstuffed sofas and chairs of the 1920s.

Castle Grounds

Meanwhile, outside the castle, the gardens, pools, the esplanade, a zoo *and* a game preserve, were growing as luxuriantly as a person watered with money. The formal gardens were designed by Hearst's childhood friend Orrin Peck, who was also a portrait painter (he did the only oil of Hearst, now hanging in the Gothic Study, which was W. R.'s command post). For two decades 20 gardeners labored to change a nearly bare hilltop into an arboretum and botanical garden. At vast cost a couple dozen 30-foot Italian cypresses were trucked across the mountains from Paso Robles. Orange and lemon trees, Spanish fan palms, and Irish yew trees, as well as less exotic pines, eucalyptus, acacia, and cedar trees were planted—perhaps 70,000 trees on 1,000 acres. During a typical year perhaps 700,000 annuals would be planted. A pergola no less than a mile long was constructed on Orchard Hill (you pass it during the drive up to the castle) and grape vines planted to cover it—Hearst liked to ride through it on horseback. The gardeners generally worked at night because Hearst disliked the sight of workmen. Since he detested death in its many guises, gardeners at this wonderland once painted green the yellowing fronds of a dying palm until Hearst was away and the tree could be replaced.

Hearst, fond of animals, wanted a zoo, and he got one that was perhaps the world's largest private menagerie: there were lions, tigers, leopards, black panthers, cheetahs, polar bears and black bears, elephants, chimpanzees and monkeys, eagles and many other birds. That was just the population of the cages and grottoes, for 2,000 acres was specially fenced to keep the camels, American bison (40 head purchased at $1,000 apiece), yaks, llamas, giraffes, elk, water buffalo, kangaroos, ostriches, and emus—some 90 species in all—from wandering. Still on the grounds today—you may see them from the tour bus as it goes up the long drive—are zebras, tahr goats, Barbary sheep.

Farther from the castle were his 10,000 head of cattle, a dairy, a poultry farm, and the horse farm that bred Arabians, palominos, Morgans, black-and-white appaloosas.

Visiting Hearst Castle Then

Hearst was able to move into La Casa Grande on Christmas Day 1924. He didn't keep this amazing place to himself. While the ordinary public got only glimpses from the coin-operated telescope on the highway and gossipy accounts in the newspapers, Hearst invited the world's famous to come and spend weekends with him. Because of his—uh—close relationship with actress Marion Davies (state park guides won't talk about this subject), on whom he spent $7 million trying to make a movie star, many of the invited were from the tinsel world.

Who came? Clark Gable, Cary Grant, Charlie Chaplin, Greta Garbo, Errol Flynn, Gary Cooper, James Stewart, Henry Fonda, David Niven, Bette Davis, Carole Lombard, Buster Keaton, Joan Crawford, Irene Dunne, Leslie Howard—they all came. So did lesser-knowns, for Hearst was not snobbish. And he was able to snag big bankers like A. P. Giannini of the Bank of America, politicians like Mayor Jimmy Walker of New York, statesmen like Bernard Baruch, foreign leaders like Winston Churchill (then out of office and writing for the Hearst press) and the last shah of Iran (then in his playboy-princeling days), celebrities like Charles Lindbergh—even George Bernard Shaw and former President Coolidge came. ("This is probably the way God would have done it if He had had the money," GBS is reported as saying.)

The real personages rated a flight from Burbank airport on Hearst's private plane, but most would take W. R.'s private train from Glendale station on Friday evening, arriving at San Luis Obispo at midnight. A fleet of limos was waiting to drive them the 40 miles to San Simeon—where the floodlit castle could be seen, rising out of the summer fog. The Chief welcomed them to his "ranch" in the huge Assembly Room, then the guests—of whom there might be 50 on a weekend—were taken to their antique-filled chambers.

The next morning they could have breakfast anytime from 9 till noon, then wander the grounds on foot or horseback, play tennis, go to the zoo, swim in either the inconceivably perfect **Neptune Pool** (filled with 345,000 gallons of heated mountain spring water, with a Venus rising from the water at one end) or the million-dollar indoor, saltwater **Roman Pool,** for which artisans were brought from Italy to lay the gold-faced Venetian tiles.

After the sit-down lunch at 2 P.M. the guests continued their play. At 7 they would gather in the **Assembly Room,** the comfortable museum room where the only drinking was allowed (Hearst wanted no genuine news of drunken orgies at Hearst Castle in his or anybody's papers). At 7:30 the host, a genial man whose high-pitched voice seemed inappropriate for his six-foot-three-inch, 230-pound frame, would descend from his **Gothic Suite** in an elevator made from an antique confessional, emerging from behind a panel to mix with starlets and statesmen.

At 9 everyone would head to the right of the sixteenth-century French mantel-over-mantel fireplace into the **Refectory,** the dining room fit for a medieval feast: below the sixteenth-century Italian carved ceiling portraying the saints were high Gothic windows, a row of antique banners from Siena (the ones used in that city's famous horseback parade and race around the Piazza del Campo), sixteenth-century Flemish tapestries depicting events in the life of Daniel, and finally, against the walls, choir stalls. The 54-foot refectory table from seventeenth-century England, would seat up to 40 diners, who might feast on, say, shrimp specially flown in from Louisiana but would use paper napkins and condiments in their original containers—Hearst's nostalgic reminder of picnics on Camp Hill.

After dinner everyone would go to the movies—in the 50-seat theater where Hearst's imperial command resulted in a showing of *Gone With The Wind* even before its premiere.

It All Ends

An appropriate movie title. San Simeon's real golden days lasted only a decade. By 1937 Hearst was spending money faster than his presses could print newspapers. His edifice was in debt $126 million and bankruptcy was imminent. A Conservation Committee stopped the building at San Simeon (leaving some bare concrete walls) and shut the zoo, surrendered the Ritz Tower in New York to a bank rather than continue paying off the mortgage, closed a few newspapers, sold off three papers plus seven radio stations, and forced the Chief to put two-thirds of the less-choice warehoused art and antiques on the market again. For a year Joe Blow was able to wander through the two acres of Gimbel's fifth floor in New York, buying up bits and pieces of Hearst's collection.

There were those who found the pity hilarious: in 1939 Aldous Huxley dissected Hearst in *After Many a Summer Dies the Swan,* and the next year Orson Welles unflatteringly portrayed Hearst in *Citizen Kane.* Welles was put at the top of the Hearst press "S-list" but the Chief couldn't stop the release of the picture.

The war partially saved Hearst's empire from total collapse. For $2 million the government bought 164,000 acres of ranchland across the mountains for troop training, but after 1941 Hearst closed his castle for two years—it was too tempting a target for Japanese submarines, he thought. Later he moved back, continued some compulsive building, and had some party weekends but rattled around an empty Xanadu during the week. Doctors forced him to move back to L.A. after a 1947 heart attack.

But it was here that, on August 14, 1951, after many a summer, the swan died, aged 88, leaving a personal estate of $59.4 million—including one castle on which as much as $50 million had been lavished. (The other permanent thing he left behind is, of course, his filmic image in *Citizen Kane,* which consistently tops lists of the best movies ever made.)

No one wanted Hearst's castle; nobody could afford it. The University of California even turned it down as a gift. The State Department of Parks and Recreation was finally persuaded to accept the castle and 123 surrounding acres in 1957. Opened to the public the next year, the castle is now visited by nearly a million people a year and turns a modest profit for the state park system.

Visiting Hearst Castle Today

La Cuesta Encantada is not run as an art museum: it is open only for guided house-tours. Those tours are conducted with military-band precision, not only to squeeze as many people as possible through scores of rooms but also to maintain adequate security. The park rangers have been on guard against vandalism and terrorism since February 1976 when, during Patty Hearst's bank-robbery trial, the New World Liberation Front set off a bomb that nearly destroyed the Casa del Sol guesthouse. Too, there are a lot of loose, fine objects that can wander off. (Only one theft of any size, a vase in 1972, is known of.)

The price of crowd handling and security is that visitors are fairly rushed through room after room, with not one idle moment to inspect any of Hearst's 5,000 treasures. Not that Hearst Castle is the Louvre, but we'll accept the conservative judgment of the guides that much of Hearst's collection is of museum quality, containing excellent Hispanic pieces and being particularly rich in the decorative arts. Visitors deserve more for their money than the present quick look around. While few of us are art scholars, neither are we all ice-cream-dripping tourists with Mickey Mouse hats and five minutes to spare for something cultural.

At present there are four two-hour tours: **Tour I***—recommended for first-time visitors—takes the largest groups (about 53) by the Neptune Pool and by the formal garden, into a sumptuous guesthouse; through the main floor of the Casa Grande—main entrance and vestibule, Assembly Room, Refectory, Morning Room, Theater (a six-minute "home movie" of San Simeon's golden days is shown); and, finally, the Roman Pool. You walk about half a mile, climb about 150 steps.

Tour II** takes the smallest group (about 12 persons) by the Neptune Pool and through the garden; into the fully equipped kitchen; then upstairs to see a Duplex Suite (whose design seems to predate split-level condominiums), the Della Robbia Room (one of the Cloister Suites, it contains many enameled terra-cotta works by the Florentine family), the Main Library (5,000 volumes, plus a collection of Greek and Etruscan urns), Hearst's Gothic Suite, including his study and bedroom, the fourth-floor Celestial Suite (matching bedrooms in each of the towers, connected by a sitting room), and the Doge's Suite; then to look at the Roman Pool. This tour moves in relatively confined spaces, requires about 300 steps of climbing.

Tour III* visits the comparatively dull North Wing guest rooms, the pools and gardens, and the other guesthouse that is open, Casa Del Monte. This also requires 300 steps and is for a small group.

Tour IV, added in 1982, visits areas not previously opened to the public, including the wine cellar and other service areas. We haven't been on it.

Generally, no wheelchairs, strollers, or pets. Cameras are allowed but not tripods or flash equipment.

Reservations are *really* advised; they are absolutely necessary in the summer, on weekends, and on holidays; don't be one of the 200,000 who have to be turned away. Casual travelers who want to tour the castle other times can sometimes get in after a little wait at the entrance complex (rest rooms, snack bar, gift shop—which sells W. A. Swanberg's *Citizen Hearst,* good reading before a visit). In that case get there early—at busy times the ticket office opens at 7:45 A.M. for first-come, first-served reservations for that day; no checks. Reservations are obtainable either through Ticketron outlets from 60 days in advance to the day before (there's a Ticketron outlet in Monterey, 230 Del Monte Center), or through the state's Hearst Reservation Office, Box 2390, Room 115, State

Department of Parks and Recreation, 1416 9th St., Sacramento 95814, between 60 and 10 days in advance; checks okay.

Admission fees: adult—$7, child 6-17—$3.50, *per tour.* Ticketron has a $1 service charge, the state 50 cents, for each ticket.

Open: daily except Thanksgiving and Christmas. In the summer and on holiday weekends, tours may leave every 10 minutes from 8-3:50; in the off-season every 20 minutes, 8:30-3:30.

If you make reservations and arrive first thing in the morning, you could perhaps squeeze in all three tours, the cost being exhaustion and a lot of round-trips up the hill on the bus. If you weren't planning that, skip Tour III. Some people find one tour quite enough; on to Hollywood!

Information: Hearst-San Simeon State Historical Monument, Box 8, San Simeon 93452; (805) 927-4621.

Oh, that dismantled Cistercian monastery that Hearst picked up, he didn't know what to do with it and San Francisco's M. H. de Young Museum finally got it. Because no extravagant millionaire was found to finance putting it together, the museum put the ornate portal on display inside (in the Hearst Court) and let Golden Gate park gardeners use some of the other stones. The leftovers are disintegrating in back of the museum.

Sic transit gloria Hearst.

PRACTICAL INFORMATION

Getting There, Getting Around

Well, you can drive or you can take a tour bus. For advice on driving Highway 1 from San Francisco or Monterey, see this section in the previous chapter. Amtrak (which runs the Coast Starlight, stopping at midafternoon in San Luis Obispo) and Great Western Tours have a rail-bus tour that can be done as a round-trip or as a stopover, with an overnight at San Simeon. Gray Line has a Hearst Castle day trip from Monterey/Carmel in the summer; see Chapter 10. The long-distance bus tours up and down the Central Coast, three days, two nights, with a Hearst Castle tour, are run by California Parlor Car Tours (offices in San Francisco, L.A.; call 800/622-0895).

There's no public transit between the Hearst Castle parking lot and the accommodation/restaurant areas at San Simeon and Cambria.

Where to Stay and Eat

Accommodations (including camping) and restaurants are listed in Part IV under the headings Hearst Castle/San Simeon and Big Sur Coast; see also all Monterey Peninsula headings.

# Part IV

Where to
Stay and Eat

Nothing is so perishable as travel information, especially hotel and restaurant listings. Name, address, telephone, price, cuisine, ownership, management, hours, credit-card acceptance, decor, style—not to mention quality—all change as frequently as the news. Although this book is primarily a sightseeing guide, we would be negligent if we failed to give readers some indication of acceptable places at which to stay and eat. Thus this concise, fallible listing of significant but perishable facts. Call or write ahead to confirm facts of concern to you.

Our emphasis in the listings below is on *choice*. We believe in that 2,000-year-old maxim of Publius': "No pleasure endures unseasoned by variety." Travel celebrates variety, thrives on it. Not every travel guide reflects this sentiment, and the tourist industry seems to think variety is positively dangerous, possibly un-American. Popular travel guides and the hotel and restaurant industries, like TV programmers, pitch their products to the lowest common denominator among American travelers: the desire to avoid unpleasantness.

The removal of risk from travel has resulted in far too many sanitized motels and wood-grain-Formica coffee shops: a Holiday Inn in every city in America, suburban strips lined with Burger King, Denny's, McDonald's, Long John Silver's, ad nauseam, all across this fair land of ours. Places to stay and eat are indistinguishable, interchangeable; inside or outside, you could as easily be in Birmingham, Michigan, as Birmingham, Alabama.

Too many travel guides reflect this uniformity rather than the variety that still exists. The publisher of the Mobil guides, Rand McNally, sends out teams of college students on vacation to take quantified, objectified, computerized inventory of accommodations ("Ck-out, noon. Coin lndry 10 blks") and restaurants ("Background music. Kiwanis, Lions meet here"). The result is homogenized listings of establishments that meet the avoid-risk criterion. Many little inns that make the Monterey Peninsula such a good weekend excursion are left out.

Choice certainly means risk. Little inns can have lumpy mattresses; rustic lodges may not have heated pools. But the inn can have individually decorated rooms, and the lodge can offer a friendly home-cooked breakfast in front of the fireplace.

To avoid risk is to forsake most of the possibility of pleasant surprise, most rustic charm, some true comfort and some interesting discomfort, a lot of relaxed communication with real people, occasional adventure, rural detours, unique experiences, and other qualities of individual travel.

Mass tourism may avoid risk. We recommend a risk a day as good for the soul. We think it is better to take a chance on a hotel or restaurant that can be wonderful or dreadful than to go to a place that can never be memorable at all.

But we're not crotchety all the time, not intolerant of Colonel Sanders and Ronald McDonald every day. We list some "surprise-free" accommodations and restaurants because even the most rigorously independent travelers don't feel like taking a risk every night and every mealtime. Even then we list a few more predictable accommodations (because it is always safer to reserve ahead) than cookie-cutter restaurants (because these are too easy to find).

Incidentally, we did not accept any free accommodations or meals, and moved about as anonymously as possible, which isn't difficult. All listings are our responsibility.

PRICE CATEGORIES

The most worthwhile guidebooks tell exactly how much things cost. Unfortunately, in times of double-digit inflation, such books are out of date as soon as they appear in the bookstore. But leaving out any indication of prices makes readers frustrated. After years of struggling with various schemes, we contrived a four-level price-category system based on a simple assumption: *While a hotel or restaurant may raise its prices, so do all its competitors—but, barring complete renovation or refurbishing, or change of cuisine or style, the place keeps the same position relative to its competitors.* Thus the Holiday Inn that charged $30 for a double five years ago may charge $60 today, but it is still moderately priced compared with the Hyatt Regency nearby. What you thought was an expensive restaurant in 1970 is likely to be expensive in 1983. We all have to run to keep up with inflation; somehow we manage, but mental adjustments and revised guidebooks are always necessary.

Here are the four price categories:

$:budget	The least expensive. A sign of welcome for those keeping a close eye on expenses.
$:intermediate	As the term implies, prices are in the middle of the range. For those whose budgets are reasonably flexible.
$:expensive	In most parts of California, though probably not in the San Francisco Bay Area or on the Monterey Peninsula, this signifies the best and most costly rooms and meals.
$:luxury	A special price category, applicable mostly to the super-hotels and super-restaurants of the Bay Area and Monterey Peninsula.

But, you ask, what is this in real money? Here we'll take a chance and give monetary definition to the terms, *based on San Francisco and Monterey Peninsula prices in late 1982* (bear in mind that lingering inflation changed this already):

Accommodations

Cost of a **typical double room** (average quality or standard for that hotel, for two persons) for one night in high season; no tax, tips, or extras included:

$:budget	less than $35
$:intermediate	$35-70
$:expensive	$71-125
$:luxury	more than $125

Restaurants

Cost per person for a **complete dinner** (soup and/or salad, aver-age-priced entrée, vegetable, potato or similar, bread and butter, coffee or other beverage); no wine, no dessert; no tax, tips, or parking included:

$:budget	less than $9
$:intermediate	$10-15
$:expensive	$16-22
$:luxury	more than $23

A mixed term, such as $:budget-intermediate, means that the hotel has two or more kinds of doubles or the restaurant dishes are priced over a wide enough range so that you can order in one price category or the other. A mixed term may also mean that the average price was, at this writing, hovering on the border between the categories.

We do not put breakfast-lunch places in price categories. The descriptions will hint at possible priciness.

We also do not indicate camping fees. In 1982 the State Parks charged about $5 per developed family campsite; commercial campgrounds typically charge a couple of dollars more.

Credit Cards

AE—American Express
CB—Carte Blanche
DC—Diners Club
MC—MasterCard
VI—Visa (BankAmericard)
Major cards—all of the above are accepted.

Where no cards are listed, there is the strong possibility that MC or VI will be accepted by the time you go there.

Reservations

If you want to be sure of eating anywhere, call ahead for reservations. Accommodations often require a deposit with reservation.

FINDING A PLACE TO STAY OR EAT

Accommodations and restaurants are grouped under the name of a principal city/town or the name of the area itself (San Mateo Coastside, for example). The cities/areas are in alphabetical order, and an introductory paragraph describes the extent of the area covered and gives telephone area code and zip codes. Under each larger city or area, listing are alphabetical and cross-referenced by cuisine type and location; for the smaller or more spread-out areas listings are geographic or by style.

A type of restaurant that is popular in California and other coastal states with big cities we call "California Continental." This elsewhere might be called "nouvelle cuisine." We mean fresh ingredients—fresh seafood from Monterey Bay or the Pacific Ocean, well-cut meats, garden- or California-grown produce—plus light sauces, a mixture of French, Italian, perhaps Oriental, and other influences, with a youthful but generally sophisticated ambiance.

The cities and areas we cover include:

The section Monterey Peninsula has general introductory remarks and cross-referenced listings for accommodations and restaurants for the entire area, and includes a section on camping.

Big Sur Coast

WHERE TO STAY

It is far better to stay a night or two along the Big Sur Coast than not. Around Big Sur proper the accommodations are mainly rustic—a campground with some cottages, typically—but there's a fancy place and an orthodox motel. Market segmentation is alive at Big Sur. By the way, there's little television hereabouts—the mountains keep it out—and hardly anyplace has phones in the rooms. Address for all below: Big Sur 93920; area code 408.

Big Sur Itself

L.A. escapes N: **Ventana Inn,** 667-2331 or 624-4812. $:luxury. AE, DC, MC, VI. The Ventana (Spanish for "window"—which early explorers thought they saw in one of the hills) is above the other accommodations in a number of ways. First, it is located well above the highway and the redwooded Big Sur Valley, on a relatively open hillside, part of 800 acres. Second, the rates are high enough to guarantee you will mix with the demographically up-scale only. Third, the architecture and interior design definitely tend toward the more tasteful, expensive, and comfortable. Fourth, when the owners wanted to expand from 24 to 60 rooms the battle before the California Coastal Commission included as participants John Denver (pro-expansion) versus Robert Redford and Johnny Rivers (anti-expansion); the CCC compromise allowed 16 more units. The now 40 guestrooms are arranged in eight aged-cedar buildings of a modern vacation-condominum design, with large rooms decorated in friendly natural wood and bright colors; the beds have handpainted carved headboards, homemade Nova Scotia quilts; all rooms have terraces, half have fireplaces, and two are actually town-house suites. Separate complex contains 90-foot heated pool, hotbaths, sauna. Also restaurant (see below) and fancy shop and, on the highway, a deli with dining terrace. Pricey, comfortable—but atypical of Big Sur: the sort of place where someone will complain of having to walk somewhere (she really *did*).

State park lodge: **Big Sur Lodge,** 667-2171. Inside Pfeiffer–Big Sur State Park. $:intermediate. No cards. The lodge, at this location since about 1935, has a beautiful site in a redwood grove and on an open hillside. The 61 rooms, which include rooms and housekeeping cottages for up to six people, are scattered around the grounds in clusters, creating a lot of breathing space. While the decor and furnishings are tacky, that is perhaps another reason to stay outside and enjoy Big Sur. Swimming pool (heated), recreation building, dining room (closed October-Easter), store, and—all around—Pfeiffer–Big Sur Park. In all, good value.

Functional motels: **Glen Oaks Motel,** 667-2105. $:budget. No cards. Well-kept with somewhat different motel decor; lots of flowers outside the adobe brick cottages. Café across the street. A bargain. **River Inn,** 667-2237. $:budget *or* expensive. MC, VI. Very casual management will rent you new housekeeping room in building on the river or room in too-old motel building across the highway. Rustic inn itself has dining room and bar—Big Sur social center in evening. Store and butcher shop. Mellow place but old units not worth it, highway location undesirable; new units overpriced.

Funky, laid-back, and overpriced: **Deetjen's Big Sur Inn,** 667-2377. $:budget. No cards. If you have never stayed here before, the management insists that you look at a room prior to staying, and well you should. Rooms like Lower Creek and Champagne are rustic but not endearing, situated in Norwegian inn-style cabins perched among the redwoods and clinging to ferny creeksides. Dining room has two sittings nightly.

Little resorts with rooms, cabins, and/or camping: **Fernwood Lodge and Park,** 667-2422. $:budget. MC, VI. 12-unit motel building, also restaurant, bar, store. **Ripplewood Resort,** 667-2242. $:budget-intermediate. MC, VI. 13 rustic cabins, on Big Sur River. Also pizza restaurant, store. **Riverside Campground and Cabins,** 667-2414. Some cabins on the river under redwoods.

Camping: **Pfeiffer–Big Sur State Park** has 218 fair sites grouped along the river, with good facilities; reservations through Ticketron are best. All the following have hookups, full facilities: **Ventana Campground,** below the inn, has 100 shaded sites. **Fernwood's** campground, with 105 sites, caters more to RVs. **Riverside Campground** has 40 sites, some shaded. The best walk-in camping for backpackers that is not too far from the highway is at **Andrew Molera State Park,** whose primitive campsites are on a first-come, first-served basis. There are, of course, many trail camps in Los Padres National Forest, mostly in the Ventana Wilderness, but check the Forest Service on these.

Tassajara Zen Mountain Center, a hot-springs resort or retreat for the earth-bound, is described under "What to See and Do," Chapter 11.

South of Big Sur

The accommodations are more scattered south of the Big Sur village area. In Lucia is the **Lucia Lodge,** 667-2476, which has 10 units and a café. Just south, **Limekiln Beach Redwoods Campground,** 667-2403, has sites for tents, RVs, or both, including sites on the beach at the mouth of the creek. The **Forest Service campgrounds,** at Plaskett Creek and Kirk Creek, have 33 and 44 sites respectively, with toilets the only facilities.

WHERE TO EAT

Big Sur Itself

High on the hill: **Ventana Restaurant,** 667-2331: 30 miles S of Carmel. California Continental. $:expensive. AE, DC, MC, VI. High on the hills with views of the Ventana Wilderness, Pacific Ocean, and neighbor Nepenthe, the Ventana features fresh food served indoors in the high-ceilinged cedar dining room and outdoors on the spacious patios. À la carte dinners may include fresh oysters on the half shell, spinach salad, fresh grilled trout, veal doré, roast glazed duckling, seasonal seafood. Save room for the rich dessert tarts and cakes. Lunch also served. By the way, the Ventana deli, on the highway, can fill your picnic order.

Tourist attraction: **Nepenthe,** 667-2345: 31 miles S of Carmel. American. $:budget-intermediate. AE, MC, VI. Full bar. The attractions at this magnetic place are the scenery (the view from 808 feet above sea level), the people (drawn from all over, including the local hills), the architecture (terraced hillside with adobe and redwood structure designed by a Frank Lloyd Wright student), interior design (warm, comfortable) and the ambiance (calm). Downstairs the Café Amphora serves brunch and lunch on the patio. Upstairs the Nepenthe features Lolly's tasty baked chicken, steaks, fresh seafood, and overrated Ambroisia burger. Go for lunch or supper for the view. Monterey–Salinas Transit bus #22 stops here for those without cars. Phoenix gift shop sells hand-hewn crafts and other items.

Homey, with a Big Sur riverbanks view: **River Inn,** 667-2234; 26 miles S of Carmel. American. $:intermediate. MC, VI. Bar. River Inn differs from the previous two in featuring hearty home cooking: well-aged beef dishes, whatever fish is fresh from Monterey, and such basics as meat loaf with mashed potatoes. The hungry can't lose. Decor is American log-cabin, fitting right into the Big Sur Valley redwoods. Breakfast is served practically all day, lunch till 5. If it's not foggy or otherwise miserable out, you can sit on a big terrace.

For families: **Big Sur Lodge Dining Room,** 667-2171. 28 miles S of Carmel. American. $:budget-intermediate. Beer, wine. Large, clean, just right for families, with standard fare such as broiled chicken, New York steak, roast beef. There's sit-down service inside and out on the patio, also counter service.

Woodsy, personal: **Deetjen's Big Sur Inn,** 667-2377; 32 miles S of Carmel. American. $:budget-intermediate. No cards, no alcohol, but BYO. By no surprise, the dining room is run like the inn: informal, publicity-shy, personal, with reservations advised. The menu is short, ranging from a vegetarian plate to a daily special to New York steak. Lots of objects to observe in the homey dining rooms, and one or two sittings nightly.

Other Big Sur: **Glen Oaks Restaurant,** 667-2623. $:budget-intermediate. MC, VI. Cl. Wed. Open for breakfast, lunch, dinner, with a varied menu including trout and eggs, crepes, seafood, pasta. **Ripplewood Resort.** Pizza, salad, beer in a cozy, wood place.

Crashing waves: **Rocky Point Restaurant,** 624-2933; about 12 miles S of Carmel. Steak, seafood. $:intermediate-expensive. No cards. Bar. Cl. Mon. Situated on a cliff with a view of a gorgeous rock cove (floodlit at night) and Rocky Creek Bridge. The menu emphasizes charcoal-broiled chicken, steaks, seafood. No tablecloths but bring your camera.

South Coast: **Sorta Gorda,** the café at the Kidco-owned, gas-station town of Gorda, which may serve Mexican food and organic pumpkin pie still.

Carmel

Carmel's accommodations are inns, low-rise hotels, discreet motels, cottages, and bed-and-breakfasts. To best enjoy Carmel's charm, we recommend parking your car, staying at a centrally located inn or bed-and-breakfast, and walking to shops, restaurants, and the beach. Since the names are not necessarily descriptive of the ambiance, here is our classification of Carmel hostelries:

Inns: Carmel Fireplace Inn, Carriage House Inn,
Cypress Inn, Lobos Lodge, Normandy Inn, Rosita
Lodge, San Antonio House, Sandpiper Inn, Sundial
Lodge, Vagabond House Inn
Hotels: La Playa Hotel, Pine Inn
Motels: Carmel Sands Lodge, Jade Tree Inn
Cottages: Cottages-by-the-Sea, Lamp Lighters Inn
Bed-and-Breakfast: Stonehouse Guest Lodge.

If you have problems locating a room, try Carmel's Room Find-er Service, Mission/Ocean; (408) 624-1711.

Carmel's restaurants are equally diverse, with selections avail-able ranging from expensive French, to very fresh seafood, to high tech Italian, to intimate pastry shops and tea houses. Just bring your credit cards and lots of cash. A selection of several of Carmel's cuisines include:

American: Hog's Breath Inn, Studio Theater and
Restaurant
California Continental: Anton & Michel, Casanova,
General Store
Creole: Toots Lagoon
English: Sticky Wicket, Tuck Box
French: Chez Felix, French Poodle, La Bohème, Le
Coq d'Or, L'Escargot, Moulin de Carmel, Patisserie
Boissière, Saint Tropez
Italian: Paolina Pasta, Raffaello
Japanese: Shabu-Shabu
Scandinavian: Scandia, Swedish Restaurant
Seafood: Clam Box, Fishhouse on the Park, Flaherty's
Oyster Bar & Grill; most of the other restaurants
also serve seafood dishes
Steak and Seafood: Butcher Shop, Simpson's
Swiss: Swiss Tavern

For further help in finding the best places to stay and eat, see under the heading Monterey Peninsula, and the listings for Car-mel Highlands and Highway, Carmel Valley, Monterey, Pacific Grove, and Pebble Beach.

Area code: 408. Zip code: Carmel 93921.

WHERE TO STAY

Carmel Fireplace Inn, San Carlos & 4th (Box 4082), Carmel; 624-4862. $:budget-intermediate. AE, MC, VI. Small (16 rooms in cottages), quiet. Fireplaces in 8 rooms, coffee in all. Cozy garden.

Carmel Sands Lodge, San Carlos & 5th (Box 951), Carmel; 624-1255. $:intermediate. MC, VI. Associated with Simpson's (see "Where to Eat"), this is mainly a motel (38 rooms with either balcony or patio) oriented around the heated pool; 6 rooms have kitchens, 8 have fireplaces. Complimentary continental breakfast. Not extraordinary, but central.

Carriage House Inn, Junipero (7th/8th) (Box 101), Carmel; 625-2585. $:intermediate-expensive. AE, MC, VI. No children. One of the newest, a modern inn with clean lines, brass beds with homemade quilted comforters, other old/new antique furnishings, beamed ceilings in upstairs rooms, nice prints and plants, fireplaces, refrigerators, sunken Japanese baths; most rooms have bay windows. Much class here but they do charge for it.

Cottages-by-the-Sea, San Antonio (7th/8th) (Box 726), Carmel; 624-4086. In residential area, a block from Carmel Beach. $:intermediate; reasonable rates for 3-9 persons and 7 or more days and families with two or more kids under 15. Five cottages around the garden vary in size and decor, but all have kitchens and private patios, all but one a living room with fireplace. Good for vacationing couples or families.

Cypress Inn, Lincoln & 7th (Box Y), Carmel; 624-3871. $:intermediate. AE, MC, VI. A 33-room inn with Spanish Colonial architecture, including a garden courtyard, and spirit. Comfortable, congenial—we like it a lot. Complimentary continental breakfast.

Jade Tree Inn, Junipero (5th/6th) (Box 3715), Carmel: 624-1831. $:intermediate. AE, MC, VI. A former Best Western but with Oriental motif, somewhat better designed, and well landscaped. Otherwise ordinary. Pool.

Lamp Lighters Inn, Ocean & Camino Real (Box 604), Carmel; 624-7372. $:intermediate-expensive. No cards. Tiny inn—only 9 units in cottages that fit in with Carmel's fairy-tale architecture; Hansel and Gretel Cottage, for up to five persons, has most facilities, with bedroom, living room with fireplace, hand-loomed rugs, kitchen; Tree-Top Room is smallest, for a couple. Cute Carmel garden.

La Playa Hotel, Camino Real & 8th (Box 900), Carmel; 624-6476. $:intermediate. AE, MC, VI. Carmel-by-the Sea's largest hotel (72 rooms), La Playa is also one of the oldest and one of the closest to the beach (2 blocks). The Mediterranean-white resort is a large L-shaped building, mostly 4 stories high, with a large lawn and pool-cabana area. The general decor underwhelms us but the rooms are personal and tasteful enough. Terrazo del Mar dining room has a good view. Also bar, meeting rooms.

Lobos Lodge, Ocean & Monte Verde (Drawer L1), Carmel; 624-3874. $:intermediate-expensive. MC, VI. 1924 cottages built by the Pine Inn were almost completely rebuilt in 1974 into 27 units connected by wandering paths and stairways, and there are a couple of specialty shops along the way. Brightly furnished, green-and-white rooms have private patios, fireplaces. Continental breakfast is complimentary. Exceedingly nice.

Normandy Inn, Ocean (Monte Verde/Casanova) (Box 1706), Carmel; 624-3825. $:intermediate-expensive. No cards. The owners, an architect and his wife, formerly a *House Beautiful* editor, have created a cheerful, neat place whose 48 units are in the main inn or cottages; a dozen have fireplaces. Decor varies but tends to Colonial maple. Good-looking little country-restaurant dining room serves free continental breakfast. There's a flower-filled garden around a small heated pool. Cottages can accommodate up to 9 persons. Good central location if you're a mad-keen shopper.

Pine Inn, Ocean near Lincoln (Box 250), Carmel; 624-3851. $:intermediate-expensive. AE, MC, VI. The Pine Inn has been a Carmel establishment since the 1920s and we hope it'll last until the 2020s, at least. Elegantly Victorian, with a preponderance of red in the carpets, upholstery, curtains, wallpaper, bed spreads—though, funny enough, the least red room is the Red Parlor bar. The Garden Room is the main dining room but the smart place to dine is the Gazebo, a glassed-in, domed courtyard. 49 rooms mostly feature brass beds, other antiquey furnishings; poshest is the top-floor penthouse (sleeps 8).

Rosita Lodge, 4th & Torres (Box 2077), Carmel; 624-6926.

$:intermediate. AE, CB, DC, MC, VI. Of the 9 units, 6 have kitchens, all have fireplaces, antiques, flowers, afternoon wine, and morning Continental breakfast and newspaper.

San Antonio House, San Antonio (Ocean/7th) (Box 3683), Carmel; 624-4334. $:budget-intermediate. This small inn is located on a quiet residential street 1 block from the beach, about 3 downhill from the village. Two and 3-room suites open onto the patios and gardens, and rooms have antiques, fridge, morning coffee, and paper.

Sandpiper Inn, 2408 Bayview at Martin Way, Carmel; 624-6433. On Carmel Point, 50 yards from ocean, a good 10 blocks from downtown. $:intermediate. MC, VI. No children under 10. Homey 15-room inn, not quaint or antiquey but comfortable enough, and recently remodeled. Free continental breakfast served by the fireplace in the lounge. Some rooms have fireplaces, others views. Most expensive are large corner rooms with king beds.

Stonehouse Guest Lodge, 8th (Monte Verde/Casanova) (Box 2517), Carmel; 624-4569. Run by the same people who have the Green Gables and Gosby House Inn in Pacific Grove, the Stonehouse was originally built in 1906 with the exterior hand-shaped by local Indians. The first owner, Mrs. "Nana" Foster frequently invited San Francisco Bay Area artists and writers to stay, including Sinclair Lewis, Jack London, and Lotta Crabtree. Guests today sleep in one of 6 rooms that share 2 baths, personally decorated with antiques, quilts, silk flowers, and fresh fruit. Continental breakfast is in the dining room or garden.

Sundial Lodge, Monte Verde at 7th (Box J), Carmel; 624-8578. $:intermediate. No cards. The 20 rooms, each with a different decor—wicker, Victorian, early American—mostly face the intimate garden courtyard (with sundial); some have views as well. Guests can use pool, other facilities of La Playa Hotel 3 blocks away. The lobby, where continental breakfast is served, is particularly well decorated. Cheerful, congenial accommodations at good rates.

Vagabond House Inn, 4th & Dolores (Box 2747), Carmel; 624-7738. $:intermediate-expensive. MC, VI. Surrounding a flagstone garden are 11 rooms, 8 with kitchens, most with fireplaces, all with fresh flowers, wine, Continental breakfast, newspaper.

WHERE TO EAT

Anton & Michel, Mission (Ocean/7th); 624-2406. California Continental. $:intermediate-expensive. AE, CB, DC, MC, VI. Full bar. Formerly called Briar House, it is still located at the Court of the Fountain, but the menu has changed from steak and seafood to California Continental. Specialties include smoked Monterey salmon, chicken Jerusalem (with artichokes in winy cream sauce), paupiettes de veau langoustine (lobster tail rolled in thin veal), Armenian lamb chops, plus filet mignon and other steaks. Ask for a table by the fountain courtyard.

Butcher Shop, Ocean (Dolores/Lincoln); 624-2569. Steak, seafood. $:intermediate-expensive. AE, CB, DC, MC, VI. Full bar. A popular restaurant with a modern decor, accented by a glassed-in fireplace; the Carmel Butcher Shop menu has much in the way of prime rib, 20-oz. porterhouse steaks, and Australian lobster tail, but also has some different concoctions, such as butcher's ribs, veal chop Marsala sautéed with shallots and mushrooms, and scallops en bouchées (scallops sautéed with mushrooms in sherry cream sauce in puff pastry). Early-bird specials are served 4:30-6, and dinner is served until 11 P.M. should Carmel somehow keep you up that late.

Casanova, 5th (Mission/San Carlos); 625-0501. California Continental. $:intermediate-expensive. MC, VI. Wine, beer. In a small house with a charming garden and patio, the Casanova has a friendly European country-farm ambiance. Three-course dinners include entrées such as rack of lamb with fresh tarragon and red wine sauce, filet mignon with béarnaise sauce, veal baked in cheese and mustard cream sauce, and filet of sole with fresh sorrel and dry vermouth sauce.

Charlie-O, Dolores (Ocean/7th); 625-0575. International. $:intermediate. AE, DC, MC, VI. Wine, beer. No res. Cl. Tues., Wed. Charlie-O has an à la carte menu from which you can put together a light meal or a multicourse dinner, beginning with a soup (hot like French onion or cold—gazpacho with tiny shrimps), then a first course (artichoke with various sauces, quiche, snow crab in pocket bread, or other things), a plate of steamed vegetables or a salad (for example, watercress, endive, and sprout salad), a second-course sandwich (how about a Mexican burger or jack cheese and sprout burger?) or omelet, then a third course (for example, Chinese spareribs, cannelloni, or other things), and finally a dessert (Black Forest cherry roll, hot deep-dish apple pie, and more). There's a nightly prix-fixe dinner, also Sunday brunch.

Chez Felix, Monte Verde (Ocean/7th); 624-4707. French. $:intermediate-expensive. Wine, beer. Cl. Sun. In the same building as the Sundial Lodge, Chez Felix is now better located in Carmel than it was on Monterey's Cannery Row. Its French provincial atmosphere is enhanced with the very personal, professional service. Delicious starters may be thick crab bisque or onion soup, followed by Monterey salmon steamed with white wine and butter in parchment, served with hollandaise sauce, scampi in a light tomato sauce, steak au poivre (double rib with green pepper), or chicken with 5 kinds of mushrooms. If you have room for dessert, try chestnut and chocolate mousse.

Clam Box, Mission (5th/6th); 624-8597. Seafood. $:budget-intermediate. No cards. Full bar. No res. Cl. Mon., half December. Like the Tuck Box, the Clam Box may have been so named for being small. On second thought, maybe it should have been called the Fishing Line, for it often has a line outside. No wonder: the Clam Box offers a memorably good seafood meal at a reasonable price. What's more, the atmosphere is better than at Monterey's Fisherman's Wharf. Take your pick from a lengthy menu that includes clam chowder with herbs (the specialty), poached salmon, stuffed clams on the half shell, rainbow trout meunière, prawns Newburg flavored with sherry, curried Alaska shrimp, and a big Captain's Plate heaped with seafood. The weekend special is, peculiarly, a Polish dish, breast of chicken Wieliczka. For dessert there's cherry cream or blueberry cream pie. All in all, one of our favorites.

Fishhouse on the Park, Junipero & 6th; 624-1766. Seafood. $:intermediate-expensive. AE, CB, DC, MC, VI. Full bar. Located directly across the street from Devendorf Plaza, Carmel's popular downtown park, the Fishhouse serves dinner in several dining rooms and maybe even on the roof. Seafood specialities include broiled swordfish steak, abalone steak doré, shrimp curry, baked deviled crab, bouillabaisse Marseillaise, and steak and lobster.

Flaherty's Oyster Bar and Seafood Grill, 6th (San Carlos/Dolores); 624-0311, 625-1500. Seafood. $:budget-expensive. MC,

VI at Grill. Connected to Flaherty's Fish Market, the blue-and-white-tiled Oyster Bar really has a marble counter and a brass rail; you sit at the stools to eat the seafood cocktails, mussels, oysters on the half shell, crab, and other fresh local and flown-in eastern fish. Next door dinners are served at regular tables and include lobster, abalone, petrale, cioppino, linguini, steak pescatori (smothered in shrimp, scallops, clams, mussels).

French Poodle, Junipero & 5th; 624-8643. French. $:intermediate-expensive. AE, DC. Wine. Cl. Sun., also Feb. or Mar. An intimate, jacket-and-tie restaurant popular with Peninsula residents. Specialties include tournedos Rossini, sautéed veal and mushroom in cream sauce, filet of sole Vedrinette, California lamb with potatoes, giant prawns sautéed with shallots and tomatoes, and veal piccata. Ranks 4 stars in the Mobil guide.

General Store, 5th & Junipero; 624-2233. California Continental. $:intermediate. AE, DC, MC, VI. Full bar. Like the Hog's Breath Inn with its popular bar, the General Store has the Forge-in-the-Forest and its western theme and outdoor patio with sunshine for lunch and a fireplace for dinner and drinks. Dinners include steamed mussels in white wine and tomato sauce, roast duckling with garlic sauce, salmon in red wine and butter sauce, New York steak, double pork chops.

Hog's Breath Inn, San Carlos (5th/6th); 625-1044. American. $:intermediate. MC, VI. Full bar. No res. Other than its name, the Hog's Breath is well known locally because of its co-owner, actor Clint Eastwood. Forewarned, you should not be surprised to find Dirty Harry's Burger, the Eiger Sandwich, or Coogan's Bluff on the menu, joined by the more prosaic rack of lamb, prime rib, Garrapata Creek trout, barbecued spareribs, roast wild pig, and chicken 'n whiskey, which is chicken sautéed in Scotch with a light wine cream sauce. A onetime stable, then an antique shop, the Hog's Breath is dark, woody, intimate but okay for families. Nice on coolish days is the outdoor patio with overhead heaters.

La Bohème, Dolores (Ocean/7th); 624-7500. French. $:intermediate. MC, VI. Wine, beer. A casual, petite French cafe à la Mimi, La Bohème serves one meal nightly. That may be veal piccata, lamb with capers and cream sauce, roast duckling in fresh raspberry and strawberry sauce.

La Playa Hotel, 8th & Camino Real; 624-6476. American.

$:intermediate. AE, MC, VI. Full bar. Old-line Carmel hotel with an ocean view (the sea is 2 blocks away) has some 1907 grace and Spanish California decor left. There's breakfast and lunch, while the dinner menu features prime rib, Monterey Bay salmon, steaks, chicken, and a daily special, such as duckling. A cocktail supper is served 5-10 in La Taberna.

Le Coq d'Or, Mission (4th/5th); 624-4613. French. $:intermediate. No cards. Wine, beer. Cl. Sun., also most Dec. A family-run French restaurant that locals like for its good value. The one small dining room has a mural, flowers on the tables. Chicken—no surprise—is the specialty of the house, and it comes in various ways: flambéed with diced ham and fresh mushrooms, in wine sauce, or in a madeira and cream sauce with mushrooms; you can also get chicken livers with mushrooms and sherry. Steak in sherry sauce, pork chops, and salmon are also available. The desserts come fresh from the Patisserie Boissière (see below).

L'Escargot, Mission near 4th; 624-4914. French: $:expensive. AE, DC, MC, VI. Wine, beer. Cl. Sun., also Dec. One of Carmel's more expensive French establishments, L'Escargot gets good reviews from many diners. The à la carte menu features salmon cured and smoked by "André", Belons oysters when available, chicken with foie gras and truffles in cream, sweetbreads with cream Madeira and mushrooms, and homemade raspberry or strawberry tarts. The decor is dressy French provincial with white tablecloths, beamed ceiling, pewter, copper, porcelain, and prints.

Moulin de Carmel, 7th & Dolores; 625-0951. French. $:intermediate. MC, VI. Cl. Tues. Wine, beer. Moulin de Carmel, owned by the Grafts, has son Charles as chef, after his apprenticeship at French restaurants in Napa and Mill Valley, and graduation from the Culinary Institute in Hyde Park, New York. A dressy French provincial atmosphere is created with cane furniture, attractive wallpaper, white tablecloths. Entrées include stuffed salmon poached in wine with Béarnaise sauce, rack of lamb and mint, milk-fed veal with mushrooms and sauce champagne, trout and almond sauce, tenderloin of beef in sauce Merchand de vin, plus tempting fresh pastries.

Paolina Pasta, in Doud Craft Studios, San Carlos (Ocean/7th); 624-5599. Italian. $:budget-intermediate. MC, VI. A high-tech, casual Italian restaurant, with pasta made before your very eyes while you sit on high stools at a counter or at tables, Paolina Pasta can roll out pasta primavera with Alfredo sauce, fettucine Alfredo, quattro formaggi (white linguini with spinach and 4 cheeses), as well as seafood fra Diavlo—shellfish sautéed in white wine, red pepper, with marinara sauce and linguini.

Patisserie Boissière, Mission (Ocean/7th); 624-5008. French. $:budget or better. No cards. Wine, beer. No res. Cl. Wed. This elegant little place, whose French provincial decor (low beamed ceiling, white plaster walls) has Louis XIV touches, is the French version of the Tuck Box a block away. There are eat-here or take-out nibblies—if we may call them that—such as quiche Lorraine or pork and veal in pastry rolls, and there are more substantial dishes: poulet Provençale (chicken breast in white wine sauce with tomatoes and olives, served with rice in butter), curried shrimp and mushrooms, sweetbreads and mushrooms with cream sauce in a pastry shell, coquilles St. Jacques, and roulade de céleri (heart of celery wrapped with ham, with cream sauce and Swiss cheese). The specialties are the Parisian patisseries—lemon cheese cake, chocolate eclairs, chocolate butter creams with meringue, babas au rhum, and other sweet things. Nice that it's okay to stop in for Camembert on French bread and a glass of (California) wine.

Pine Inn, Ocean (Monte Verde/Lincoln); 624-3851. American. $:intermediate-expensive. AE, MC, VI. Full bar. One of the best hotels in Carmel also offers one of the most stylish meals around, either in the Crystal Room (large globe chandeliers, stained glass, crisp white tablecloths) or the Gazebo (quasi-outdoors courtyard with a skylight that opens if it is mild outside). This being the inn's dining room, there's breakfast and lunch (Sunday brunch) and on Friday there's a special seafood buffet. The regular dinner menu features hefty plates like beef Wellington and leg of lamb or merely tasty ones like veal Oskar (sautéed in butter, topped with crabmeat, served with asparagus and Béarnaise sauce), scampi Pine Inn (sautéed in butter with shallots, spices, and wine), or sand dabs almondine. Drinks are in the Red Parlor.

Raffaello Carmel Restaurant, Mission & Ocean; 624-1541. Italian. $:expensive. VI. Wine, beer. Cl. Tues., also Dec. Elegant, expensive, Raffaello's is not your corner Italian restaurant but it is as popular—and we suggest you call for a reservation ahead. Featuring mainly northern Italian cuisine, Raffaello's offers veal as the house specialty—with tomato sauce, or lemon sauce, or fontina cheese and truffles. Other dishes include duck with brandied orange sauce, chicken Jerusalem (with cream sauce and artichoke bottom), filet of sole poached in champagne with shrimp, and homemade pasta, of which the fettuccine alla Romana (in cream with grated cheese) is well known. Jacket and tie are required in this formal dining room, which has chandeliers, a fireplace, paintings, and fresh flowers and candles on the dozen tables.

Saint Tropez, Junipero (5th/6th); 624-9018. French. $:intermediate. No cards. Wine, beer. Cl. Tues. A French provincial feeling is created within the small spaces with copper utensils on the wall, fresh flowers on the a-little-too-cozy tables, and attentive service from Simone, whose husband is the chef. Specialties are chicken à l'orange, chicken St. Tropez (with squash, eggplant, bell pepper, and tomatoes), fresh vegetable plate, and pastries by Chef Christian.

Scandia, Ocean (Lincoln/Monte Verde); 624-5659. Scandinavian, American. $:budget-intermediate. AE, MC, VI. Wine, beer. Cl. late Dec. Quiet but busy, plain but attractive, the Scandia is a fresh breeze if you've had too much of the "turf and surf" type of restaurant. While the Scandia does have prime rib, that does not typify a menu on which poached salmon with pickled cucumbers, or weiner schnitzel, or frikadeller (Danish meatballs with pickled red cabbage and lingonberries) are more likely to get your attention. There's also roast leg of lamb, veal, shish kebab, stuffed Cornish hens, kalvefilet Oscar, and some concessions to non-Scandinavian tastes served in moderate portions on blue Scandinavian china. Friendly, relaxed, the Scandia is one of our favorites in Carmel. They do their own baking here.

Shabu-Shabu Japanese Country Restaurant, Mission (Ocean/7th); 625-2828. Japanese. $:intermediate. AE, MC, VI. Wine, beer. The Shabu-Shabu has gained a loyal following from among those who couldn't abide the touristy Ginza at Monterey's Fisherman's Wharf. Things are simpler and country-elegant here, with redwood walls and Japanese kites, stoneware and hemp-rope curtains. You have a choice of sitting in rattan chairs at high Western tables or on cushions at low Japanese tables. There's candlelight and Japanese classical music no matter how you sit. The big attraction on the short (11 entrées) menu is the authentic Japanese bouillabaisse called shabu-shabu ("swish-swish"). Cooked in a ceramic pot over an electric grill at your table are fresh clams, scallops, shrimps, chunks of lobster, rock cod, spinach, Chinese cabbage, mushrooms, and other ingredients. When cooked, a selection of these is served to you for dipping in various sauces—and the cooking broth becomes seafood soup. For dessert: bananas deep-fried in tempura batter, served with green-tea ice cream. Definitely a meal out of the ordinary.

Simpson's, San Carlos & 5th; 624-1238. Steak, seafood. $:expensive. MC, VI. Full bar. An old-line restaurant with a loyal set of customers for the specialties (prime rib, fresh salmon, cheese soufflé, and jumbo shrimps stuffed with crab and tiny shrimps, fried and served in spiced butter sauce), daily specials (poached filets of sole Marguery, chicken Burgundy, or deviled crab au gratin), standard items (pot roast, abalone steak), and homemade desserts (southern pecan pie, lemon chiffon, coconut cream, and chocolate fudge cake). Hard not to be satisfied here.

Sticky Wicket, Ocean & Lincoln; 625-4908. English. $:budget. MC, VI. In case you didn't have your fill at the Tuck Box or you couldn't get in their door, you can have tea here—homemade scones with strawberries topped with Devon cream, English sausage in pastry, daily specials such as Cornish pasties. Then run down to the beach and back to work up an appetite for dinner.

Studio Theater Restaurant, Dolores (Ocean/7th); 624-8688. American. $:intermediate including show. No cards. No bar (BYO from next door). Cl. Mon., Tues., and Wed. Scarcely a gourmet restaurant, the Studio offers a choice at dinner of roast beef or roast turkey with salad, vegetable, and baked potato—and a play at 8:30 Fri. and Sat., 7:30 on Sun. all year plus Thurs. during the summer. Lunch is simple, too—sandwiches, spaghetti and meatballs, pot roast, chicken with wine sauce, beef stew—but plainness in a town of rich food is an attraction.

Swedish Restaurant, Dolores (Ocean/7th); 624-3723. Swedish. $:budget. No cards. Wine, beer. For breakfast have Swedish pancakes, then come back for Swedish meatballs and lingonberries, poached salmon, and other hearty dishes for lunch or dinner. A cheerful homelike atmosphere, and Scandinavian imports are for sale in the shop next door.

Swiss Tavern, Lincoln (5th/6th); 624-5994. Swiss. $:budget-intermediate. MC, VI. Wine, beer. Cl. Mon. Skiers who yearn for the slopes and après-ski fondue can find some happiness here. Fondues include beef Bourguignon for two, cheese, and chocolate, plus other Swiss and American entrées—veal cordon bleu, filet of beef, seafood.

Toots Lagoon, Dolores (Ocean/7th); 625-1915. Creole. $:intermediate. AE, DC, MC, VI. Full bar. Toots Lagoon is the only Creole restaurant in this neck of the woods, and has ceiling fans and other New Orleans touches. A special 7-course Creole dinner is prepared nightly. Other dinner entrées include redfish court bouillon with saffron, fresh gulf prawns royale, chicken Rochambeau over Holland rusk and with Béarnaise sauce, and New York steak served en flambé with green peppercorn sauce. Also breakfast, lunch, oyster bar.

Tuck Box, Dolores (Ocean/7th); 624-6365. English, varied. $:budget. No cards. No res. No bar. Open til 4 P.M. Cl. Mon., Tues. Housed in one of Carmel's 20 fairy-tale houses, with wavy tile roof, stucco and beamed exterior, flowers, fireplace, and all that, the Tuck Box is, not surprisingly, an English tearoom. People line up all the time for breakfast, morning snacks, lunch, or afternoon tea—or whenever they want black English tea with scones and homemade preserves or strawberry pastries or apple walnut cake. The lunch menu has 3 entrées—for example, shepherd's pie, beef and Yorkshire pudding, chicken pie, curried shrimp, cheese soufflé, meat loaf. The Tuck Box isn't to everyone's taste, but it is entirely at home in Carmel-by-the-Sea.

Bakeries: You can buy your breakfast, lunch, tea, or dessert at **Hector DeSmet Bakery,** Ocean near Lincoln, 624-6265, American yummies; **Patisserie Boissière,** Mission (Ocean/7th), 624-5008, French delectables and irresistibles. Also **Wishart's Bakery,** Ocean (Mission/San Carlos), 624-6250; and **Cookie Place,** Ocean (Mission/San Carlos), 625-3853.

Delicatessens, gourmet markets: Pack your picnic lunch and head for the beach or Big Sur with the help of the **Mediterranean Market,** Ocean & Mission, 624-2022, and Del Monte Center in Monterey; **Nielsen Bros. Market,** Dolores & 7th, 624-6441; and **Peter's Gourmet Foods,** 5th next to the post office, 625-2688.

Carmel Highlands and Highway

If you choose to stay in Carmel Highlands or other accommodations just off Highway 1, you will need a car to get around to other places for variety in restaurants. This area of the Monterey Peninsula features a large hillside resort, a convention hotel, motels, cottages, and rental condominiums. Dining is at the Highlands Inn dining room or elsewhere.

For further help, see Monterey Peninsula, Carmel, Carmel Valley, Monterey, Pacific Grove, and Pebble Beach.

Area code: 408. Zip code: 93921.

WHERE TO STAY

Carmel River Inn, 26600 Oliver Rd., Carmel; 624-1575. On 10 acres near Hwy. 1 at Carmel River. $:budget (motel), $:intermediate (cottages). AE, MC, VI. Motel building has 19 rooms with decks, while 22 cottages under the trees range from queen double to cottage with 2 bedrooms, living room, kitchen; 12 tiny or full kitchens; 6 have fireplaces. Free coffee. Heated pool.

Highlands Inn, Highland Dr., Carmel Highlands (Box 1700, Carmel); 624-3801. 4 miles south of Carmel on Hwy. 1. $:expensive-luxury; rates include 2 meals. AE, CB, DC, MC, VI. Located on 13 acres looking over the whitecaps and rocky coast, the Highlands Inn may be unique in California because it has a wedding chapel—scene of more than a thousand weddings per year—and the resulting activity has given the inn an air of the Poconos. But it's also a popular weekend resort. It was originally built in 1916–17 by Carmel's founders, was later expanded and given its Scottish motif. The cottages (fireplaces in all, honeymooners in many) are here and there on the well-landscaped grounds, the newer lanai rooms in a long building; some cottages and all the lanai rooms have ocean views over or between the trees. Dining room, bar, pool; snacking on the Yankee Point Terrace. Early December through New Year's is Scottish Merry Month, with bagpipes, Scottish country dancing, laying the yule log, and so forth. The Highlands Inn is, we would say, somewhere between swinging and staid, and maybe a bit old-fashioned, but it has terrific views.

Holiday Inn–Carmel, Hwy. 1 & Rio Road (Box 5048), Carmel; 624-1841, or any Holiday Inn for reservations. $:expensive.

AE, DC, MC, VI. No surprises here. (Note: There's a Holiday Inn–Monterey, too, but they planted it smack dab on the Monterey Bay beach, which we find so offensive that we're not recommending it.)

Tickle Pink Motor Inn, 155 Highlands Dr., Carmel Highlands (Box 3276, Carmel); 624-1244. $:expensive. MC, VI. No children under 12. An atypical motor lodge with truly spectacular views from each of the 29 rooms, which are arranged in a 3-faced, 3-story block above the trees on the Carmel Highlands hillside. What's more, the degree of quality in decor and the comfort are high in this modern, cheerful, very quiet rural motel. Suites have living room, larger balcony, fireplace. Continental breakfast comes with a morning newspaper. By the way, the name is honestly derived from a couple of the original landholders and operators of the Highlands Inn (next door), State Sen. and Mrs. Edward H. Tickle. The present lodge is on the site of their stone cottage. Red and pink predominate in the decor, but not excessively so. Exceptional accommodations for adults seeking quiet and views.

Condominiums: **Riverwood,** 4000 Rio Rd., Carmel (reservations to Sullivan Properties, 26555 Carmel Rancho Blvd., Carmel 93923; 624-9099), is a town-house development in the mouth of the Carmel Valley, half a mile off Hwy. 1. Rates range from $180 for a 1-bedroom condo for 3 nights to $1,050 for a 3-bedroom unit for a month. Heated pool, tennis courts available.

Carmel Valley

Carmel Valley is long, linear, dry after the Carmel Valley Golf and Country Club, and for travelers with cars who want to stay at a resort or motel and cottages. Dining is sparsely located, although things are picking up at the west end where the Barnyard and Crossroads are developing.

For more information, see also Monterey Peninsula, Carmel, Carmel Highlands and Highway, Monterey, Pacific Grove, and Pebble Beach.

Area code: 408. Zip codes: 93923, 93924.

WHERE TO STAY

Canary Cottages Resort Motel, Via Contenta, Carmel Valley Village (Box 87, Carmel Valley 93924); 659-2297. Located just off

Carmel Valley Rd., 13 miles E of Carmel. $:intermediate. MC, VI. No children under 16. We've included this resort motel because it's very quiet. The 17 rooms all face the heated pool, have private patios. Complimentary coffee, also morning newspaper. No meals here but Carmel Valley Village has several restaurants.

Quail Lodge, 8205 Valley Greens Dr., Carmel 93923; 624-1581. At the Carmel Valley Golf and Country Club, 3 mi. along Carmel Valley Rd. from Hwy. 1. $:luxury. AE, CB, DC, MC, VI. Quail Lodge is justifiably proud of the many stars bestowed on it: AAA's 5 stars (the lodge is one of 3 resorts in California thus honored) and Mobil's 5 stars (one of 5 hotels in the state, the only resort). Without overdoing anything, Quail Lodge manages to be beautifully situated, well designed, modern, comfortable, and deluxe—and they don't even seem snooty about their achievement. Only the design of their standard brochure and tariff sheet seem mundane, though the rates are admirable. The 96 rooms are either facing the pool or have balconies with valley views, or are in 4-bedroom-and-sitting-room cottages on the little lake, which is crossed by a charming arched bridge. Guests have golf and tennis privileges. Covey restaurants (see "Where to Eat"). Free continental breakfast. The only thing Quail Lodge doesn't have that the Lodge at Pebble Beach does is the patina of age and the seaside location. Avid golfers may want to take two vacations—one at each place.

Valley Lodge, Carmel Valley Rd. at Ford Rd. (Box 93), Carmel Valley 93924; 659-2261. Quite near Carmel Valley Village. $:intermediate-expensive. AE, MC, VI. The 19 units (12 with kitchens) are either garden-patio rooms or 1- or 2-bedroom cottages with fireplace. 3 acres of garden, pool, sauna. Quality of interior decor isn't high, but this is a quiet, reasonably priced resort.

WHERE TO EAT

André's, Hwy. 1 and Rio Rd., in the Barnyard; 625-0447. California Continental. $:intermediate-expensive. AE, DC, MC, VI. Cl. Tues. Andrés in the Barnyard has different rooms that create different moods—Crystal Room, whose booths come each with its own crystal chandelier, Garden Room filled with plants, and more. Lunch, Sun. brunch, and dinners are served. Dinners feature sole

Marguéry, duck à l'Orange, seafood Provençale, scampi André, prawns Camarguaise (in garlic, herbs, white wine, tomatoes), tournedos Henri IV, and specials nightly.

The Covey, Quail Lodge, Carmel Valley; 624-1581. 3.5 miles up Carmel Valley Rd. Continental. $:expensive-luxury. AE, CB, DC, MC, VI. Full bar. Like Club XIX at the Lodge at Pebble Beach, The Covey is for luxury dinners in a dressy, country-club atmosphere. The dining room is exquisitely decorated in brown, beige, black, and barnwood, with Belgian linen, pewter, and fresh flowers on each table. The dining room overlooks Quail Lodge's man-made lake and arched footbridge. Menu items: poulet à l'orange; fresh trout amandine; steak au poivre flambé; abalone steak sautéed in light egg batter; sautéed veal medallions in a light cream sauce with mushrooms; and crêpes filled with crab, mushrooms, and cheese in a wine sauce.

Thunderbird Bookshop, The Barnyard, Hwy. 1 and Rio Rd., Carmel; 624-1803. Near Holiday Inn; enter from Carmel Rancho Blvd. Varied menu. $:budget. MC, VI. Wine, beer. Cl. dinner Sun., Mon. We've had restaurants in cellars, gardens, Queen Anne mansions, country clubs, fish markets, adobe houses, old sardine factory canteens, and a theater—and now we have a bookshop in a restaurant. The Thunderbird must be unique, if only for the owners' courage in letting people eat things with gravy while perusing art books. The old California barn is filled with 50,000 (new) books; the decor is natural wood, of course, with stone fireplaces, antiques, ferns, paintings for sale. Classical music fills up the rest of the space. Outside is a patio with Cinzano umbrellas and a view of the Carmel Valley. For lunch there's mostly sandwiches, a soup, salad; for dinner the buffet inclines to American country dishes— roast prime rib au jus, beef stroganoff, barbecued beef ribs, breast of chicken and mushrooms in a patty shell, and so forth, plus desserts like chocolate mousse, cheesecake, and Apfelstrudel. Early-bird special. Don't spend too much on books!

Bakeries: **Sylvia's Danish Pastry Shop,** 3650 The Barnyard, 624-1198.

Delicatessens: **Joseph's Oak Deli & Bakery,** Oak Bldg., Carmel Valley Village, 659-3416. **Yavor's Deli & Wines,** Mid Valley Shopping Center, 625-2260.

Hearst Castle/San Simeon

The accommodations around San Simeon are generally modern motels, plus cabins and campsites, in clusters about 3 and 6 miles S of the town. Reservations should be made well ahead of time.

Area code: 804. Zip codes: Cambria 93428, San Simeon 93452.

WHERE TO STAY

Representative modern motels near San Simeon: **Best Western Cavalier Inn,** Box 18-X, 927-4688. $:intermediate. AE, CB, DC, MC, VI. Located near ocean. 66 rooms with balconies, some with fireplaces, also heated pool, coffee shop, bar. **Castle Inn,** Box 95, 927-4850. $:intermediate. MC, VI. 30 rooms with ocean views. Heated pool. **San Simeon Pines Resort Motel,** Box 115, 927-4648. AE, MC, VI. $:intermediate. Nicely landscaped, across from Moonstone Cove beach, with golf course, heated pool. Rooms not extraordinary, but in general a good deal.

Cottages among the pines: **Cambria Pines Lodge,** 2905 Burton Dr., 927-4200. $:intermediate. MC, VI. A long-time establishment with 50 cottages and 9 lodge rooms, pools for swimming, wading, whirling, plus sauna, picnic tables, dining room.

Camping: **San Simeon State Beach,** very popular, is 5 miles S of Hearst Castle, has 134 sites, also toilets; reserve through Ticketron. There are more campgrounds S, near Morro Bay.

WHERE TO EAT

The restaurants here, like the accommodations, are far more standardized, but the choice of the choosy must be the **Brambles Dinner House,** Burton Dr., Cambria, (805) 927-4716. Steak, seafood. $:intermediate. AE, VI. Wine, beer. The inside of this English cottage complex is Victorian, with the owner's antiques here and there. The food, primarily rib-eye steak, prime rib, whatever fish is in season, and lobster, is served with attractive, home-baked bread and dessert, and with friendly, efficient service.

Alternatives: **Grey Fox Inn,** 4095 Burton Dr. & Center, Cambria, 927-3305. American. $:intermediate. MC, VI. Wine, beer. Open for Sun. brunch and dinner, the Grey Fox offers fresh seafood, steak, its own baking, with some outdoor tables. **San Simeon Restaurant,** Hwy. 1, San Simeon, 927-4604. Italian. $:intermediate. Full bar. Serving breakfast, lunch, and dinner, the San Simeon features Italian pastas, Wisconsin milk-fed veal, fresh seafood. . . . At the Hearst Castle entrance gate is a snack bar and picnic area; if you're coming from the N, you may want to get some gourmet deli items and eat richly not far from this American palace, since it is likely you won't be invited to dinner in the castle's Refectory.

Monterey

Motels are the primary accommodation in Monterey, although there are also a resort, hotel, and inn. Motel row is along Munras. Developing downtown around the Monterey Conference Center are more facilities that tie into the Fisherman's Wharf and Cannery Row action. A splendid inn (a former mayor's house) is in a lovely residential area. Up on the hill is a Hyatt resort. Here is our classification of Monterey hostelries:

> Inn: Merritt House (also motel), Old Monterey Inn
> Hotel: Doubletree Inn
> Motels: Casa Munras Garden Hotel, Cypress Gardens
>   Motel, Hilton Inn Resort, Ireland's Park Crest
>   Motel, Merritt House (also an inn), Motel 6,
>   Monterey Motor Lodge, Reef Motel, West Wind
>   Lodge
> Resort: Hyatt Del Monte Hotel
> Camping: Veterans Memorial Park campground

Monterey's restaurants are clustered in Fisherman's Wharf, Cannery Row, and downtown, and include:

> American: Alvarado Café
> California Continental: Cellar, Clock Garden
> French: Fresh Cream
> Italian: Salvatore's
> Mexican: Casa Maria
> Seafood: Abalonetti, Neil de Vaughn's, Outrigger,
>   Rappa's, Rogue, Whaling Station Inn,
>   Windjammer; also most of the other restaurants
>   serve seafood dishes
> Steak and seafood: Neil de Vaughn's, Rogue

For more information, see the listings under Monterey Peninsula, Carmel Highlands and Highway, Carmel Valley, Pacific Grove, and Pebble Beach.

Area code: 408. Zip code: 93940.

WHERE TO STAY

Casa Munras Garden Hotel, 700 Munras at Fremont (Box 1351); 375-2411. $:expensive. AE, CB, DC, MC, VI. One of the nicer full-service commercial motels—130 rooms, meeting rooms, big coffee shop, dining room with dancing and entertainment, heated pool and nice grounds. The rooms are in 2-story, balconied Monterey Colonial-style buildings—indeed, the lobby in some way incorporates the old Casa Munras (1824). The standard rooms have typical motel decor; the suites are better. Good location for those planning to look at Monterey's adobes.

Cypress Gardens Motel, 1150 Munras; 373-2761. On Carmel Hill, 1.5 mi. from downtown. $:intermediate. AE, MC, VI. Extremely bland motel rooms have Jacuzzi baths, private balconies, free continental breakfast and free coffee. Heated pool but no other facilities.

Doubletree Inn, 2 Portola Plaza (Box 3260); 649-4511. In the Monterey Convention Center complex near Custom House Plaza and Fisherman's Wharf. $:expensive. AE, CB, DC, MC, VI. New in 1978, this is the big (375 rooms), modern, multilevel convention hotel in the city's Custom House Plaza redevelopment area. The rooms are standard in design and decor. 2-story greenhouse lobby with shopping arcade—Doubletree Lane—plus 2 restaurants, 2 bars, tennis courts, health spa, pool. But vacationers (as opposed to convention-goers) would be better off at a less urban location, we think.

Hilton Inn Resort, 100 Aguajito Rd.; 373-6141, or Hilton Reservation Service. Off Hwy. 1 at Fremont Blvd. $:expensive. AE, CB, DC, MC, VI. Formerly the Royal Inn, now misnamed "resort"—it's really a pretty average, overpriced, 200-room, commercial motor lodge on the highway. The rooms have twin queen-size beds, at the least, also private balconies; suites are, of course, larger, more comfortable. Harvest Grille, Lobby Bar, heated pool, putting green.

Hyatt Del Monte Hotel, 1 Old Golf Course Rd.; 372-7171 or (800) 228-9000 for reservations. Off Mark Thomas Dr. not far from Hwys. 1 and 68. $:expensive. AE, CB, DC, MC, VI. Well-forged link in the Hyatt chain, and located on the links—that is, the Old Del Monte Golf Course (the old hotel is across Hwy. 1 and belongs to the navy). 420 rooms in rambling complex on land-scaped acreage. Rooms larger than normal, best ones facing the golf course. Full facilities, including shops, services, meeting rooms, tennis courts, putting green, 2 pools, bar, restaurant (Pirate's Cove), coffee shop. If you can afford it, the President's House is a small mansion with 4 bedrooms, 5 baths, living room, den, kitchen, pool, patios.

Ireland's Park Crest Motel, 1100 Munras; 372-4576, or (800) 528-1234 for reservations. $:budget-intermediate. AE, CB, DC, MC, VI. A Best Western motel, extremely typical of its class: modern, clean, respectable, and utterly boring. Pool.

Merritt House, 386 Pacific St. at Del Monte Ave.; 646-9686. Downtown, across the street from Monterey Conference Center. $:expensive. Merritt House, one of Monterey's Path of History buildings, was built in 1830 as a 2-story adobe house for Josiah Merritt, a former county judge who helped organize Monterey County. This structure is incorporated as a section of the 25 rooms that compose this inn (old) and motel (new), with fireplaces, antique touches, and fresh coffee included.

Monterey Motor Lodge, 55 Camino Aguajito; 372-8057. Faces El Estero a block off Del Monte Blvd., near Monterey State Beach. $:intermediate. AE, CB, DC, MC, VI. 37 rooms in 2-story buildings oriented around the heated pool. Elegant Rooster restaurant, bar. Unexceptional but well located.

Motel 6, 2124 Fremont; 373-3500. 2.5 miles from downtown. $:budget. No cards. The bare accommodations, at a bare price. Heated pool.

Old Monterey Inn, 500 Martin St. at Fountain; 375-8284. In a residential area, about a mile from downtown. $:expensive. Truly elegant, the Old Monterey Inn was built in 1929 for Carmel Martin, Monterey's mayor for whom this street was named. Currently owned by the Swetts, who raised their family here and 3 years ago moved into the rooms above the garage, the spacious, gracious house and 1.5-acre gardens were turned into an inn. The 8 bed-rooms and cottage include the Library, Creekside, and Windsong, some of which share baths. Stroll through the rose garden, swing in the twin hammocks (but don't fall in the creek!), sip your wine, enjoy your continental breakfast. But leave home your kids, pets, cigars.

Reef Motel, 1300 Munras; 373-3203. Near Hwy. 1. $:interme-diate. MC, VI. A Best Western motel with 32 rooms in 2-story block, but somewhat more distinctive than others of the type, with an attractive South Seas decor, rattan and basket furniture, etc. Pool.

West Wind Lodge, 1046 Munras; 373-1337. $:intermediate. AE, CB, DC, MC, VI. Some of the rooms are Gaudy Motel Mod-ern but there's an attractively designed indoor pool (heated) to counterbalance the ordinariness. 52 units, 10 with kitchens.

WHERE TO EAT

Abalonetti, 53 Fisherman's Wharf; 375-5941. Seafood. $:inter-mediate. No cards. Wine, beer. No res. Cl. Tues. Abalonetti has a claim to the attention of anyone who fancies squid. Those who were frightened to death by the squid in *20,000 Leagues Under the Sea* may wish to think remotely of calamari, which is what squid is called on most menus. The squid at Abalonetti, an unpretentious 9-table harborview restaurant located in the Liberty Fish Market, comes not naked to the table but dressed in a variety of more appe-tizing ways. The Sicilian-style squid cutlet comes fried with garlic and parsley. The Neapolitan style is to simmer it in tomato sauce and serve it over spaghetti. The house fashion (Marty's Special) is to serve it with eggplant, tomato sauce, and Parmesan cheese. The style that gives the Abalonetti its name, however, is to pound and flatten the squid, bread the resulting tender fillet (abalonetti), then sauté it in butter. The menu features other seafood—shellfish is well done here—and some standard Italian dishes. Very popular: you'll have to stand in line in order to sample some of the 20 tons of squid Abalonetti prepares each year.

Alvarado Café, Alvarado/Bonifacio Plaza; 375-4533. Ameri-can. $:budget-intermediate. MC, VI. Wine, beer. The Alvarado Café is open for breakfast, lunch, and dinner to serve all-American food like ranch eggs, waffles, artichoke heart salad, barbecued beef ribs, fried chicken, New York steak, and a Monterey variety steak 'n squid. Kids menu. They close early, at 8 P.M.

Casa Maria, 600 Cannery Row/Hoffman; 373-0611. Mexican. $:budget-intermediate. AE, MC, VI. Full bar. Set in the middle of Cannery Row with a view of Monterey Bay, Casa Maria is open for lunch, brunch, and dinner, with entertainment Wednesday-Sunday. Traditional Mexican decor and menu.

The Cellar Restaurant, 150 W. Franklin; 375-4477. Italian, California Continental. $:intermediate. AE, CB, DC, MC, VI. Wine, beer. Cl. Sun. Stepping down into this long-established Monterey restaurant, you find a Victorian elegance, with mahogany and etched glass, but there's a menuful of home-cooked Italian specialties: veal scallopini, linguini with mussels and clams in garlic butter, cannelloni, calamari, and scampi. Also noteworthy are chicken breast casserole, tournedos of beef with sauce Béarnaise, teriyaki steak, lamb chops Bombay, and Garrapata trout.

Clock Garden, 565 Abrego (Pearl/Webster); 375-6100. California Continental. $:intermediate. AE, MC, VI. Full Bar. Res. dinner only. Another of our favorites—and it would be a favorite even if it were in a big city. The Clock Garden (the clock is a blue jeweler's clock at the gate, the garden is a brick patio with lots of flowers around) is very popular, especially on nice days, and reservations are a must. Inside the decor is very personal, or maybe weird and funky, with more clocks, partitions made of empty wine bottles, paper collages, etc. And the food is very good, starting with the Greek lemon soup and the Salinas Valley salad (chilled wedge of iceberg lettuce with green goddess dressing or the half-chilled Castroville artichoke), through the few entrées (for example, broiled filet teriyaki, veal Vallarta, shrimp crepes, pork tenderloin en brochette) to the desserts (pecan pie, cheesecake, minted sherbet Cointreau). Lunch and Sunday brunch have some of the same selections plus crepes Carlotta—of spinach, turkey, and cheese—cold poached salmon, and other things. Hard to miss a good time here.

Consuelo's, 361 Lighthouse near Dickman; 372-8111. Mexican. $:budget-intermediate. AE, MC, VI. Wine, beer. Criticized by some for being too showy, Consuelo's is at least unusual in that it *does* have some style: for one thing, it's located in an 1880 Victorian, with the Indian pine by the patio being credited to Luther Burbank (1885). The quesadilla with hot cheese is complimentary while you scan the unsurprising Mexican menu.

Domenico's, 50 Fisherman's Wharf; 372-3655. Seafood. $:intermediate-expensive. AE, DC, MC, VI. Full bar. Open for lunch and dinner with excellent views of Monterey's wharf, Domenico's features an oyster bar, mesquite barbecued fresh fish and steaks, homemade pastas, and homemade ice cream. Crisp blues and white tablecloths go with the bay and boats outside.

Fresh Cream, 807 Cannery Row; 375-9798. French. $:intermediate-expensive. MC, VI. Wine. Cl. Tues. Fresh Cream is located upstairs in the Trading Co. Building, and was started by owner-chef Robert Kincaid, after he worked around the world in high-quality restaurants and hotels in Portland, Seattle, Tokyo, Munich, and San Francisco. The menu uses fresh ingredients and changes nightly, and may feature quenelle de poisson beurre rouge (very fine chicken dumplings with shellfish coral butter), roast rack of lamb Dijon, or sliced sirloin with Madeira and Béarnaise sauces, plus soufflé grand Marnier, and steamed chocolate cake sauce Anglaise.

Neil de Vaughn's, 654 Cannery Row; 372-2141. Steak, seafood. $:intermediate-expensive. MC, VI. Wine, beer. Neil de Vaughn's, one of the original restaurants (1953) on Cannery Row, is popular with tourists, less so with food critics. What it offers is a lot of San Francisco–style Victorian decor, heavy on the red, and a lot of red meat and fresh fish. The specialties are shad roe, beef brochette, beef Stroganoff, and sole Felipe; also on the menu are jumbo prawns, crab Sargon, lobster thermidor, sand dabs, red snapper, filet of rock bass, poached salmon, prime rib, and charcoal-broiled steaks.

The Outrigger, 700 Cannery Row; 372-8543. Polynesian; steak, seafood. $:intermediate. AE, CB, DC, MC, VI. Yes, one more overdecorated imitation Trader Vic's. There are no fewer than 141 of those exotic and expensive South Seas alcoholic concoctions plus blazing tiki torches and peacock chairs, and cuisine to match. A complete dinner: puu puus (appetizers like egg rolls and fried shrimp), Hawaiian honey pork, Islander soup, Polynesian steak Kew, prawns Cantonese, chicken Hawaiian, and fried rice. Reserve in plenty of time for the window tables on Monterey Bay. Entertainment (comedy and song or cabaret guitar) 6 nights. Weekday buffet lunch.

Rappa's, far end of Old Fisherman's Wharf #1; 372-7562. Seafood. $:intermediate. MC, VI. Full bar. Situated since 1953 on the far bay end of Fisherman's Wharf with a view on 3 sides, Rappa's serves seafood and Italian dishes on red-checkered tablecloths without many frills. Specialties include calamari cioppino, combination bouillabaisse, fresh baked red snapper, spaghetti with baby shrimp, linguini with combination fish and shellfish, steaks. Earlybird dinner specials.

Rogue, Monterey Marina Wharf #2; 372-4586. Steaks, seafood. $:intermediate-expensive. AE, CB, DC, MC, VI. Full bar. Located in a large free-standing building between the 2 long wharves, the Rogue is upstairs with a view of the bay and boats. Complete dinner entrées include choices like halibut stuffed with crab meat and tomatoes, salmon Wellington, lobster Nantua, sole hollandaise, cioppino, scampi, steaks, chicken.

Salvatore's, 710 Cannery Row; 373-4492. Italian. $:intermediate. MC, VI. Full bar. The Rappas expanded from Fisherman's Wharf seafood to Cannery Row provincial, family-style Italian, complete with hanging grapes. Entrées may include cioppino Siciliano, pasta di casa (with garlic, mushrooms, parsley, egg and Parmesan cheese), oven-baked lasagna, veal piccata, chicken cacciatore, and cannelloni.

Sardine Factory, 701 Wave at Prescott; 373-3775. In block above Cannery Row. Continental, steaks and seafood. $:intermediate-luxury. AE, CB, DC, MC, VI. Full bar. They're not kidding around with restaurateuring at the Sardine Factory. In quality it rises far above the Cannery Row tourist traps. Appropriately, it's located on a hill above the Row, in a building that 50 years ago was the canteen of a sardine cannery. Up the steps under an awning and inside is an interior that fills you up before you've sat down. Not modest, there's red and gilt Victorian *and* nautical decor (hurricane lamps and velvet drapes with tassels), plus some Old California mementoes and a 110-year-old bar in case your interest wanders. The menu is heavy with choices, running from well-aged beef in various styles to varieties of fresh seafood to a number of pasta dishes. The specialties include sole Vannessi (rolled filet of sole stuffed with cheese and crab, baked in sauce with shrimp), veal Cardinal (Wisconsin veal slices and lobster in lemon sauce), prawns St. James (baked in hollandaise sauce),

Monterey Bay prawns, lobster Wellington (lobster tail baked in light pastry, served with cognac sauce), and veal piccata. Take your choice of sitting in the Cannery, Captain's Conservatory, or Wine Cellar rooms, because you'll be there a long time. In sum, not a place for those with light wallets or appetites. But worth it.

Whaling Station Inn, 763 Wave near Prescott; 373-3778. In block above Cannery Row. Seafood. $:intermediate-expensive. AE, DC, MC, VI. Full bar. Cl. lunch. Next door to the Sardine Factory, the Whaling Station Inn successfully competes with its neighbor and rival. Sumptuously decorated with wood paneling, Tiffany lamps, plants, early California artifacts, the restaurant is cozy and dark—and popular enough that it's got an annex. The pride of the kitchen staff is the large selection of seafood, some of it grilled over oakwood: crab cioppino, salmon, clams and linguine, clams and mussels (the latter flown in from the East Coast), sturgeon, abalone with sherry and walnuts, bouillabaise, and more, plus nonbriny entrées like lamb and eggplant. The building went up about 1900 and was a Chinese grocery store in Steinbeck's day—the whaling station was down the street on the waterfront.

The Windjammer, Municipal Wharf #2; 373-2818. Seafood. $:intermediate-expensive. AE, DC, MC, VI. Full bar. The Windjammer occupies the middle quality and price range among Monterey's seafood restaurants but it excels in its location overlooking the small-craft harbor next to one of the city's wharfs, and has a retractable roof for nice days and evenings. For dining down among the boats, you can choose from broiled salmon steak (in season), grilled oysters, Monterey sand dabs, broiled lobster tail, calamari in several ways (deep-fried, tempura, Italian, with eggplant, sweet and sour), and other fresh seafood. There's a Sunday brunch 11-2, and in the late afternoon there may be jazz on the wharf. The Windjammer is situated picturesquely enough to have been photographed by the *National Geographic,* and we'll agree.

Bakeries: **Hector de Smet Bakery,** 675 Lighthouse Ave., 372-9588. **Del Monte Pastry Shop,** Del Monte Shopping Center, 375-4222.

Delicatessens: **Bavarian Delicatessen and Gift Shop,** 422 Tyler St., 372-8426. **Mediterranean Market,** 390 Del Monte Shopping Center, 373-0555. **Troia's Market,** 350 Pacific, 375-9819.

Monterey Peninsula

WHERE TO STAY

The Monterey Peninsula is never so popular as when you're trying to obtain reservations—which is one reason we've listed 46 hotels, motels, inns, and resorts in the 6 principal areas. You can expect horrible difficulties in getting reservations on weekends, in the summer, during vacation times, on holidays, during special events (such as the Bing Crosby golf tournament), in fine weather . . . And it *is* nearly impossible to come during the summer and find reservations anywhere within a hundred miles. So decide when you want to be there and start writing or calling. You'll not only be required to put down a deposit or pay in full in advance but you may have to reserve 2 nights (for weekends) or 3 nights (for 3-day weekends, special events). The only break you may get is that rates are lower in the off-season, which is only November to March in any case.

If you *have* arrived without reservations, either tool along Munras Avenue in Monterey, where there's a long line of standard motels, or phone any Carmel accommodation to hook into their information network of vacancies.

Accommodations in Carmel tend to be small inns and cleverly disguised motels; few have facilities beyond morning coffee.

Color television is the norm, as are heated pools; a surprising number of tiny Carmel inns have pools.

A fireplace is, we would say, the most desirable extra you can get. It can get chilly when the fog's in.

Area code for all: 408. Zip codes: Monterey 93940, Pacific Grove 93950, Pebble Beach 93953, Carmel 93921, Carmel Valley 93924.

Locations

Our detailed alphabetical lists of Monterey Peninsula accommodations are found in Part IV under each separate area—Carmel, Carmel Highlands and Highway, Carmel Valley, Monterey, Pacific Grove, Pebble Beach. What follows is a quick summary:

Monterey—downtown, Fisherman's Wharf: Casa
Munras Garden Hotel, Doubletree Inn, Merritt

House, Monterey Motor Lodge

Monterey—outskirts and highways: Cypress Gardens Motel, Hilton Inn Resort, Hyatt Del Monte Hotel, Ireland's Park Crest Motel, Motel 6, Old Monterey Inn, Reef Motel, West Wind Lodge; Veterans Memorial Park campground (see below)

Carmel—downtown (on and a couple blocks off Ocean Ave.): Carmel Fireplace Inn, Carmel Sands Lodge, Carriage House Inn, Cypress Inn, Jade Tree Inn, Lamp Lighters Inn, Lobos Lodge, Normandy Inn, Pine Inn, Rosita Lodge, San Antonio House, Stonehouse Guest Lodge, Sundial Lodge, Vagabond House Inn

Carmel—away from downtown: Cottages-by-the-Sea, La Playa Hotel, Sandpiper Inn

Carmel—outskirts and highway (also Carmel Highlands and mouth of Carmel Valley): Carmel River Inn, Highlands Inn, Holiday Inn–Carmel, Tickle Pink Motor Inn; Riverwood condo

Carmel Valley: Canary Cottages, Quail Lodge, Valley Lodge; Riverside and Saddle Mountain campgrounds (see below)

Pacific Grove: Asilomar Conference Grounds, Gosby House Inn, Green Gables Guest House, House of the Seven Gables; 17-Mile Dr. Village (RVs; see below)

Pebble Beach: Lodge at Pebble Beach; Ocean Pines condos

Categories

Good for families: Carmel River Inn, Cottages-by-the-Sea, Monterey Motor Lodge

Good for low-budget travelers: Asilomar Conference Grounds, Carmel River Inn, Motel 6, Sundial Lodge

Best for the rich and/or picky: Lobos Lodge, Lodge at Pebble Beach, Quail Lodge, Tickle Pink Motor Inn

All-purpose commercial hotels with all facilities: Casa Munras Garden Hotel, Doubletree Inn, Holiday Inn–Carmel, Hyatt Del Monte Hotel

Most stunning: Lodge at Pebble Beach, Quail Lodge
Most elegant: Carriage House Inn, Lobos Lodge,
   Lodge at Pebble Beach, Old Monterey Inn, Quail
   Lodge
Quietest: Canary Cottages, Carmel Fireplace Inn,
   Sandpiper Inn, Tickle Pink Motor Inn
Best views: Asilomar Conference Grounds, Green
   Gables Guest House, Highlands Inn, Lodge at
   Pebble Beach, Sandpiper Inn, Tickle Pink Motor
   Inn
Most intimate: Green Gables Guest House, House of
   the Seven Gables, Lamp Lighters Inn, Stonehouse
   Guest Lodge
Best for honeymooners: Highlands Inn
Resorts: Hyatt Del Monte Hotel, Lodge at Pebble
   Beach, Quail Lodge
Authors' choices: Asilomar Conference Grounds,
   Cypress Inn, Hyatt Del Monte Hotel, Lobos Lodge,
   Pine Inn, Quail Lodge, Sundial Lodge

Camping

There are no decent **campgrounds**—probably because the Local
Establishment regards camping as Common and campers as the
Unwashed and thus a Threat. At any rate, it's a bit easier for RVs
and trailers, who can try **17-Mile Dr. Village,** 1000 Sinex, Pacific
Grove, 373-2721, which has 75 spaces, or the low-grade **Riverside
Park and Campground,** Schulte Rd. (Rte. 2, Box 827), off Car-
mel Valley Rd., 624-9329, which has 35 spaces.

Tenters don't have much choice: **Saddle Mountain Recreation
Park** is also on Schulte Rd. (Rte. 2, Box 816), 624-1617, but the
ratio of tents to RVs is still unacceptable. More accommodating
but disorganized and sometimes muddy is Monterey's **Veterans
Memorial Park** (to get there drive straight up Jefferson St.),
which has space for 40 tents or RVs (no trailer hookups). Farther
out is **Laguna Seca Recreation Area,** Hwy. 68, 10 miles E of
Monterey (Salinas 424-1971), with 85 RV and 95 tent sites. Alter-
natively you could commute from Andrew Molera or Pfeiffer–Big
Sur State Park or Los Padres National Forest campsites. Or you
could surrender and stay at an inn.

WHERE TO EAT

After San Francisco, the Monterey Peninsula has the finest selection of restaurants in Northern California. The 53 we list are not all the restaurants, but the very best are included along with some of the more exotic, inexpensive, atmospheric, and popular. As indicated, some are tourist traps, but even they can be fun.

Except for some of the more casual restaurants, we'd advise calling a restaurant to make sure it's open and to make reservations, if they take them. You'll need a shoehorn to get into some of these, they're so popular, so don't hesitate to call the top restaurants days ahead of time from out of town.

Locations

Our detailed alphabetical lists of Monterey Peninsula restaurants are under each separate area—Carmel, Carmel Highlands and Highway, Carmel Valley, Monterey, Pacific Grove, Pebble Beach. What follows is a quick summary:

> Carmel—all 1 or 2 blocks from Ocean Ave.: Anton & Michel, Butcher Shop, Casanova, Charlie-O, Chez Felix, Clam Box, Fishhouse on the Park, Flaherty's Oyster Bar, French Poodle, General Store, Hog's Breath Inn, La Bohème, La Playa, Le Coq d'Or, L'Escargot, Moulin de Carmel, Paolina Pasta, Patisserie Boissière, Pine Inn, Raffaello, Saint Tropez, Scandia, Shabu-Shabu, Simpson's, Sticky Wicket, Studio Theater Restaurant, Swedish Restaurant, Swiss Tavern, Toots Lagoon, Tuck Box
> Carmel Valley and outskirts: André's (Barnyard), The Covey (Quail Lodge), Thunderbird Bookshop
> Pacific Grove: Maison Bergerac, Old Bath House, Willie Lum's
> Pebble Beach: Club XIX (Lodge at Pebble Beach)
> Monterey—Cannery Row: Casa Maria, Consuelo's, Fresh Cream, Neil de Vaughn's, Outrigger, Salvatore's, Sardine Factory, Whaling Station Inn
> Monterey—Fisherman's Wharf: Abalonetti, Domenico's, Rappa's, Rogue, Windjammer
> Monterey—in town: Alvarado Café, Cellar Restaurant, Clock Garden

Cuisine Categories

American: Alvarado Café, Hog's Breath Inn, La Playa
Hotel, Pine Inn, Studio Theater Restaurant,
Thunderbird Bookshop (See also Steak and seafood.)

Chinese: Willie Lum's

California Continental: Anton & Michel, André's,
Casanova, Cellar, Clock Garden, General Store, Old
Bath House

Continental: The Covey, Sardine Factory

English: Sticky Wicket, Tuck Box

French: Chez Felix, Club XIX, French Poodle, La
Bohème, Le Coq d'Or, L'Escargot, Maison
Bergerac, Moulin de Carmel, Patisserie Boissière,
St. Tropez

Italian: Paolina Pasta, Raffaello, Salvatore's

Japanese: Shabu-Shabu

Mexican: Casa Maria, Consuelo's

Scandinavian: Scandia (also American), Swedish
Restaurant

Seafood: Abalonetti, Clam Box, Fishhouse on the
Park, Flaherty's Oyster Bar, Rappa's, Rogue,
Whaling Station Inn, Windjammer. (See also next
category.)

Steak and seafood: Butcher Shop, Neil de Vaughn's,
Outrigger, Rogue, Simpson's

Varies/international: Charlie-O, Clock Garden,
Thunderbird Bookstore

Other Categories

Breakfast: Alvarado Café, La Playa Hotel, Pine Inn,
Sticky Wicket, Tuck Box

Sunday brunch: André's, Casanova, Charlie-O, Clock
Garden, Hog's Breath Inn, Old Bath House,
Outrigger, Pine Inn, Windjammer

Light meals: Charlie-O, Patisserie Boissière, Sticky
Wicket, Thunderbird Bookshop, Tuck Box (no
dinner)

Less-expensive dinners: Abalonetti, Alvarado Café,
Cellar Restaurant, Clam Box, Flaherty's Oyster
Bay, La Bohème, Patisserie Boissière, Scandia, St.
Tropez

Big productions: Club XIX, Neil de Vaughn's,
   Outrigger, Raffaello, Sardine Factory
Best for families: Alvarado Café, Butcher Shop, Clam
   Box, Consuelo's, Hog's Breath Inn, Patisserie
   Boissière, Scandia, Thunderbird Bookshop
Authors' choices: Casanova, Chez Felix, Clam Box,
   Clock Garden, Flaherty's Oyster Bar, Patisserie
   Boissière, Thunderbird Bookshop, Tuck Box
   (afternoon tea)

Pacific Grove

Pacific Grove has one of the most beautiful state park facilities in California—Asilomar—plus picturesque gabled inns and bed-and-breakfast homes facing out to the Pacific Ocean. Stay here for long walks along the coast right outside. But your car will be necessary for dining variety, because the selection here is limited. Standard motels are along Lighthouse Ave., in case you can't get reservations for the listings that follow.

For further help, see Monterey Peninsula, plus Carmel, Carmel Highlands and Highway, Carmel Valley, Monterey, and Pebble Beach.

Area code: 408. Zip code: 93950.

WHERE TO STAY

Asilomar Conference Grounds, 800 Asilomar Blvd. (Box 537); 372-8016. Located at Asilomar State Beach, end of Hwy. 68. $:intermediate. No cards. A unit of the state park system, Asilomar (coined Spanish, "refuge by the sea") is used mainly for conferences but ordinary visitors can be accommodated to the limit of the space, and you can even reserve up to a week in advance. Besides the sand, pines, and cypresses, the conference grounds include 3 principal buildings for meetings, three semi-cafeteria dining rooms (table d'hôte meals at 7:30, noon, and 6), a social hall, heated swimming pool and other recreational facilities, and a dozen accommodation buildings, ranging from small rustic cottages and lodges to larger condominium-style buildings, with a total of 315 rooms. Surf and Sand, with sea views, has won architectural awards. Several lodges have rooms with 3 or 4 beds, or connecting doubles and triples; the Sea Galaxy complex, Fireside, and Forest

Lodge have rooms with fireplaces—a nice extra on this foggy peninsula, we'd say. Asilomar makes a good discovery for visitors. (See also "What to See," Chapter 7.)

Gosby House Inn, 643 Lighthouse Ave.; 375-1287. Downtown Pacific Grove. $:intermediate. No cards. 2 Queen Anne Victorians grace this block—the Gosby House and the Maison Bergerac—both tastefully refurbished, redecorated, and put to work, one as a tasteful inn, the other as a restaurant. Mr. J. F. Gosby, cobbler and citizen, built his home in 1886 and expanded it to rent rooms to folks on retreat. Renovated in 1978, the inn has 17 individually decorated rooms, 1 with fireplace, 1 with cat (Margaret Rose), 11 with bath. Sherry, continental breakfast, warm hospitality, conversation, no smoking.

Green Gables Guest House, 104 5th St.; 375-2095. On Ocean View Blvd., 1 block N of Central Ave. $:intermediate. No cards. The Green Gables is an extremely well maintained Victorian house, has only 4 guest rooms, is very homey—mainly because it is the owners' home—and has no facilities to speak of. The Chapel Room and Gable Room are particularly well decorated. It's charming but, we know, not for everybody—guests may feel inhibited in their movements for fear of disturbing the household calm. The Posts also own the Gosby House here and the Stonehouse Guest Lodge in Carmel, both larger.

House of the Seven Gables, 555 Ocean View Blvd.; 372-4341. $:intermediate-expensive. Perfectly situated across the street from the Pacific Ocean, House of the Seven Gables was built in 1888, amply expanded by Mrs. Lucie Chase, and bought by the Flatleys (who used to own the Green Gables and sold that to the Posts). The several bedrooms have private baths, antiques, and some views of the ocean. Continental breakfast is served in the stately dining room or cheery sun porch.

WHERE TO EAT

Maison Bergerac, 649 Lighthouse at 19th; 373-6996. French. $:luxury. No cards. Wine. Dr. Hart's 1892 Queen Anne mansion now has an equally gracefully restored but hard-working next door neighbor, the Gosby House Inn. The former French chef, Raymond Bergerac, has retired but advises the current Chinese owners, who continue the Victorian ambiance and award-winning

French cuisine. There are 2 seatings nightly (5:30, 7:30), and the prix-fixe dinner menu changes about every 3-4 weeks. Several courses are served and may include a light pasta, homemade soup such as garden sorrel, choice of entrée (e.g., duckling braised with orange and liqueur or pork loin roasted with green peppercorns), with each course served with a different wine; house salad, Grand Marnier soufflé or other dessert, coffee or tea. Reservations are required.

Old Bath House, 620 Ocean View Blvd., Lover's Point Park; 373-5195. California Continental. $:intermediate-expensive. AE, CB, DC, MC, VI. Superbly located at the site of Pacific Grove's historic bath house at the curved end of a sheltered bay popular still with swimmers and toddlers, the Old Bath House presides over the scenery like a well-dressed, blue-and-white matron. Sunday brunchers can best enjoy the views, though the dinner menu is much broader. Entrées include beef Wellington, veal piccata, Monterey Bay salmon, sole Cardinale, canneloni Romana, New York steak, and other steak and seafood dishes. After dinner take a stroll in Lover's Point Park or along the shoreline.

Willie Lum's, 125 Ocean View Blvd.; 373-8494. Chinese—Cantonese, Mandarin, Szechwan. $:budget-intermediate. AE, DC, MC, VI. Full bar. Try Willie Lum's if you like a Hollywood-style Chinatown setting with rickshaws and gongs, and other paraphernalia. The menu ranges across several styles of Chinese cuisine. Early-bird specials at dinner. Lunch also served. Located in the American Tin Cannery.

Bakeries: **Hector De Smet Bakery,** 591 Lighthouse Ave., 373-1592. **Scotch Bakery,** 545 Lighthouse Ave., 375-3569.

Delicatessens: **Grand Deli,** 306 Grand Ave., 373-6868. **Mrs. Olsen's Delicatessen,** 197 Country Club Gate Center, 375-5577.

Pebble Beach

Pebble Beach has very limited, but exclusive, accommodations: one resort—the Lodge at Pebble Beach. That has a dining room, fancy Club XIX, 3 bars, and the Tap Room for sandwiches. If you are lucky enough to stay here, drive to Carmel, Monterey, or elsewhere for dining variety.

For more information, also see Monterey Peninsula, and Carmel, Carmel Highlands and Highway, Carmel Valley, Monterey, and Pacific Grove.

Area code: 408. Zip code: 93953.

WHERE TO STAY

Lodge at Pebble Beach, Box 627; 624-3811. Mile from the Carmel Gate, on 17-Mile Dr. $:luxury. AE, CB, DC, MC, VI. The Hyatt Del Monte is nice, but the Lodge at Pebble Beach (successor to the old Del Monte resort and then hotel) is definitely a first-class resort, outpointed locally only by Quail Lodge. The 151 rooms are in 4- to 18-room buildings here and there between the 1st tee and the famous 18th green of the Pebble Beach Golf links. Close by (see "What to See," Chapter 8) are tennis, Olympic-size pool, riding stables, more golf courses, etc. The lodge has a dining room (3 meals, dinner dancing Fri.-Sun.), fancy Club XIX (lunch, dinner, entertainment Wed.-Sat.), 3 bars—including the Beach and Tennis Club (open to lodge guests) and the Tap Room (sandwiches), which has golfing memorabilia. Also shops, meeting space, post office. Nobody could be unhappy staying here.

If you're interested in longer-term accommodations—a week to a couple of months—there are some **condominiums** available. **Ocean Pines,** 19 Ocean Pines La., Ebbtide N, 625-2279, has 2-person rates ranging from $210 for a 1-bedroom condo for a week to $850 for 2 bedrooms and a den for a month (the weekly rate decreases with time, as does the monthly rate).

WHERE TO EAT

Club XIX, Lodge at Pebble Beach; 625-1880. French. $:lunch—intermediate, dinner—expensive-luxury. AE, CB, DC, MC, VI. Full bar. Reservations necessary. The Club XIX, named of course for the 19th hole on the world-famous Pebble Beach golf course, has a split personality. By day it's lunch on the terrace of the luxurious Lodge at Pebble Beach, with a sweeping view of the Pacific Ocean and the meticulously manicured golf course. The more casual menu features seafood salads, chicken served various ways, and so forth. The $4 17-Mile Dr. admission fee is deducted from the bill, which may be an inducement to stop for lunch. Things change at dinnertime—it's tie and jacket time and they light the candles. The menu becomes expensive and à la carte: fresh Monterey Bay salmon (in season) with hollandaise sauce, Maine lobster with Nantua sauce, veal sweetbreads in creamy white wine sauce, Cornish hen with mushrooms and lardons and onions, medaillons of veal with morel sauce, veal piccata, filet mignon, duck à l'orange, and more. The dining room is richly done in oak paneling.

Salinas/Inland Monterey County and San Juan Bautista

Driving up or down Hwy. 101 or inland from Monterey, the 2 main centers for dining, less so for staying, are Salinas, a working agricultural and small industry city, and San Juan Bautista, a mission and state park town. Since the Monterey Peninsula is so close, there's really no reason to stay inland unless you are a business traveler, too tired to go to the coast, or just like the convenience. Restaurants offer surprising variety, particularly for lunch.

Area code: 408. Zip codes: Salinas 93906, San Juan Bautista 95045.

WHERE TO STAY

There are no destination accommodations like resorts, one country inn we know of, the only other unique—not to say incredible and eccentric—place being the **Madonna Inn** outside San Luis Obispo (100 Madonna Rd.; 804/543-3000), just beyond the range of this guide. There each of the 109 rooms is individually decorated in the style of some period or exotic locale. $:intermediate-expensive.

Salinas

Salinas has a number of motels, including chains, that will do as well as any: **Best Western Hi-Way Center Lodge,** 556 Airport Blvd., 424-1741. $:intermediate. AE, CB, DC, MC, VI. Of the 96 rooms, all have color TV, 12 have steambaths, some have balconies, waterbeds, or oversize beds. There are also a heated pool and putting green, coffee shop on premises, airport and 18-hole golf course nearby. **Laurel Inn Motel,** 801 W. Laurel Dr., 449-2474. $:intermediate. AE, CB, DC, MC, VI. Off Hwy. 101 a bit, the Laurel is an unsurprising motel with a pool and adjacent restaurant. **Motel 6,** 1010 Fairview, 758-2791. $:budget. Mediocre standard.

San Juan Bautista

For the more personal style, try **Bed & Breakfast San Juan,** 315 the Alameda, San Juan Bautista, 623-4101. $:intermediate. A newish entry to the B&B circuit, B&B SJ is in the Wilcox-Lang House, built in 1858 and in the National Register as of 1982. Run by Jeanne and Todd Cleave, you may stay in *the* (and we do mean the only) place in San Juan with reservations, so plan ahead for this step backward in time.

Pinnacles

Camping is principally at the Pinnacles National Monument, Fremont Peak State Park and adjacent Hollister Hills SVRA, the county areas at San Antonio Lake and Nacimiento Reservoir, and Arroyo Seco and other primitive tenting grounds in Los Padres National Forest (Santa Lucia Mountains). Just outside the eastern park boundary is the private **Pinnacles Campground,** about 35 miles S of Hollister off Hwy. 25, 389-4462, with 78 tent, 14 group, and 36 RV sites on 375 acres. RVs and others may stay at the **Cabana Holiday Motel & Trailer,** 8710 Prunedale Rd., Salinas, 663-2886, with its pool, restaurant, and cabin units to rent. Also see Monterey Peninsula camping listings, including Laguna Seca Recreation Area on Hwy. 68.

WHERE TO EAT

The restaurant choices are actually quite good inland, with several in Salinas and more than a half-dozen in San Juan. We'd recommend lunch at any of them, but head to the Monterey Peninsula for dinner and a view.

Salinas

One of our favorites: the **Steinbeck House,** 132 Central at Stone, 424-2735, is run by Valley Guild, an organization of women interested in gourmet cooking who were looking for a place in which to open a restaurant when the novelist's home of youth was threatened with demolition. The two came together; proceeds go to charity and further restoration. Table d'hôte luncheons only, with 2 sittings (11:45, 1:15) Mon.-Fri. only; reservations required. Lunch is $:budget. No cards. The menu is California Continental but features the best fresh produce from the Salinas Valley—big green salads of lettuce and spinach (not cooked). The entrées include, for example, green chili quiche, chicken Maxim, poulet de broccoli, crab soufflé, ratatouille crepe, "Cowbelle Enchilada," shrimp-stuffed artichoke, and sole Florentine. Mouth-watering desserts include strawberry parfait pie, tropical ambrosia pie, almond chocolate mousse, mocha nut torte, brandy Alexander pie, and raspberry cheesecake—but only one at a time. . . . Another interesting place to eat is **East of Eden,** 327 Pajaro St., 424-0819, located in a landmark square-towered 1875 Presbyterian church. Steak, seafood. $:intermediate. AE, MC, VI. Full bar. Cl. for lunch Sat.-Sun. The interior is quite remodeled, the ambiance youthful. There's entertainment on occasion. **Italian Villa,** 64 Monterey Hwy. (68), 424-6266. Italian, American. $:intermediate. AE, CB, DC, MC, VI. Full bar. Not too much atmosphere, but what there is is air-conditioned or is warmed by the fireplace—and filled with organ music from the bar. The specialties are steak barbecued over oakwood, chops, veal scallopini.

Steak and seafood: **The Pub's Prime Rib,** 227 Monterey St., 424-2261. Both steak and seafood here. **Smalley's Roundup,** 700 W. Market, 758-0511. $:intermediate. MC, VI. Meat lovers come here for the 32-oz. porterhouse, 24-oz. T-bone, 16-oz. ribeye, 12-oz. New York, and one-half side of barbecued pork ribs. Roll up your sleeves and dig in. **Quality Inn Townehouse,** 808 N. Main St., 424-8661. $:intermediate. While the motel coffee shop serves breakfast and lunch, the restaurant offers New York steak, prime rib, filet of sole Véronique, shrimp.

Others in Salinas on Main St.: **Saeed's,** 319 S. Main St., 422-4611, has Mediterranean and Middle Eastern specialties, including shish kebab and falafel. Also has deli items to take out. Open until 7 weekdays, closed Sunday. **The Windfall,** 228 Main St., 646-8272. California Continental. $:intermediate-expensive. AE, MC, VI. In a century-old brick building, the Windfall has a varied menu for brunch, lunch, and dinner, including veal (Oscar, schnitzel, piccata, Murat), steaks, prime rib, sole amandine, scampi Windfall, broiled snapper, and more.

Salinas sandwiches and perishables: **Garden Café,** 172 Main St., 758-0882. MC, VI. Cl. Sun. How about an Irvine (breast of turkey with avocado, jack cheese), Smith (tuna and almonds, chestnuts), Walsh (hot pastrami, Swiss cheese, tomato), or plain old roast beef, ham, salami? **International Market,** 343 Main St., 424-5575.

San Juan Bautista

Italian-American: **Cademartori's Casa Maria,** 1st St./San Jose, 623-4511. $:intermediate-expensive. AE, MC, VI. Full bar. Cl. Mon. Located in the old parish hall of the Mission San Juan Bautista, on the old mission grounds, this restaurant shares the mission's wonderful hillside location and view of the valley below. Atmosphere is doubly enjoyable if you can eat in the patio. The big menu has lots of pasta (canneloni is a specialty) plus veal parmigiana, saltimbocca (which is prosciutto and veal sautéed in butter), abalone, steaks. Family-run restaurant since 1927.

German: **Faultline,** 11 Franklin, 623-2117. $:budget-intermediate. Cl. Tues., Wed. A strange name for a German restaurant, right? Only in California could you have a blue-and-white German establishment with a patio and gazebo perched on the edge of and overlooking the San Andreas Fault, with a sweeping view of the rodeo ring in the foreground and the well-irrigated agricultural fields and Gabilan Mountains in the background, *and* a Rapazzini wine-tasting room next door, state park adjacent, and working mission church across the street. The menu here really does feature wiener schnitzel, sauerbraten, kassler rippchen, undsoweiter, plus sandwiches and other things for lunch. What more could you want?

Mexican and Early Californian: **La Casa Rosa,** 107 3rd St. (which, by the way, is "restaurant row"), 623-4563. $:budget. Wine, beer. No cards. Cl. Tues. Nicely, not to say charmingly located antique-filled restaurant in an 1858 house painted pink with an herb garden. It's for lunch only and there's a choice of two entrées—chicken soufflé or the Early California Casserole of corn, cheese, and meat—each served with a salad with house-special herb dressing and dessert, such as cheesecake or macadamia nut ice cream. The chef also makes wine and preserves, including chutneys. **Felipe's California Cuisine,** 313 3rd St., 623-2161. $:budget. Cl. Tues. Both Mexican and Salvadoran food are served for lunch and dinner indoors. One state park ranger recommends it highly. **Jardines de San Juan,** 115 3rd St., 623-4466. $:budget-intermediate. MC, VI. Full bar. Cl. Mon. True to its name, Jardines has a popular patio garden as well as an indoor room that serve Mexican and Spanish dishes, including standard tacos, enchiladas, combinations, and specials, such as red snapper. Tourists love this place. **Dona Esther,** 25 Franklin St., has Mexican food also.

California Continental: **Mariposa House,** 37 Mariposa St., 623-4666. $:intermediate. Wine, beer. Cl. Mon. The Mariposa House is in an 1891 Queen Anne Victorian that has 2 indoor dining rooms in lavender and gray and a sunny outdoor patio deck. The co-owners and chefs, Wanda Styron and Rebecca McGovern, use fresh ingredients, change the menu with the seasons, and may serve fettucine Wanda, veal piperade (veal layered with ham, mozzarella cheese and baked with tomatoes and peppers), young rabbit braised and with creamy mustard sauce, trout Mariposa breaded in ground walnuts, lemon mousse.

Steaks and seafood: **Cutting Horse,** 307 3rd St., 623-4549. $:intermediate. Full bar. Cl. Mon. In an old-time western façaded-front building, the Cutting Horse offers steaks, seafood, and Italian entrées.

Market and bakery: **Plaza Market,** 319 3rd St., and **San Juan Bakery,** 203 3rd St.

Ice cream: **Cindy's,** 211 3rd St., and **Jolly Frostie,** 100 3rd St.

San Mateo Coastside

The San Mateo Coastside does not have a good mixture of places to stay, because most visitors drive through here on their way somewhere else (e.g., Monterey, Santa Cruz) or only go for the day. A few motels, an inn, hostels, and camping are about it. Restaurants are better, offering brunch or lunch for Sunday drivers, dinners of various kinds for residents, and travelers, and beachcombers.

Area code: 415. Zip codes: Half Moon Bay 94019, Montara 94037, Moss Beach 94038, Pacifica 94044, Pescadero 94060, San Gregorio 94074.

WHERE TO STAY

Visitors to the San Mateo Coast typically come for the day, thus accommodations are sparse. Standard motels: Pacifica—**Marine View Motel,** 2040 Francisco Blvd., 355-2543. $:intermediate. 12 units about 2 blocks from the beach, some with kitchens. Also **Rockaway Motel,** Hwy. 1, 355-9976; and **Sea Breeze Motel,** 100 Rockaway Beach Ave., 359-3903. Moss Beach—**Dan's Motel,** Cabrillo Highway, 728-3786. Half Moon Bay—**Best Western Half Moon Bay Lodge,** 2400 Cabrillo Highway, 726-6301. $:intermediate. AE, CB, DC, MC, VI. The 55 rooms include 12 with kitchens, some with fireplaces, and the facilities have a view of the 18-hole golf course (guest privileges for a fee).

A small inn and restaurant: **San Benito House,** Main/Mill, Half Moon Bay, 726-3425. $:intermediate. What was the former 1904 Mosconi Hotel was purchased in 1976 and restored by owner Carol Regan and craftsman Marco Hnatt. Of the 10 French-country-inn, period-style rooms, 8 have bath and 2 share. Sundeck, sauna, continental breakfast. Reserve in advance for weekends. Also see "Where to Eat," below.

The adventurous might try the **Jesse James Redwood Inn,** La Honda Road, La Honda, 747-9994.

Hostels are slowly developing as part of a plan to have a series of coastal hiking and/or biking trails with 38 eventual Oregon-Mexico hostels. In California the impetus for this partially came as a result of the 1974 Collier-Keene State Hostel Facilities Act, with the hostels co-sponsored by national, state, local, and private agencies. 3 hostels are on or near the San Mateo Coast now. Closest to San Francisco is the **Montara Lighthouse Hostel,** 16th/Cabrillo Hwy., Montara, 728-7177, where there are 6-person dorms in renovated turn-of-the-century buildings, and a now-automated lighthouse circa 1928. **Pigeon Point Lighthouse Hostel** is along Hwy. 1 about 50 mi. S of San Francisco. Named, like the Point, after the Clipper ship *Carrier Pigeon,* wrecked off the coast here in 1852, the hostel has 50 beds, dining and living room, bike storage, and a beautiful coastal view, which it's enjoyed since 1871. Information: American Youth Hostels–Golden Gate Council, Building 240, Fort Mason, San Francisco, 771-4647. The third hostel open is in **Sam McDonald Park** up the redwoods off La Honda Road. This building was imported from Denmark, erected by the Sierra Club, and opened in the 850 hillside acres of the park in 1977. Reserve a bunk space here by calling 327-8111 Mon.-Fri. afternoons.

Camping is primarily at county and state parks in the redwoods, such as at Butano State Park near Pescadero (our choice), and Portola State Park about 25 mi. uphill from the coast; reserve both through Ticketron. On the coast are state or local campgrounds at Thornton State Beach, Pillar Point Harbor in Princeton (overnight RVs), and Francis Beach in Half Moon Bay.

WHERE TO EAT

While the San Mateo Coastside has no distinguished restaurants, it has several interesting places and several that should be passed by in favor of San Francisco's, Santa Cruz's, or Carmel's, even if you're starving.

Our favorite: **Duarte's,** 202 Stage Rd., Pescadero, 879-0464. American. $:budget-intermediate. MC, VI. Full bar. This Formica-and-pine tavern is the town's social center, which makes it good for absorbing local atmosphere. Three generations of Duartes have presided since 1894, with the artichoke as focal point of the menu, and their own 3-acre farm to raise produce. Rising before the sun, the Duartes make their menu change with the seasons and with what's available locally from the fields and the ocean. Artichoke specialties include cream of artichoke soup, artichoke-heart salad, fried artichokes, artichokes Béarnaise. Other American dishes include omelets, steaks, sandwiches, pork chops, grilled fresh fish, and Pigeon Point oysters. But don't leave without trying the homemade pies—rhubarb, apple, apricot, and more. During crab season cioppino feeds are every other Sat., and call ahead for these.

In Moss Beach: One of the pleasantest places for view dining is the **Moss Beach Distillery,** Beach/Ocean, 728-5434. It's in the Old Galway Bay Inn, so named by someone who thought of that scenic Irish harbor. Naturally they serve fresh fish, plus aged eastern grain-fed beef. Entertainment is Sat. nights and jazz Sun. afternoons.

Princeton-by-the-Sea's four to choose from: **Shore Bird,** 390 Capistrano Rd., 728-5541. Steak and seafood. $:intermediate-expensive. AE, MC, VI. Full bar. The fanciest of the four here, the Shore Bird has the air of a New England fishing-port inn, with a white picket fence, shuttered windows, and, inside, a view of Pillar Point, fresh flowers, and lots of blue details. The menu features steak, lobster, crab, clams, abalone (when available), and other fish in season. Weekend brunch really packs people in for orange juice, fruit bowl, entrée choice, perhaps buttermilk biscuits, downed with coffee. **Princeton Inn,** Capistrano Rd./Prospect Rd., 728-7311. Seafood. $:intermediate. Full bar. Cl. Mon. Built in 1906 and having survived a checkered career, the Princeton Inn was restored and reopened in 1976, with a distant bay view through arched windows, and charming country touches. Seafood dinners may cover Dover sole, shark Benito, salmon Wellington, Pacific snapper. Sun. brunch is very popular, as it is at the neighboring Shore Bird. **Ida's Seafood Restaurant,** 4230 Cabrillo Hwy., 726-2822. Seafood. $:intermediate. Wine, beer. Cl. Mon. Ida's son nets the fish and the abalone, which is the specialty when it's available. **Hazel's Seafood Parlor,** County Wharf, 728-9984. Seafood. $:budget. Wine, beer. Hazel's is known for its friendly ambiance and well-prepared seafood plates.

El Granada's English contribution: **Village Green,** 89 Portola Ave., 726-3690. British. Wine, beer. While you wait you can examine (but not too closely) the Tudoresque styling, hanging flower baskets, lace curtains, and veddy British menu. Anglophiles can order fried bread, Cornish pastie (like beef stew in a crust), bubble and squeak (cabbage and fried potatoes—guaranteed the only time this dish appears in this book!), sausage roll, Welsh rarebit, and bread from the Half Moon Bay Bakery. Breakfast and lunch are also served, as is afternoon tea with scones, jam and clotted cream.

Half Moon Bay's two popular spots: **San Benito House,** Main/Mill, 726-3425. California Continental. $:intermediate-expensive. Full bar. Both an inn (see "Where to Stay") and restaurant with French county atmosphere San Benito House caters to locals for weekday lunches, residents, guests, and excursion brunchers and dinner crowds on weekends. Gardens cheerfully invite diners in with sidewalk planters, enhance views from the decks, and actually feed people with freshly grown snow peas, zucchini, herbs, and more. The menu is changed constantly by chef and owner Carol Regan, who sharpens her culinary skills with further training occasionally in France (e.g., under Roger Verge at Moulin des Mougins near Nice—sounds like a tasty working vacation). Entrées may include poached salmon, salmon mousse, roast pork in orange sauce, with rich desserts. Call ahead for the menu and a reservation for 1 of the 2 seatings Fri. or Sat. (about 6:30, 8:30). Sun. brunch on the decks are nice, especially when the sun shines through the fog. **Moon Garden,** 4230 Hwy. 1, 726-2454. Chinese (northern). $:budget-intermediate. Wine, beer. How many Chinese restaurants do you know of with a view into the Pacific Ocean, nearly to China on the other side? Here's one in Half Moon Bay. You can order with or without MSG such à la carte dishes as pot stickers, hot and sour soup, Mongolian beef, Hunan Gen. Tauo's chicken, fresh fish.

Santa Cruz and Coast

Santa Cruz has traditionally been a day-tripper destination for thousands of Bay Area people looking for sun, sand, surf, a roller coaster, and casual food. With the growth of the U.C. campus and Santa Cruz and environs—Capitola, Seacliff, Aptos, over to Watsonville—as an extended bedroom community and escape from Silicon Valley, the demand for variety in dining deepened and became more sophisticated, and today the selection of restaurants is pretty good. Accommodations have not developed as well, with still funky or spruced-up beach cottage units, modern motels, rental condominiums, and a rare inn the situation around this coastal area.

We'd recommend spending the day leisurely in Santa Cruz, with dinner on the bay or among the redwoods, then overnight on the other side of Monterey Bay.

Area code: 408. Zip codes: Aptos 95003, Capitola 95010, Davenport 95017, Santa Cruz 95060-66, Soquel 95073, Watsonville 95076.

WHERE TO STAY

The city of Santa Cruz lacks accommodations with depth of character. It has no good city hotel, no nice country resort, and several old-time and new motel or cottage units near the beach and boardwalk.

Standard motels: **Dream Inn,** 175 West Cliff Dr., 426-4330. $:expensive. MC, VI. Located (objectionably) right on the beach, the Dream Inn's 164 garishly decorated rooms all command an ocean view. Heated pool, lanai, coffee shop. **Holiday Inn,** 611 Ocean, 426-7100. $:expensive. AE, DC, MC, VI. About a mile from the beach on one of the main streets, this Holiday Inn has a pool, and Dietrich's for buffet and à la carte meals overlooking the garden and pool. **Sandpiper Lodge,** 111 Ocean St., 429-8244. $:intermediate. AE, DC, MC, VI. A newer motel on the San Lorenzo River and closer to the beach, the Sandpiper has 25 units and 4 hot tubs (bring your own peacock feathers).

Older and/or budget motels or cottages: **Best Western Torch-Lite Inn,** 500 Riverside Ave. 426-7575. $:budget. About 5 blocks from the Boardwalk across the San Lorenzo River. **Blackburn House Motel,** 152 Center St., 423-1804. $:budget. Centrally located 2 blocks from the beach, 2 blocks from Pacific Garden Mall downtown, the 32 kitchen units are around the Judge Blackburn house and garden, or in the 2-story modern addition. **Casablanca Motel,** 101 Main St., 423-1570. $:intermediate. AE, MC, VI. With its "country inn atmosphere," the Casablanca's units are nearly on top of the beach and bay. The restaurant by the same name is listed below.

Aptos has our choice among area hotels: **Bayview Hotel,** 8041 Soquel Dr., 688-1928. 8 miles from Santa Cruz, a few blocks from Seacliff State Beach. $:budget. Once popular beach-resort hotel (Lillian Russell and King David Kalakaua of Hawaii were guests) closed in 1915, reopened in the '40s apparently with the original furnishings, which remain to charm willing guests. Only 18 rooms but all have baths. Dining room. By the way, there's no bay view. Reasonable motel is the **Rio Sands,** 150 Stephen Rd., 688-3207. Block from beach. $:budget-intermediate. MC, VI. Rooms are standard but grounds, with pool, barbecues, picnic tables, are unexpected.

In Capitola, the **Capitola Venetian Hotel,** 1500 Wharf Rd., 476-6471, is a recently restored Mediterranean villa on the beach; it looks good but we haven't checked it out. Comments welcome.

Condominiums are for rent at Seascape, 1 Seascape Blvd., Aptos, 688-6491, and Pajaro Dunes, 2661 Beach Rd., Watsonville,

722-9201. Pajaro Dunes has 17 tennis courts but its brochure talks of the "unstructured beach life" on this attractive sand spit at the mouth of the Pajaro River. Seascape has tennis courts and Racquet Club restaurant, an 18-hole golf course with restaurant, also sauna, Jacuzzi, and pool, and the beach is 3 blocks away. Pajaro Dunes has the more interesting architecture and is the more rural. Minimum stay at either is 2 nights; for 2 people rates are $:luxury for a weekend stay only, $:expensive for an entire week.

Youth hostel: Summertime youth may be interested in the 60-bed hostel run by the Santa Cruz Hostel Society, 423-8304, at 717 Pacific near downtown. Cost is $:bare budget (a couple of bucks). The disadvantage: it's not open until 8 P.M. and you have to leave at 8 A.M.

Camping: Other than private trailer parks, campers mostly go to New Brighton State Beach, which has 115 spaces for tents or RVs, and Sunset State Beach, which has 90 spaces. Seacliff State Beach has 26 RV spaces only.

WHERE TO EAT

In the decades B.C. (Before the Campus), visitors to Santa Cruz had to be content to eat at some creaky resort hotel, Boardwalk hot-dog stand, an Italian or seafood joint—and that was it. Now there are some new categories: a savoring of natural-food restaurants; a gathering of food-and-drink places where the mellow crowd and entertainment are more important; a trumpery of New Lifestyle restaurants with lots of international culinary or historical period image and decor, each one equipped with an arch name carved in redwood or spelled in stained glass; and a minority of new good restaurants. Some Santa Cruz people journey across the mountains to Los Gatos or save their appetites and splurge in San Francisco or Carmel. But at least you don't have to choose between Denny's and Sambo's. Here's a sampling of what Santa Cruz and its neighbors on the shore have to offer:

Locations

Davenport: New Davenport Cash Store & Pottery
　　Gallery
Santa Cruz: Broken Egg, Caffè Pergolesi, Casablanca,
　　Castagnola, Catalyst, Cocoanut Grove Sun Room,

Crow's Nest, Heavenly Goose, Hilarie's, Hollins
House, Ideal Fish Company, La Chaumiere,
Miramar, Pearl Alley Bistro, Santa Cruz Hotel and
Bar & Grill, Whole Earth
Capitola: Shadowbrook, Suzanne's by the Sea, Zelda's
Soquel: Courtyard, Greenhouse at the Farm, Theo's,
La Trattoria
Aptos: Café Rio, Charles Dickens, Redwood Grove
Watsonville: Mansion House

Cuisines

American: Broken Egg, Cocoanut Grove Sun Room,
Greenhouse at the Farm, New Davenport Cash
Store; also see Steak & seafood, Seafood, and
California Continental
California Continental: Courtyard, Hilarie's, Mansion
House, Redwood Grove
Chinese: Heavenly Goose
Continental: Hollins House
French: La Chaumiere, Pearl Alley Bistro, Theo's
Italian: La Trattoria, Santa Cruz Hotel
Seafood: Charles Dickens, Ideal Fish Company,
Miramar, Zelda's; also Steak and seafood below
Spanish: Suzanne's by the Sea
Steak and seafood: Café Rio, Casablanca, Castagnola,
Crow's Nest, Shadowbrook
Snacks, sandwiches: Caffè Pergolesi, Catalyst

Broken Egg, 605 Front, Santa Cruz; 426-0157. Snacks. $:budget. No cards. No bar. The menu at this informal place features lots of different omelets, sandwiches, fresh fruit, and cider. Open till midnight.

Café Rio, 131 Esplanade, Rio Del Mar, Aptos; 688-8917. Steak and seafood. $:intermediate-expensive. AE, MC, VI. Full bar. From the woody airy interior you can look out beyond Seacliff State Beach to Monterey Bay, and have a drink on the courtyard while you watch the sun set. Entrées include fresh fish, perhaps flounder amandine, Pacific snapper, abalone (if available), and fettucine Alfredo, New York steak, steak teriyaki. The good life and the views are open for dinners only.

Caffè Pergolesi, 1547 Pacific, Santa Cruz; 426-1775. Snacks.

$:budget. No cards. No bar. Located in a brick-walled space behind the Bookshop Santa Cruz, the Caffè serves up 6 espresso coffees, 13 teas, pastries, and ice cream. There's classical music and international newspapers for whiling away the time, or a deck for catching some bennies (beneficent sun rays). Open till midnight.

Casablanca, Beach/Main, Santa Cruz; 426-9063. Steak and seafood. $:intermediate. AE, MC, VI. Wine, beer. From the 2nd-story vantage point the Casablanca has an excellent view of Santa Cruz Harbor and Municipal Pier, not to mention palm trees to add to the Humphrey-and-Ingrid setting. Steak and seafood are on the menu.

Castagnola's, 119 River Street S., Santa Cruz; 426-4222. Continental, Italian. $:intermediate. AE, MC, VI. Full bar. Cl. Mon. Located on the river opposite San Lorenzo Park. One of the fancier restaurants with plush color-coordinated decor; outside is a garden terrace. The indoor dinner menu includes halibut steak stuffed with avocado, mushrooms, and tomato; jumbo prawns; veal scallopini Marsala; cannelloni; and other Italian dishes. The outdoor menu is lighter and less expensive but you get classical music with your meal.

Catalyst, 1011 Pacific, Santa Cruz; 423-1336. Varied. $:budget. No cards. Wine, beer. A gathering place for the campus crowd and those wandering through Santa Cruz. There are deli sandwiches plus steaks and hamburgers. Sat.-night entertainment.

Charles Dickens, 9051 Soquel Dr., Aptos; 688-7800. Seafood. $:intermediate. AE, MC, VI. Wine, beer. One of Aptos's older houses was charmingly remodeled into a Dickensian dining room with striped wallpaper, old prints, fireplace, and high-backed chairs, with an outdoor deck and patio. Seafood lunch and dinner.

Cocoanut Grove Sun Room, 400 Beach St., Santa Cruz; 423-5590. Sunday brunch. MC, VI. $:intermediate. Upstairs on the 2nd story of the Cocoanut Grove is the covered patio dining area, with a retracting curved roof to let the warm air in, or keep the cool air out, while you brunch at linen colored tables complete with umbrellas. Brunch is either buffet or à la carte, and is served 9:30-2 (November 9:30-12).

Courtyard, 2591 Main St., Soquel; 476-2529. California Continental. $:intermediate. AE, MC, VI. Wine, beer. The Courtyard diners can overlook Soquel Creek for Sun. champagne brunch, beggar's banquet and other lunches, and California Continental dinners, with entertainment weekend evenings.

Crow's Nest, 2218 East Cliff Dr., Santa Cruz; 476-4560. Steak, seafood. $:intermediate. No cards. Full bar. From indoors and a glass-protected deck, you've got a nice view over the Santa Cruz Yacht Harbor. Standard menu of well-aged beef, Australian lobster, etc., and there's an oyster bar and a salad bar.

Greenhouse Restaurant at the Farm, 5555 Soquel Dr., Soquel; 476-5613. $:intermediate. MC, VI. Wine, beer. Here you can dine either in the greenhouse attached to the farmhouse or outside under striped umbrellas, with trees to one side, crops to the other. Take what you want from the salad bar to accompany your char-broiled steak or hamburger; there are also some soups and omelets. Breakfast, Sunday brunch.

Heavenly Goose, 1538 Pacific Ave., Santa Cruz; 425-8988. Chinese (Szechwan). $:intermediate. Wine, beer. Exposed brick and a pine bar plus art on the walls compose the simple decor to watch while you wait (no reservations taken). Typically very hot Szechwan dishes to choose from include Hunan beef, hot and sour beef, pork shreds in hot garlic sauce, as well as milder cashew shrimp, Kung Pao chicken, or vegetables various ways. Be ready to drink lots of water, ginger ale, and beer.

Hilarie's, 821 Front St., Santa Cruz; 426-8335. California Continental. $:intermediate. MC, VI. Wine, beer. Hilarie's is proudly located in the historic St. George Hotel. Crisp green and beige linen, cane-backed chairs, ferns, and fans surround the fountain under the peaked, totally skylit roof. Weekday lunch, Sun. brunch, and nightly dinners of fresh ingredients, and a wine bar.

Hollins House, 20 Clubhouse Dr., Pasatiempo Golf Course, Santa Cruz, 425-1244. Continental. MC, VI. $:intermediate-expensive. Full bar. Cl. Mon. For a higher-altitude change of pace, go up to the Pasatiempo Golf Course for lunch, Sun. brunch, or a standard continental dinner overlooking the beautiful gardens, golf course, and distant Monterey Bay.

Ideal Fish Company, Wharf, Santa Cruz; 423-5271. Seafood. $:intermediate. AE, MC, VI. Full bar. Located at the entrance to the Municipal Wharf at Santa Cruz and open since 1917, the Ideal Fish Company is one of the old-time seafood establishments, with bay and boardwalk views and an indoor aquarium. Fresh seafood may include cracked crab, scampi, clams, sole, oysters, salmon, cioppino, shrimp, prawns. Steak, chicken, and children's plates also available.

La Trattoria, 2807 Porter, Soquel; 476-0599. Italian. $:intermediate. No cards. Wine. Cl. Tues.-Thur., also Sept.-May. Every day there's a different 5-course dinner, with entrée mainly northern Italian, plus antipasto, salad, vegetable, dessert. Good for families.

Mansion House, 418 Main St., Watsonville; 724-2495. California Continental. $:intermediate-expensive. AE, MC, VI. Full bar. True to its name and showing off one of Watsonville's many Victorians, the Mansion House is an 1871 former hotel by that name that has been restored on the outside and is in the National Registry of Historic Buildings. The inside is equally elegantly but contemporarily decorated, and has three dining rooms and a heated courtyard for brunch, lunch, dinner. Entrées include sole Mansion House (with light tomato and crème fraîche sauce), calamari Monterey, prawns Pernod, New York strip St. Michel (in shallot sauce), veal piccata, roast duckling Perignon. Fresh ingredients are used from locally grown artichokes, lettuce, and other produce from Watsonville, Castroville, plus fish from Monterey Bay.

Miramar, Municipal Wharf, Santa Cruz; 423-4441. Seafood. $:expensive. AE, MC, VI. Full bar. The decor in here is cocktail-lounge flashy and the prices are steep, but the menu has a lot to select from: seafood—calamari, oysters, scallops, abalone, rock cod, halibut, salmon, and more—plus chicken, steaks, prime rib, and lobster.

New Davenport Cash Store, 1 Davenport Ave., Davenport; 426-4122. Organic American. $:budget. MC, VI. Wine. Why "New"? Because the functional "Old" burned down in the 1950s, and the counterculture new took its place, hence today's combination bakery, restaurant, and crafts store. The menu, served from 7 A.M. to 5 P.M. starts with homemade pancakes, big omelets, baked breads and muffins, freshly squeezed orange juice, and moves on to burgers, tostadas, sandwiches, cheesecake, and apple pie out of the oven.

Pearl Alley Bistro, 110 Pearl Alley (off Pacific), Santa Cruz; 429-8070. French. $:budget-intermediate. No cards. Wine, beer. Cl. Sun. Hidden in a building behind Woolworth's, the Bistro delights with its personal service and different-every-night table d'hôte meals, which sample the cuisines of France and Switzerland. The Bistro has served coquilles St. Jacques, ratatouille, mushroom and ham crepes, coq au vin, chicken in pastry shell, veal in white sauce in mushrooms, baked red snapper. There's cheese fondue every night, a choice of 3 soups, different appetizers and desserts. California wines. The decor is eclectic, with booths, a Victorian buffet, handmade placemats and napkins.

Redwood Grove, 9099 Soquel Dr., Aptos; 688-0621. California Continental. $:intermediate-expensive. AE, MC, VI. Cl. Mon. Tucked into the redwoods in Aptos with a view into the greenery, the Redwood Grove serves Provimi veal, rack of lamb, steaks, and fresh seafood.

Santa Cruz Hotel and Bar & Grill, Cedar & Locust, Santa Cruz; Hotel, 423-1152; Bar & Grill, 429-1000. $:intermediate. MC, VI. Full bar. The hotel is very popular for its button-popping 7-course Italian dinners; the Bar & Grill is a more pretentious addition with a broader menu and fancier decor—oak paneling and stained glass. Both have lunch most days, the Bar & Grill a Sun. brunch with champagne. The Santa Cruz Hotel calls itself the oldest restaurant in Santa Cruz; no surprise it has lasted.

Shadowbrook, 1750 Wharf Rd., Capitola; 475-1511. Steak, seafood. $:expensive. AE, MC, VI. Full bar. Long one of the smartest places to eat in the Santa Cruz area. There's a very mini-funicular railroad to transport you from the parking lot down to the restaurant, located in a lush setting on a wooded hillside over Soquel Creek. The chalet-style dining room has a rock garden, and there's a deck down below for daytime and Sat. night dining outside. Entertainment, dancing Fri.-Sat. The menu, not extraordinary, has abalone, scampi, and prime rib as specialties. A place to go without sand in your shoes or Frisbee under your arm.

Suzanne's by the Sea, 427 Capitola Ave., Capitola; 476-9923. Northern Spanish. $:intermediate. Wine, beer. No cards. Cl. Mon. The decor is Iberian and food Catalán—paella, gazpacho, and other specialties plus hot soups, sandwiches, salads, and fresh seafood. Very nice.

Theo's, 3101 N. Main St., Soquel; 462-3657. French. $:intermediate-expensive. AE, MC, VI. Cl. Sun. White tablecloths on pink, fresh flowers, and a fresh menu every 2 weeks. Call ahead for the menu and reservations.

Whole Earth, Redwood Bldg. (near the library), UC–Santa

Cruz Campus; 426-8285. Vegetarian. $:budget. No cards. No bar. Cl. Sun. dinner. A most casual campus hangout for fanciers of avocado, bean sprout, egg, cheese, and other nonmeat sandwiches. The nightly dinners, with soup and salad, are a bargain. Sun. brunch.

Zelda's, 203 Esplanade, Capitola; 475-4900. Seafood. $:intermediate. MC, VI. Full bar. Along the Capitola Beach esplanade, Zelda's has a 1930s air kept moving with overhead fans. Seafood is served for both lunch and dinner, and diners can choose the patio overlooking the bay.

Bakeries: **Gayle's Fine Pastry & Bread,** 504 Bay Ave., Capitola, 462-1127. **Kelly's French Pastry,** 1547C Pacific Ave., Santa Cruz, 423-9059. **Maddock's,** 4628 Soquel Dr., Soquel, 475-1408. **Old Theatre Café,** 106 Walnut Ave., Santa Cruz, 426-0544. **Pajaro Valley Bakery,** 523 Main St., Watsonville, 724-1361. **Plaza,** Pacific/Front, Santa Cruz, 423–1330. **Staff of Life Natural Foods,** 1305 Water St., Santa Cruz, 423-8065. **Wine Barrel at the Farm,** 5555 Soquel Dr., Soquel, 476-9921.

Delicatessens: **Apple City Deli,** 323 Main, Watsonville, 728-3354. **Chachie's,** 2106 Mission, Santa Cruz, 426-0944. **Continental,** 7492 Soquel Dr., Aptos, 688-1366. **Cooperhouse Deli & Wines,** 110 Cooper, Santa Cruz, 429-9004. **Erik's,** 712 Front, Santa Cruz, 425-5353; also Aptos, Capitola, other locations. **Piggie Market,** 3000 Valencia, Aptos, 688-4397. **Yosef's,** 190 Rancho Del Mar Shopping Center, Aptos, 688-1388. **Zoccoli's,** 1534 Pacific Ave., Santa Cruz, 423-1711.

Santa Cruz Mountains

The Santa Cruz Mountains are favored by backwoods and redwood aficionados, families who like to camp, folks on retreat or at camp, and commuters who like the hairpin Hwy. 9 turns on a daily basis. Accommodations include a country-type club, a few motels and lodges, and camping in Henry Cowell and Big Basin State Parks. Dining is equally spread out between Felton, Ben Lomond, and Boulder Creek, with the basics and a few frills offered.

Area code: 408. Zip codes: Ben Lomond 95005, Boulder Creek 95006, Brookdale 95007, Felton 95018, Mount Herman 95041.

WHERE TO STAY

Boulder Creek Golf and Country Club, 16901 Big Basin Hwy., Boulder Creek; 338-2111. $:expensive. MC, VI. Not really a resort but a golf and racquet club with condominium villas for rent. 1-, 2-, or 3-bedroom condos have beamed ceilings, full kitchens, fireplaces, and decks that overlook the links. Extra charge for tennis, swimming, 18-hole golf. Redwood Room restaurant.

Ben Lomond Hylton, P.O., Ben Lomond; 336-5643. On Hwy. 9, 9 mi. N of town. $:intermediate. "Hylton" is a 21-room motel building plus cottages, mostly in the shade of the redwoods, on the San Lorenzo River. The pool is heated, the rooms are very motel-like. Free continental breakfast; nearest restaurant is half a mile away.

Merrybrook Lodge, P.O. Box 845, Boulder Creek; 338-6813. 3 blocks from town center on Big Basin Hwy. $:budget-intermediate. MC, VI. Homey, knotty-pine-walled cottage or motel units amid the redwoods and ferns on Boulder Creek. Six cottages have living room with fireplace, fully equipped kitchen, bedroom(s) with electric blankets (there's heat, too). Less expensive motel units have small fridge, also morning coffee. All in all, quite pleasant.

Camping: Henry Cowell and Big Basin State Parks have family campsites and Big Basin has a walk-in campground for tenters as well as the 6 trail camps on the Skyline-to-the-Sea Trail. Reservations through Ticketron for regular campsites. Among the commercial campgrounds that are better for big RVs and trailers: River Grove Park, 4980 Hwy. 9, Felton, 335-4511; and Smithwoods Resort, 4770 Hwy. 9, Felton, 335-4321.

WHERE TO EAT

No great eating in this neck of the woods. **Felton Guild,** the arts and crafts gallery at 5447 Hwy. 9, 335-3464, has a casual, $:budget restaurant serving Bible-bread sandwiches, soups, omelets, Fri.-night all-you-can-eat spaghetti, and some Mexican food, served either indoors in the gallery or outside under the trees. Cl. Tues. More basically Mexican is the $:budget **El Rancho Tampico,** 6231 Graham Hill Rd., Felton (in Felton Shopping Center), connected with the long-running Tampico Kitchen in Santa Cruz. The Sun. brunch is, however, not Tampican. A much bigger deal is **Scopazzi's Inn,** Big Basin Way, Boulder Creek, 338-4444. Italian. $:intermediate. MC, VI. Full bar. Cl. Mon.-Tues. Rustically decorated dining room in a 1904 mountain lodge has such Italian dishes as cannelloni, semi-Italian ones as lamb chops Toscana, and non-Italian ones as pepper steak flambé. If the drinks don't keep you warm, the lounge fireplace will. Another popular place is **Costella's Chalet,** 6275 Hwy. 9, Felton, 335-4307. American. $:intermediate-expensive. AE, CB, DC, MC, VI. Full bar. Cl. Mon.-Tues. Steak, seafood, and prime rib; background music, entertainment, and dancing; and no bare feet. **Wild Goose,** 100 Main St., Ben Lomond, 336-2248. California Continental. $:intermediate-expensive. MC, VI. Full bar. An earthy, casual backwoods mien is a contrast to the varied menu, which may include veal piccata, tournedos Massena (with Bordelaise and artichoke hearts), rack of lamb, steaks, mocha cheesecake, and other made-there desserts. Also open for Sun. brunch.

Index